CONFEDERATE EXODUS

CONFEDERATE EXODUS

Social and Environmental Forces in the Migration of U.S. Southerners to Brazil

ALAN P. MARCUS

UNIVERSITY OF NEBRASKA PRESS   LINCOLN

© 2021 by the Board of Regents of
the University of Nebraska

All rights reserved

Library of Congress Cataloging-in-Publication Data
Names: Marcus, Alan P., 1967– author.
Title: Confederate exodus: social and
environmental forces in the migration of U.S.
Southerners to Brazil / Alan P. Marcus.
Other titles: Social and environmental forces in
the migration of U.S. southerners to Brazil
Description: Lincoln, Nebraska: University
of Nebraska Press, 2021. | Includes
bibliographical references and index.
Identifiers: LCCN 2020024023
ISBN 9781496224156 (hardback)
ISBN 9781496225245 (epub)
ISBN 9781496225252 (mobi)
ISBN 9781496225269 (pdf)
Subjects: LCSH: American Confederate voluntary
exiles—Brazil—History—19th century. | Whites—
Southern States—Attitudes—History—19th century. |
United States—History—Civil War, 1861–1865—
Refugees. | Southern States—Emigration and
immigration—History—19th century. | Brazil—
Emigration and immigration—History—19th century.
Classification: LCC F2659.A5 M37
2021 | DDC 981/.00413—dc23
LC record available at
https://lccn.loc.gov/2020024023

Set in New Baskerville ITC by Laura Buis.
Designed by N. Putens.

For Debbie Marcus

CONTENTS

List of Illustrations ix

Preface xi

Acknowledgments xvii

Introduction 1

1. The Baltimore Connection 33

2. Moving to Brazil 58

3. The Importance of Agricultural, Social, and Economic Conditions in Brazil 97

4. Ideologies of Race, Religion, Politics, and Science 126

5. Protestantism, Education, and the Campo Cemetery Grounds 157

Conclusion 181

Notes 189

Bibliography 221

Index 237

ILLUSTRATIONS

MAPS

1. The major Confederado settlement clusters in Brazil. 79

PHOTOGRAPHS

Following page 180

1. Col. William Hutchinson Norris's grave at Cemitério do Campo
2. Igreja do Campo, the first Methodist church in Brazil
3. Grounds of the cemetery pavilion
4. Obelisk monument at Cemitério do Campo
5. Monument honoring Col. William Norris
6. An elevated Confederado tombstone
7. View of the Campo grounds
8. The Backwoods at Cemitério do Campo

PREFACE

A few years ago, a colleague of mine at Towson University loaned me a book, *The Graves of Tarim*, written by Enseng Ho in 2006. Ho explained how the graves of pious ancestors have played an important symbolic role in the religious and social lives of Hadhramis in Tarim, Yemen, and between Hadhrami communities and the Indian Ocean diaspora. His discussions on genealogy and mobility, the significance of *presence* and *absence*, and the interplay between kinship and memory reminded me of the Confederate cemetery in Brazil—a legacy of the migration of thousands of U.S. Southerners to Brazil after the U.S. Civil War.

Located on the outskirts of Santa Bárbara d'Oeste in the western interior of the Brazilian state of São Paulo, the Confederate cemetery (Cemitério do Campo, known as "Campo"), conspicuously reflects the exodus that took place over a century and a half ago.[1] Twenty Confederate soldiers who fought in the U.S. Civil War are among the 430 U.S. Southern immigrants and their descendants buried there.[2] Here, similar to the narrative in *The Graves of Tarim*, Campo and the U.S. Southern diaspora played an important role in the recording of family genealogies as well as in the ties of kinship and memory between the U.S. South and Brazil. According to Ho, graves and visits to them are meaningful, taking up "discourses of mobility" and "frequently becom[ing] the object of movement itself, the destination of pilgrimages."[3] More important, experiences of mobility involve "complex and subtle interplays, and societies, cultures, and religions that have been mobile for a long time."[4] These conceptions about mobilities and the complex migration networks at hand led me to revisit the trajectories of the Confederados in Brazil (*Confederado* is a term used in Brazil that refers to the U.S. Southerners who migrated to Brazil).

The story of U.S. Southern migration to Brazil is a familiar one to me personally and professionally. As I began to write this book, I came to realize that I have a few personal connections to the phenomenon, especially as they relate to concepts of mobility and ideas of presence and absence. Although I was born in Rio de Janeiro, raised in São Paulo, Brazil, and went to bilingual British private schools in Rio and São Paulo, I attended a bilingual American school in São Paulo my last four years of high school. However, I am not a Confederado descendant.

I came to learn that one of Charles Nathan's siblings (Nathan being one of the most well-known immigration agents) was buried at the same cemetery as my maternal English-born grandfather Edward Hughes: the Cemitério dos Ingleses (the English Cemetery) in Gamboa, Rio de Janeiro.[5] I also came to learn that Brazilian politician Quintino Bocaiúva—coincidently, the namesake of the street I used to live on in São Paulo (Rua Quintino Bocaiúva)—was an important Brazilian immigration agent stationed in New York as well as the Brazilian Minister of Foreign Affairs; he later became the president of the province of Rio de Janeiro.

Finally, as a Baltimore resident since 2008, I began to take further interest in Baltimore and its role in the Confederado migration story. One of the important Baltimorean figures discussed in this book, William Henry DeCourcy Wright—who was involved in the nineteenth-century flour and coffee trade with Brazil and who cofounded the firm Maxwell, Wright & Co.—is buried among other Wright family members at Greenmount Cemetery, just about five miles from where I currently reside.[6] As it turns out, there are more connections between Baltimore and Brazil than I had previously imagined.

My interest in this study of the Confederados also stems from my professional research work as a geographer, starting well over a decade ago under the tutelage and supervision of Dr. Richard W. Wilkie at the

Geography program at the Department of Geosciences, University of Massachusetts Amherst. Dr. Wilkie had conducted his own research on migration patterns of the Volga-Deutsch communities just outside of Buenos Aires, Argentina, in the late 1960s.[7] Through his mentoring, my doctoral dissertation research centered on Brazilian migration studies, focusing on contemporary Brazilian immigrants in Georgia and Massachusetts in the United States. I also examined the salience of immigrants' places of origin in Brazil in the states of Minas Gerais and Goiás—from whence many Brazilian immigrants hail. I conducted research fieldwork with Brazilian immigrants in Massachusetts and Georgia, as well as with immigrants who had returned to their homes in Minas Gerais (Governador Valadares) and Goiás (Piracanjuba).[8] Curiously, that research involved the same two countries in which this story takes place, except with a *reversed* migration trajectory—Americans who migrated to Brazil—under completely different circumstances almost a century and a half ago. The time I spent in Georgia conducting interviews as well as meeting and talking with both immigrants and locals provided me with an insightful preview of "U.S. Southern culture," which I would revisit when writing this book.

More recently I was exposed to another perspective into U.S. Southern culture in the heart of the Mississippi Delta. For four years in a row (2009–12) as a guest scholar partially supported by Towson University's Faculty Fellowship offered by the College of Liberal Arts, I was kindly invited to join a field course, "Race, Blues, Rock 'N' Roll and the Geography of the Mississippi Delta: A Field Experience," by geographer Dr. John B. Strait at Sam Houston University, Texas.[9] This fieldwork trip offered me insight into the African American experience in the Deep U.S. South, set at the polar opposite of white supremacy.

Immersing his students in the sweltering hundred-degree Delta heat on a weeklong field experience in August, Dr. Strait and his group of students began their field trip by meeting on Beale Street in Memphis, Tennessee. Then they headed south, weaving their way through the extensive, flat Delta cotton fields and the desolate byways and blues juke joints of the Mississippi Delta, making stops along the way at several important blues landmarks and sites that spurred the U.S. Civil Rights movement, eventually ending the trip in Indianola, Mississippi.[10]

The Mississippi Delta, as a sociocultural region, lies at the crossroads of several U.S. historical events that have significantly shaped U.S. racial politics over the past 150 years. This is, of course, where the Delta blues emerged, in a land of sharp racial contrasts of white privilege and black disenfranchisement, described by Will D. Campbell as "a land of garish opulence and mean poverty."[11] Near Clarksdale, Mississippi, we stayed overnight at former sharecropper cabins (now refurbished rentals), surrounded by mosquitoes the size of hummingbirds in the scorching heat, and overlooking relentless and seemingly endless rows of cotton. I could not imagine what life had been like for the hundreds of thousands of cotton sharecroppers who worked every day under such oppressive and appalling conditions in Mississippi and the rest of the U.S. South. It was a macabre glimpse into the human capital involved behind the wealth created by cotton—in a land where "Cotton was King."

Moreover, this was a land where another exodus had taken place, albeit during the twentieth century. Over six million blacks from the U.S. South moved to U.S. northern, northeastern, and western cities during "the Great Migration," which occurred in waves between 1910 and the early 1970s—the demographics and infrastructure in several major U.S. cities would dramatically change as a result.[12]

These Mississippi Delta experiences offered me vital in situ perspicuity into the broader socioeconomic conditions in the U.S. South, past and present. The knowledge gained from this immersion experience brought me to think more closely about the wider implications of nineteenth-century global capitalism, its inherent connection to cotton in the U.S. South, and its imbalanced power structures, produced by the socioeconomic system in the Delta.

When I began researching this story of the Confederados, I was examining themes already familiar to me personally and professionally, relating to migration studies, geography, Brazil, and the U.S. South. This professional and personal background may help to explain any of this book's biases and its choice of examples.

Reading Laura Jarnagin's book *A Confluence of Transatlantic Networks: Elites, Capitalism, and Confederate Migration to Brazil*, published in 2008, inspired and influenced me to focus on the Confederados. I realized, through her work, how the broader interrelationships of kinship genealogies and networks available are instrumental to understanding the various important transatlantic connections within the Confederado migration process. Jarnagin aptly explores the prominent confluences of family and trade connections between Baltimorean entrepreneurs in Brazil as commercial ties in that country were forged. I decided to advance and highlight this "Baltimorean connection" in Jarnagin's work, expanding the role of Baltimoreans as they became one of the major stakeholders in this migration story. In particular, I was inspired by the concept of the geographical imagination, which had lured individuals and families to move from their homeland to Brazil—a "geo-seduction" of sorts.

After reading recent newspaper issues (e.g., in the *New York Times* and the *Washington Post*) with feature stories about Confederado family reunions at the cemetery grounds of Santa Bárbara d'Oeste, I noticed how they tended to depict Confederados as a bizarre "oddity." This portrayal has received even more attention with current U.S. controversies over the removal of Confederate monuments and the Confederate flag, which have sparked increased inflammatory political and racial debates over their symbolic meaning. I also noticed that most media coverage on Confederados mistook the city of Americana for Santa Bárbara (where Campo and the Confederado descendant grounds are located), much to the chagrin of Santa Bárbara locals.

Of course, I will never be able to interview an immigrant from the U.S. South circa 1865 and ask questions such as, "Why did you leave your homeland?" or "Where is *home* to you?" Though I was trained in contemporary social science methodologies, which have informed and shaped my own fieldwork research experience, I realized that this was evidently not possible here. Though I spoke informally with a handful of Confederado descendants, I did not conduct formal interviews with them. Nonetheless, the process of understanding this U.S. Southern trajectory to Brazil is interpreted here through my weaving in and out of excerpts from various historical sources, stitching snippets and glimpses from the past, and establishing connections left from an archeology of archival fragments. In the words of John Lewis Gaddis, "by the time we've become aware of what has happened it's already inaccessible to us: we cannot relive, retrieve, or return it as we might some laboratory experiment or computer simulation. We can only represent it."[13]

As with any analysis of migration patterns, we should not merely quantify the subjective nature of human phenomena and human agency or simply reduce the reasons in the migration decision-making process down to any single motivation. Reducing human behavior down to bare quantitative figures is akin to examining mere predictable automatons, and migrants' reasons and intentions for moving are often ambiguous and contradictory, frequently subjected to broad, complex, interrelated, arbitrary, unquantifiable circumstances and contexts. I therefore have chosen to take a closer look in this book at the strategic influence of stakeholders who were invested in the migration of Confederados to Brazil.

Questions emerged as I began to examine the migration initiative of thousands of U.S. Southerners heading for Brazil. Why Brazil? What was the life of an American immigrant in Brazil like? Where did U.S. Southerners settle in Brazil? Which settlements failed, and why? Why was Santa Bárbara the settlement that thrived best in Brazil? These are among the questions that I address here. As the story unfolds, I examine various factors and circumstances, individuals, networks, institutions, and communities, as well as multiple actors who engaged with the aid, facilitation, and encouragement of U.S. Southern mobility to and within Brazil.

ACKNOWLEDGMENTS

This research project was partially funded by two grants awarded by the College of Liberal Arts Faculty Research Grants at Towson University, Maryland, which helped to defray travel expenses and allowed me to travel to Brazil in 2017 and 2018. I was able to conduct archival research work in Rio de Janeiro, São Paulo, Santa Bárbara d'Oeste, and the Confederate cemetery (in Santa Bárbara d'Oeste in the interior of the state of São Paulo, Brazil). Most Brazilian monographs are not accessible online, and some are available only in print. I had access to master's theses and doctoral dissertations on the Confederados, completed in Brazil and available at the Museu da Memória (Memory Museum) in Santa Bárbara d'Oeste. Copies of local newspapers, original letters, and documents were found at the Arquivo Nacional do Rio de Janeiro and the Arquivo do Estado de São Paulo. I was also awarded the Lord Baltimore Fellowship by the Maryland Historical Society in 2018, which allowed me access to various documents, letters, and books available at the H. Furlong Baldwin Library of the Maryland Historical Society, Baltimore.

Several people have helped me throughout the writing process, and without them the completion of this book would not have been possible. I want to thank my friends and colleagues at the Department of Geography and Environmental Planning and the College of Liberal Arts at Towson University; Bridget Barry, who took on my project, and Emily Wendell, Elizabeth Zaleski, Kenneth Wee, and the staff at the University of Nebraska Press who helped me with the process of publishing this book; Paporn Thebpanya for producing the maps and helping with the formatting of the photographs; Charles Schmitz, David McCreery, and Derrick Marcus for reading early drafts and for making helpful suggestions and comments; and Josette Marcus for her assistance in facilitating contact with Confederado descendant Penny Algramm in São Paulo. On that note, I am thankful to Penny for loaning me two rare book copies of the Miller and Hall families of Santa Bárbara. I am also thankful to Cyrus B. Dawsey, Brian Godfrey, and Christian Brannstrom for their ongoing support and input, as well as Edward Heimiller, curator at the Stephen J. Ponzillo, Jr. Memorial Library & Museum of the Grand Lodge of A. F. & A. M. of Maryland (Maryland Masonic Museum).

I want to thank Laura Jarnagin Pang, who kindly took the time to read an early draft and a newer version of my manuscript. She pointed me to many vital sources and was generous enough to share several comments and suggestions that were extremely helpful.

Last but not least, I am indebted to my wife, Debbie Marcus, who read several early drafts of this manuscript, provided input, and assisted me throughout the writing process of this book. I am grateful for her unending encouragement; the completion of this book would not have been possible without her patience and support, and I dedicate this book to her.

Although I received assistance in the writing process, any missteps and errors here are entirely mine. The spelling of Portuguese words in this text conforms to modern orthography, and the names of people and places have been modernized.

CONFEDERATE EXODUS

Introduction

In 1857 Reverends Daniel Parish Kidder and James Cooley Fletcher colorfully described Rio de Janeiro in their widely read publication *Brazil and the Brazilians*. They claimed, "Probably no city in the world can compare with Rio de Janeiro in the variety of sublime and interesting scenery in its immediate vicinity. The semi-circular Bay of Botafogo and the group of mountains surrounding it form one of the most picturesque view[s] ever beheld."[1]

A decade later the geographical imagination of the tropics would spread throughout the U.S. South, enticing U.S. Southerners to head below the equator to Rio. In 1868 the *Gazette & Comet* in Baton Rouge, Louisiana, reported, "A lull has, for some time past been observable in the interest which was so lively manifested the past year or two among the Southern people for emigrating to Brazil."[2] The time was right to relocate to another place, and that ideal place was Brazil. By 1871 the *New York Times* had labeled U.S. Southern emigration a "fever," and "entire counties were almost depopulated by the great exodus of reputable emigrants and disreputable adventurers, who were alike infected with the fever for Brazilian colonization."[3]

The majority of U.S. Southerners who left the country went to Brazil and were known there as the Confederados. Many were former U.S. Civil War Confederate veterans, mostly from Alabama, Mississippi, Louisiana, Texas, Georgia, Kentucky, Virginia, Missouri, North Carolina, and

South Carolina, and several were doctors, dentists, and agriculturalists. Although a few roustabouts jumped on the proverbial bandwagon at that time, for the most part Confederados belonged not to the poorest or most affluent families in the U.S. South but families somewhere in between (albeit certainly privileged).

The United States is typically known as a destination for immigrants, not as the land of emigrants departing to another place. Today the terms "refugees" and "immigrants" are commonly heard in the whirlwind of global current affairs, and the topic of immigration has appeared at the forefront of most recent U.S. political debates. Yet the topic of emigration *out* of the United States—that is, the emigration of an estimated ten thousand Confederates who left the country after the U.S. Civil War (1861–65)—remains conspicuously absent.

However, of the thousands of U.S. Southerners who went to Brazil, only a very small portion stayed. While the number of U.S. immigrants pales in size compared to the number of immigrants of other nationalities who arrived in Brazil at that same time, Confederados were the largest organized group of white Americans to ever voluntarily emigrate *out* of the United States. The voluntary emigration of large groups numbering in the thousands out of the United States is an anomaly.[4]

This act of leaving was the result of a carefully thought out and calculated move, driven by a combination of push and pull factors. Furthermore, this migration to Brazil would not have happened at such a large scale without access to various networks available or multiple stakeholders who were invested in the migration enterprise.

This project is not a comprehensive study of *all* Confederate immigrants who went to Brazil, nor is it about the U.S. Civil War, the Confederacy, or the Lost Cause. Rather, this study focuses on the strategic maneuvering of several stakeholders and the ways in which they promoted, facilitated, aided, and financed U.S. Southern mobility to and within Brazil.

Race is treated as an important dimension here, as it inherently merges with this migration story.[5] While comparative studies of race in Brazil and the United States are widely available and extensive, with few exceptions critical discussions on race have been noticeably absent in publications that specifically deal with the Confederados.[6] In this case, discussions of race emerge as a paradox: former Confederates went to Brazil, a land where slavery was still a legal institution yet one with "no official color line divide." The inclusion of race is also relevant here, especially since the salience of ideologies disseminated by mid-nineteenth-century politicians, scientists, and religious leaders dovetailed simultaneously to promote immigration to Brazil.

Moreover, publications in the past have tended to focus on the migration of Confederados unilaterally and in isolation—in a temporal, geographical, and sociopolitical vacuum—thus ignoring various synergies and broader global scenarios. Take, for example, the influx of thousands of immigrants from other nationalities flocking to Brazil at the same time, the new racial and scientific ideologies of the time, and the agricultural lag and chronic labor shortage that Brazil faced during the mid-nineteenth century—all of which I discuss here.

More than a mere oddity or exotic curiosity, the synthesis of Confederado immigration is a valuable case study within the broader fields of U.S. Civil War and U.S. Southern studies, migration studies, and Brazilian studies.

Nonetheless this phenomenon, one of the largest human migration movements out of the United States, remains largely unknown to most of the U.S. public and, surprisingly, within the discipline of geography (despite migration being a quintessential geographical topic). With very few exceptions, most academic publications on this topic have been written by historians. Publications written by geographers are scant. In *Ordem e progresso*, published in 1949, Gilberto Freyre mistakenly referred several times to L. E. Elliott as a "male cultural geographer" (*o geógrafo cultural*); in fact, Lillian Elwyn Elliott (Joyce) was a woman and a travel writer.[7] Nonetheless, her detailed geographical focus on Brazil features several sections devoted to the Confederados in *Brazil of Today and Tomorrow*, published in 1917, that offer valuable insights here. While in 1972 geographer T. Lynn Smith included sections with perspicacious commentaries on U.S. Southern immigration to Brazil in *Brazil: People and Institutions*, the topic itself was not the focus of his research.

The renowned geographer Mark Jefferson published a short article in *Geographical Review* after his visit to the Santa Bárbara settlement in 1928 during his South American expedition. However, his articulations on race were clearly anachronistic at best, even for that time. For example, he referred to a local Confederado youngster, surmising, "The infusion of American blood in the Brazilian race was worthwhile"—an unsettling statement even in 1928.[8] Finally, his conclusion that the Santa Bárbara settlement was a failure is patently untrue—it was *the* most successful of all the Confederado settlements.

The last publication written by a geographer to focus on this topic was by Cyrus B. Dawsey and his brother, anthropologist James M. Dawsey, in an edited volume in 1995. Before that, the only other geographer to publish any work on the Confederados was Mark Jefferson in 1928, more than ninety years ago. This project seeks to fill this gap.

By examining the strategic significance of the several stakeholders involved in the Confederado immigration plan, this book offers a new lens through which to view and explore the interconnected relationships in the Confederado story. Its framework includes multiple approaches and considerations (historical, geographical, ideological, sociopolitical, agricultural, and economic). While the underlying Freemasonry connections explored here remain inconclusive, they emerge as a strong network with broader linkages to this migration enterprise. For example, settlers (Charles G. Gunther, William H. Norris, and the latter's son Robert Cicero Norris), immigration agents (Charles Nathan and Quintino Bocaiúva), Brazilian political elites (Tavares Bastos, Dom Pedro II), and Baltimoreans in Brazil (Robert Clinton Wright, William Henry DeCourcy Wright) were all Freemasons. Understanding the deeper importance of Freemasonry in this migration story—a largely unstudied yet compelling topic—requires conclusive results, perhaps a task for future scholarship.

To gain a better understanding of this migration process, the following five features provide a basic framework to help follow the various angles discussed in this book. These features are not mutually exclusive; much to the contrary, they are inherently intertwined.

1. The importance of Baltimore in the mid-nineteenth-century mercantile Atlantic world, and the sociopolitical influence of Baltimorean entrepreneurs who had already been well-established in Brazil prior to the exodus of U.S. Southerners to that country. The salience of U.S. flour exports from Baltimore and the reciprocal Brazilian coffee import trade relationship that was established (key figures in this area include members of the Wright family and Maxwell, Wright & Co.).
2. The influence of U.S. religious Protestant leaders, mostly U.S. Southerners, who lived and traveled to Brazil and who disseminated their knowledge about Brazil to the U.S. public. These leaders encouraged U.S. Southerners to move to Brazil and were in direct contact with Brazilian political elites as well as with scientists (key figures include Reverends Dunn, Fletcher, and Kidder).
3. The importance of propaganda and the influence of immigration agents who helped to promote, finance, and encourage the migration project to Brazil (key figures include Charles Nathan, Maj. Meriwether, Dr. Shaw, and Gen. Wood).
4. The influence of scientists and the new "scientific" vocabulary disseminated at that time. Their influence among Brazilian political and intellectual elites generated a "scientific" justification for bringing immigrants of European "stock" to Brazil (key figures include Matthew Fontaine Maury, Louis Agassiz, and Arthur de Gobineau).
5. The ideological climate in Brazil and various inducements offered to new immigrants by the Brazilian government, as well as the favorable political, agricultural, and economic conditions in Brazil at the time; theses were furnished by key political and intellectual elites (key figures include Dom Pedro II, Joaquim Nabuco, and Tavares Bastos—all Freemasons).

The Mise-en-Scène

Exactly how did trade, agriculture, ideology, scientists, and religious leaders fuel the exodus of thousands of U.S. Southerners to Brazil? What was the "Baltimore connection"? Why Brazil? To answer these questions effectively, we need to first consider the agricultural, economic, and historical contexts at play. Perhaps the best way to start is to look at the mise-en-scène of the 1820s, when trade and commercial ties between Baltimore and Brazil began to increase and strengthen. The trade and commercial vector that spanned most of the mid-nineteenth century was spearheaded by mercantilism in the Atlantic world during the "Age of Capital."[9]

Brazil was the only country in the Western hemisphere with a long-lasting emperor, Dom Pedro II, born and raised in Brazil. His empire lasted from 1831 to 1889.

This was a time when "cotton was king" in the U.S. South and when the flour trade from Baltimore marked that city's growth and development. Trade and commerce had transformed physical landscapes in both countries: cotton and flour in the United States, coffee in Brazil. Amid Brazilian fears of potential U.S. interventions and speculations, it was a time when the advent of new scientific knowledge intersected with the growing interest in Brazil, especially in the Amazon region. It was also a time when new scientific rhetoric merged with religion and scientific racial ideologies, which looked at Brazil through patronizing eyes. The period was also marked by the early stages of environmental determinism, employed to justify imperialism, racism, and political interventions.

Undoubtedly, the end of the U.S. Civil War turned out to be the catalyst that hastened and galvanized U.S. Southerners to move to Brazil. Given Brazil's chronic shortage of agricultural labor and the pending end of slavery, hundreds of thousands of immigrants from Europe moved to Brazil. To understand the context of the pull factors attracting immigrants to Brazil, it is vital to look at Brazil's commodity booms and its agricultural and economic conditions.

In the centuries that followed the first arrival of the Portuguese in 1500, Brazil underwent a number of commodity booms, Brazilwood being the first.[10] However, that boom quickly ended by the turn of the sixteenth century, and it was followed by (cane) sugar.[11] Known as "white gold," sugar became a vital export-based commodity in an economic system devised during the early Portuguese colonial years in Brazil. Throughout most of the seventeenth century, Brazil was the world's largest producer of sugar. Although sugar cultivation continued in the northeast of the country, Brazilian sugar hit a major slump in the 1690s as the gold cycle began.[12] With the discovery of gold (and later diamonds) spurring mining in the hinterlands (particularly in Minas Gerais, Mato Grosso, and Goiás), the Brazilian Gold Rush was fully on. As historian A. J. R. Russell-Wood explains, "It appears that migrants came from every walk of life, from the most diverse social backgrounds and from all sorts of places: the coastal areas of Brazil, the Atlantic islands of Madeira and Azores, and Portugal itself. There were English, Dutch, Irish and French . . . friars left monasteries in Salvador, Rio, and Maranhão, as well as Portugal, soldiers deserted from the garrisons . . . freedmen of color, slaves abandoned their owners, merchants, former planters and people with claims to nobility were all infected with gold fever."[13]

An important turn emerges here: the discovery of Brazilian gold and diamonds led to two long-lasting outcomes in Brazil: agricultural lag and the increase in the transatlantic slave trade. With this development, the Portuguese abandoned their attempts to "industrialize—and to modernize and diversify agriculture—with damaging long-term consequences" in Brazil.[14]

After the decline in the gold cycle in the 1750s, the coffee boom bolstered Brazil's economy. The first coffee seeds were brought to Brazil from French Guiana in the early eighteenth century. By the first quarter of the nineteenth century, the coffee boom had begun to flourish, and within a few decades, in the words of Stanley J. Stein, "the decade of the 1850s was the golden age of coffee."[15]

Coffee, *Coffea arabica*, is said to have developed in the city of Mocca, Yemen (although it first appeared in Ethiopia). Until the 1690s, it was grown only in Yemen "on small, steep, irrigated mountain gardens by hundreds of peasants in three coffee districts."[16] However, by the mid-nineteenth century, Brazil had become the largest producer of coffee in the world and Americans the world's largest consumers of coffee. This symbiotic relationship is an important one to consider.

Brazil began to focus on its coffee export–oriented plantation economy (*grande lavoura de exportação*), concentrated in the Paraíba Valley

(Vale do Paraíba) in the interior region of Rio de Janeiro province and, later, in the western interior of São Paulo province.[17] The first coffee from Brazil arrived in New York City in 1809, and by the 1850s Brazil supplied two-thirds of coffee imports to the United States. By the early 1900s, Yemen produced less than 1 percent of the world's coffee.[18]

Pressured by the British, Brazil prohibited the trafficking of slaves from Africa in 1850 while keeping the institution of slavery legal.[19] Overall, Brazil received the largest number of Africans brought to all the Americas throughout the entire transatlantic slave trade period.

However, with the increased demand for Brazilian sugar, gold, and then coffee, Brazil needed more laborers, subsequently supplied by the slave trade from Africa. Yet with the end of the transatlantic slave trade, high death rates among slave populations, and Brazil's shortage of labor, Brazilian politicians and agrarian elites eagerly sought alternatives to solve this labor predicament through the enterprise of immigration. In this case, U.S. Southern immigrant agriculturalists helped fulfill that demand.

Why did the Brazilian government invest in recruiting and welcoming U.S. Southern immigrants? Brazil's political and national ideologies merged with the country's critical need for skilled human capital: newly arrived immigrants would bring their own agricultural expertise to Brazil while at the same time fulfilling Brazil's attempts to bring "industrious" immigrants of "European stock" (in mid-nineteenth-century vernacular).

At first, Brazil's inducements to bring immigrants to Brazil can be interpreted as a mere "practicality," considering its shortage of the domestic labor needed to replace black slave populations that were declining in numbers. In the minds of Brazilians, this transition in the labor force signaled the natural progression from slave labor to free labor. At that time, most European immigrants were sent to work in Brazil's agricultural sectors, particularly in the interior of São Paulo, only to become indentured laborers on farm plantations who often worked alongside black slaves. However, the Brazilian national rhetoric on race gradually changed, as intellectuals and politicians became conspicuously concerned with racialized discourses (markedly, by the 1870s).[20] A new vernacular and rhetoric emerged to explain the differences between world populations, stemming from the Victorian "science" of the day.

Why were eminent scientists and writers of the day, such as Louis Agassiz, Matthew Fontaine Maury, and Arthur de Gobineau (discussed in chapter 4), so invested in U.S. Southern immigration to Brazil? First, they were ideologically consumed with environmental-deterministic worldviews. Second, they vehemently opposed racial equality and widespread miscegenation in Brazil. Third, their viewpoints looked at the world through a condescending gaze, dovetailing with racist tendencies common at the time. They believed that Brazil's only salvation, its only way to advance into modernity, was to bring white immigrants to the country; at the same time, this immigration offered a solution to the plight of U.S. Southerners. These scientists and writers popularized newly conceived racial ideologies that influenced Brazilian intellectuals and politicians. They also steered Brazilians to become increasingly uneasy with their world image. This anxiety about race concerns in Brazil would drive the implementation of official government policy strategies toward "whitening" Brazil. Such policies would contribute to later debates about Brazil's "myth of racial democracy" and to Brazil's contradictory world image as a "racial paradise." I return to this topic in chapter 4.

On the other hand, Protestant ministers and missionaries based in the United States, such as Rev. Ballard S. Dunn of Louisiana, often acted as immigration agents. They interacted directly with Brazilian politicians and scientists. For example, Rev. James C. Fletcher of Indiana had worked as an assistant for Professor Louis Agassiz of Harvard University during the Thayer Expedition to the Amazon (1865–66). Both men were actively involved with the U.S. Southern move to Brazil. As Lawrence F. Hill maintains, "in this era the fingers of 'manifest destiny' pointed southward as much as westward."[21]

Still, how was the "Baltimore connection" linked to the U.S. Southern exodus to Brazil? Long before the U.S. Civil War, dating back to the 1820s, firms such as Maxwell, Wright & Co. established strong trade and commercial relationships between Baltimore and Rio. Family members of Maxwell, Wright & Co. were among the first Americans to initiate and subsequently expand the flour export and coffee import trade with Brazil in the early to mid-nineteenth century. This firm published vital information about Brazil; it literally "wrote the book" about commerce and trade in Brazil in their reports, published in *Commercial Formalities*, between the 1820s and 1840s. The importance of this "Baltimorean connection" is highlighted in this book.

Baltimoreans also encouraged and facilitated the mobility of Confederados within Brazil, furnishing them with important contacts and knowledge of the empire. In addition, many of the Wright family members were either born or raised in Brazil, and several married into prominent Brazilian family clans.

Would U.S. Southerners have moved to Brazil without the presence of Baltimoreans in Brazil? Possibly and likely. The potential for growth in trade, commerce, and agriculture in Brazil was intrinsically tied to the interests of U.S. Southern immigrants. Nonetheless, if not for the key alliances, contacts, and associations that Baltimoreans had long established in Brazil—their close familiarity with Brazilian bureaucracy, for instance—the facilitation of U.S. Southern mobility at such a large scale to and within Brazil would not have been readily available.

These Baltimoreans optimized their potential for commercial and financial opportunities, directly positioning themselves to hedge future commercial dividends from the U.S. Southern immigration enterprise to Brazil.

How Many Migrated?

The exact number of U.S. Southerners who migrated to Brazil is unknown. The *Baltimore Sun* reported that "of [the] 8,000 and 10,000 embittered people [who] left the southland following the fall of the confederacy, more than half went to Brazil."[22] Scholars' estimates of the number of people who migrated out of the United States range between 10,000 and 20,000; of that number, possibly 4,000 to 10,000 went to Brazil.[23] Most estimates claim that the rest went to other countries, mostly Mexico, at least for a brief time.[24] One survey counted 6,691 U.S. immigrants who entered Brazil between 1890 and 1919; another survey, over a much broader period between 1884 and 1957, counted 30,686.[25] Still another survey counted 3,575 Americans living in Brazil between 1864 and 1872.[26] Figures differ widely depending on the source. Nonetheless, given the data available, it is likely that about 4,000 U.S. Southerners migrated to Brazil after the U.S. Civil War, though the question is difficult to answer with reliable accuracy.

There are several reasons for this lack of accuracy. For one, Brazil did not keep accurate immigration records until 1884.[27] The country did not conduct its first official national census until 1872, and this census did not include land or slave ownership.[28] The 1872 Brazilian Census reported that 389,459 immigrants of all nationalities were living in Brazil at the time.[29] From the data available on U.S. immigrants, Brazilian surveys made no distinction between migrants from the Union and the Confederacy. Brazilian surveys used the category *norte-americano* (North American), a vague term that does not distinguish immigrants who hailed specifically from the U.S. South.[30] For instance, many U.S. northerners had also migrated to Brazil during that same time. Many estimates also relied on immigrant entries from just one Brazilian port—for example, Rio de Janeiro. However, U.S. Southerners entered Brazil through various ports throughout the country, not just in Rio; these include Santos, Salvador, Recife, Belém, and others.

Who Were the Confederados?

The Confederados were a heterogeneous group from a variety of occupational and social backgrounds. Most of those who stayed in Brazil were agriculturalists, merchant planters, doctors, lawyers, educators, and ministers.[31]

However, the group that settled around the Santa Bárbara d'Oeste region (from here on, Santa Bárbara) shared a common trait: most were Freemasons and Protestants, and many were from the "Broad River group."[32] Laura Jarnagin identifies at least 40 percent of those U.S. Southerners who went to Brazil as descendants (either directly or by marriage) of families that had migrated intraregionally from the "Broad River" region—located on the Georgia and South Carolina border—and long established themselves as farmers and "bourgeois/gentry" in Alabama. This was a group of privileged merchant-agriculturalist families that had migrated from North Carolina and South Carolina to Georgia and Alabama at the turn of the eighteenth century. Many of the Confederado family members who were registered as residents of Alabama when they migrated to Brazil had been transplants themselves or belonged to families originally from North Carolina and South Carolina (e.g., William Hutchinson Norris, from Alabama, was born in Oglethorpe County, Georgia). Jarnagin coined the term "legacy behaviors" to describe how generation after generation of these migrants would become "the elite purveyors of capitalism throughout the Atlantic world."[33] Among the family names associated with the Broad River group were Carr, Gaston, Gunter, Hall, Meriwether, Miller, Norris, and Yancey. Many of these names reappear throughout this book.[34]

Unlike other settlers in Brazil, most Confederados who went to Santa Bárbara were not funded by immigration societies or immigration promoters but through the private efforts of William Hutchinson Norris. Other U.S. Southern families eventually joined Norris and his family, settling in or around that region (which eventually developed into the cities of Santa Bárbara and Americana). Those settlers were different from most immigrants recruited to join Rev. Ballard S. Dunn's settlement in Iguape or Lansford W. Hastings's settlement in Santarém—or the thousands of immigrants who eventually returned to the United States. James M. Dawsey characterizes the Santa Bárbara settlers as an "aristocracy of yeomen." According to Dawsey, like yeomen in the United States, the Confederados and their families worked on their own land or for others until they were able to purchase their own land. Gilberto Freyre characterizes most U.S. Southern immigrants who went and stayed in Brazil, on the other hand, as "white aristocrats" who were merely continuing their roles as "gentlemen farmers" under ideal agricultural and social conditions.[35] Jarnagin uses the term "bourgeois/gentry" to describe the majority of U.S. Southern migrants in Brazil; the term functions "as a means of reinforcing the presence of the combination of urban- and rural-based occupations and mentalities."[36] Most of these merchant-planter families had been involved in supplementary occupations to agrarian capitalism before moving to Brazil; many were engineers, bankers, diplomats, educators, lawyers, and doctors.[37]

Martha Temperance Steagall (1850–1933), wife of Robert Cicero Norris (son of William H. Norris) and daughter of H. F. Steagall of Texas (from one of the first settler families in Santa Bárbara), stated in an interview late in life that the Alabamians who settled in Brazil "were not fitted to be pioneers in any country."[38] Steagall continued, explaining that it was "not reasonable to assume that men accustomed to direct big policies and to handle progressive business firms could immediately fit themselves into those conditions which required the[ir] menial labor."[39] According to Steagall, the Confederados who settled in Santa Bárbara were already well established within the globalized antebellum U.S. South, which supports Jarnagin's claims. After all, this was a group already familiar with mobility and global capitalism.

Many Confederados became proprietors of relatively small-to-medium-sized agricultural businesses—for example, agricultural areas averaged seven acres per farm in the Santa Bárbara settlement, in contrast to the forty or fifty acres typical of Brazilian owned plantations in the interior of São Paulo. Confederado Dr. James MacFadden Gaston, a physician from South Carolina, explains: "To our Southern people the empire of Brazil embodies the character and sentiment among the better class of citizens, very much in keeping with our standard of taste and politeness."[40] Many elite agriculturalist family clans, particularly in the interior of São Paulo, shared sociocultural similarities with most U.S. Southern agricultural families, such as the traditional mores of chivalry, cordiality, patronage, patriarchal economic societies, agricultural family clans, common intermarriage between cousins—and, evidently, close familiarity with the institution of slavery.

The role of leadership as well as access to community, institutional, and political networks within Brazil are important factors to consider within each settlement. Settlement leaders' intentions and personalities likely influenced broader impacts in their respective communities, setting the tone for the recruitment of other U.S. Southern families that would later join them in Brazil.

The Freemasons appear as a network that most likely helped galvanize many U.S. Southern families to move to Brazil, most certainly those who went to Santa Bárbara. William Hutchinson Norris and his son Robert Cicero Norris inaugurated the first Freemason Lodge in Santa Bárbara, which expanded largely within that community—a legacy still conspicuous to this day (most of the grounds and headstones throughout the cemetery at Campo are marked with Freemason symbols).

It is also important to point out that many individuals identified as Confederados in the body of literature available were not, in fact, from the U.S. South or even from the United States. For example, at least four to five hundred Irish and German immigrants newly arrived in New York were known to have immediately boarded ships headed for Brazil. One manufacturer of steel-tipped plows in Santa Bárbara, John Domm, was a Dutchman, even though he is often cited as a Texan. Domm had lived in Texas before coming to Brazil with U.S. Southerners. Niels Nielsen, who also lived among Confederados, was Danish. Franz Müller (often known as "Miller" and mistakenly identified as a Confederado) was a German who came to own the textile mill in Americana, Carioba.[41] In addition, William Van Vleck Lidgerwood—whose foundry in Campinas near Santa Bárbara, "Lidgerwood Mfg. Co. Ltda[,] became a powerhouse by producing agricultural machines and setting up textile mills"—was from New Jersey.[42] Rev. Ballard Dunn was purportedly from Louisiana, though there was speculation that he was from New York; Horace Manly Lane, future director of Mackenzie College in São Paulo, was from Redfield, Maine.[43] Charles Nathan, purportedly born in Rio (to Jewish English parents) and a resident of Rio and New Orleans, is often cited as a U.S. Southerner. William Scully, a Catholic born and raised in Ireland who arrived in Brazil in the 1850s, is also often mistaken for a U.S. Southerner.[44] It is clear, from these examples, that not all individuals in this narrative were Protestants, from the U.S. South, or even from the United States. Moreover, not all individuals buried at Campo were Confederados—a few European

Protestant immigrants who lived in the community are buried there as well (see chapter 5).

As I unravel, examine, and interpret snippets of personal biographies of selected individuals, I identify additional layers and complexities in this Confederado story. As the formations of each major settlement in Brazil unfold—especially the particular success of the Santa Bárbara settlement—a clearer picture emerges, one that helps answer the question of who the Confederados were.

Scholarship

Publications on Brazil in the early to-mid-nineteenth century stimulated European and American public interest in that country. Notably, publications written by religious leaders and U.S. Southerners subsequently encouraged U.S. Southerners to move to Brazil. The nineteenth century was also a period when "travel literature" peaked in popularity in Europe and the United States, particularly literature about Brazil and the Amazon. These publications helped create an increasing public fascination with Brazil.

By the mid-nineteenth century, three publications written by Protestant leaders became hugely popular; all played an important role in galvanizing American interest in Brazil and actively promoting U.S. Southern immigration to Brazil. *Sketches of Residence and Travel in Brazil*, published in 1845 by Rev. Daniel Parish Kidder, missionary of the Methodist Episcopal Church, Louisiana, was "ranked as the best work in the English language on the subject."[45] Many "who went to Brazil during the late sixties acknowledged the influence of Kidder's book."[46] Almost a decade later Kidder coauthored with Rev. James Cooley Fletcher in 1857 *Brazil and the Brazilians*, another widely popular publication. Rev. Ballard Smith Dunn, an Episcopal Chaplain also from Louisiana, published *Brazil, the Home for Southerners* in 1866. Despite its less-than-modest literary value, Dunn's book became a particularly influential call for U.S. Southerners to move to Brazil—as the *Baltimore Sun* reported, the book "enjoyed a tremendous sale in a South which was hard-pressed to buy food, much less literature."[47] The book is replete with Rev. Dunn's anti-Semitic and racist remarks, virulent even for that time. Nonetheless, the sections he devoted to the geography of Brazil must have been useful to immigrants to Brazil. However, many of those sections were merely reprints taken from the notes of Jacob Humbird (of the Humbird family of Maryland), reprints of letters sent to Humbird by other immigrant agents, and editorials and articles previously published in the *Anglo-Brazilian Times* newspaper of Rio de Janeiro. Last, Confederado James McFadden Gaston's book *Hunting a Home in Brazil*, published in 1867, offers unique firsthand accounts and strongly favors the migration of U.S. Southerners to Brazil. I rely on all four accounts in this book.

In 1943 the Brazilian Ministry of Foreign Relations published a valuable collection of several original letters and documents—which had never been in print—from the Imperial Legation of Brazil in New York, published between 1866 and 1868 in *Revista de imigração e colonização*. This collection includes a chapter on U.S. immigration to Brazil, with several letters to and from Confederados before they left for Brazil (including Rev. Dunn, Frank McMullen, and William Bowen, among others). The letters had been documented at the archives at the Itamaraty (headquarters of the Ministry of Foreign Affairs in Brazil) and are taken from *Ofícios recebidos pela Secretaria dos Negócios Estrangeiros da Legação Imperial nos Estados Unidos (1866, 1867, and 1868)* and *Despachos expedidos à Legação Imperial nos Estados Unidos pela Secretaria dos Negócios Estrangeiros (1866, 1867–68)*. This book relies on these rarely seen letters as well.

Women played an important role in the documentation of Confederados. Judith MacKnight Jones, a Confederado descendant, published the first book manuscript on the topic in Brazil in 1967, *Soldado, descansa! Uma epopéia norte americana sob os céus do Brasil* (Rest, soldier! A North American epic under Brazilian skies). In addition, two important diaries written by daughters of U.S. Southern immigrants—Julia L. Keyes (published by Peter Brannon in 1966) and Sarah Bellona Smith Ferguson (published by Dawsey and Dawsey in 1995)—provide personal narratives with vital information. A rare publication about the Hall and Miller families' histories, *An American-Brazilian Odyssey: The Story of the Miller and Hall Families*, privately printed in 1979 by Confederado descendant

Caroline Smith Ward, offers unique insights into those families and their livelihoods in Santa Bárbara. Here I have also relied on these publications for context and content.

Today, a considerable body of scholarly literature about the Confederados is available. For an excellent annotated bibliography on the literature available, see James M. Gravois and Elizabeth J. Weisbrod's contribution to *The Confederados: Old South Immigrants in Brazil* (published by Dawsey and Dawsey in 1995). The first known scholarly article published on the Confederados was written by Lawrence Hill in 1927. Hill later wrote a three-part series in 1936 and 1937 providing a broad view of the Confederates who left for South America, and especially for Brazil. Peter A. Brannon published a vital article in 1930 (a diary he was editing was published posthumously in 1966), and Blanche Henry Clark Weaver published two important journal articles in 1952 and 1961, making substantial early scholarly contributions, particularly on the impact of education and the introduction of Protestantism in Brazil.

Two other publications merit attention, although they did not focus on the Confederados. Vera Kelsey's *Seven Keys to Brazil* (1941) and T. Lynn Smith's *Brazil: People and Institutions* (1972) both provide a wealth of important information on mid-nineteenth-century Brazil, with insightful chapter-sections devoted to U.S. Southern immigration to Brazil.

More recently, two Confederado descendants published important book manuscripts: William Clark Griggs in 1987 and Eugene Harter in 2000. Both were former U.S. diplomats. Although these publications were written in a biographical or semibiographical style, I rely on their valuable accounts while remaining careful about their personal and sentimental attachments to the topic.

Cyrus B. Dawsey and James M. Dawsey—Confederado descendants, scholars, and brothers—coedited with contributing authors a volume in 1995 titled *The Confederados: Old South Immigrants in Brazil*, which includes the complete diary of Sarah Bellona Smith Ferguson with an annotated bibliography and contributions from eminent scholars.[48] This volume is the most comprehensive book manuscript to date on the Confederados in Brazil.

Moreover, in her milestone study, *A Confluence of Transatlantic Networks*, published in 2008, Laura Jarnagin offers a unique discussion of the genealogies of mid-nineteenth-century mercantile companies and families—especially of how business and kinship networks intersected with Confederado migration. This publication is the most thorough analysis available of nineteenth-century mercantile family networks in Brazil as well as of the Maxwell, Wright & Co. firm and its respective family members.

Another publication merits brief attention here. Gerald Horne published a valuable book, *The Deepest South*, in 2007, and although U.S. Southern immigration to Brazil was not the focus of his research, he wrote one chapter about the Confederados.[49] As Horne's discussion of the Confederados evolved through a contemporary U.S.-centric racial optic, he overlooks (perhaps inadvertently) the overall heterogeneity of Brazilians and of immigrants to Brazil as well as the broader agrarian and sociocultural developments happening at that time in Brazil. Moreover, he misses the hundreds of thousands of immigrants from various other nationalities who were also flocking to Brazil—and who were certainly not seeking a "white paradise"—as I later point out.[50] Last, historian Todd W. Wahlstrom recently published *The Southern Exodus to Mexico* in 2015, a book about the exodus of U.S. Southerners who went to Mexico (including white and black populations), however, his discussion naturally focused on the migration to Mexico, not Brazil.

The story of these Confederados is not new, clearly. So, what differentiates this book from past publications? Here, the synthesis of the migration of former Confederates to Brazil has been given a fresh, contemporary perspective by a geographer. This book offers a broad context by looking at the interconnecting synergies that galvanized, financed, and encouraged U.S. Southerners to migrate to Brazil. I rectify several misconceptions on the issue in this book and rely on secondary and primary sources (including original letters, documents, and newspaper articles), many of which, to the best of my knowledge, have never been used before. Furthermore, discussions on race are examined here in the specific context of Confederado migration.

The Backdrop of Race

Why another a discussion about race? The current literature on race is immensely broad and has been extensively studied in both the United States and Brazil.[51] Nonetheless, it is fitting to comparatively contextualize nineteenth-century racial politics in Brazil against that in the United States in order to understand and interpret the often convoluted narratives in this migration story.

Widespread racism was (and still is) a political reality in Brazil; statistics have clearly shown that *race matters* in Brazil as much as it does in the United States. Racism in Brazil, however, is also a paradox. While both countries were slaveholding nations, Brazil did not experience the horrors of the Ku Klux Klan, racially motivated lynchings, Jim Crow, and legal institutional segregation. Moreover, in nineteenth-century Brazil medical, law, and theological colleges as well as schools, restaurants, public transportation, and even opera houses were not segregated, in sharp contrast to the United States at that time—it is known that in Brazil then, no institutionalized distinction was made by color alone.[52] Nonetheless, it took Brazil two more decades after slavery had ended in the United States to abolish that institution.

Consequently, some scholars have unraveled the "myth of racial democracy" in Brazil to counter the widespread global perception that Brazil was a "racial paradise." For example, Abdias do Nascimento argued in 1978 that Brazil's diverse populations had developed through rape and violence over time rather than through consensual miscegenation or benign displacement.[53] Nancy Scheper-Hughes states, albeit in postmodernist jargon, that "racism is a disallowed and submerged discourse in Brazil."[54]

Hence, discussions about race are fraught with challenges, particularly when comparisons are made between Brazil and the United States at different points in time. For one, the traditional biracial approach (black/white) used in the United States to examine racial politics is problematic when applied to Brazil, especially considering the diverse varieties and nuances of Brazilian conceptions of color, which Brazilians have long used to self-identify (and with the benefit of hindsight and twenty-first-century vernacular).[55] That is, the range and variation of "colors" used in

Brazilian population surveys often do not correspond to the traditional U.S. black/white racial divide.[56] Unlike the clear-cut racial boundaries predicated by law in the United States, the existence of various "mixed" and "quasi-ethnic" groups (e.g., *caboclo, cafuzo, mameluco, ribeirinho, mulato, mestiço, pardo, caiçara*, etc.) geographically spread around Brazil may have easily confused the nineteenth-century traveler or immigrant, who may have overlooked Brazil's complex population makeup through an oversimplified black/white lens.

Furthermore, the rural peasantry in Brazil had developed into regionalized and conflated groupings that are not easily defined by U.S. racial categories, either (e.g., *caipira, forreiro, roçeiro, lavrador, matuto*).[57] Therefore, the process of examining population groups in Brazil in different regions and at different points in time merits careful attention. Brazilian populations have been historically marked by extreme heterogeneity, and using monolithic U.S. optics to examine Brazilian populations only opens the door to potential misinterpretations.

Consider that before the arrival of Europeans and African slaves, an estimated two to three million Indigenous populations were living in Brazil.[58] Hundreds of thousands of immigrants from other countries, such as Portugal, Italy, Germany, Russia, Spain, Switzerland, Belgium, Austria, and later Armenia, Japan, Syria, Turkey, and Lebanon, also migrated to Brazil throughout the nineteenth and twentieth centuries. These immigrants included Jews (e.g., Sephardic Jews from Portugal, Spain, and Morocco as well as Ashkenazi Jews from Eastern Europe) and Arabs (mostly from Syria and Lebanon). Intermarriage between these diverse populations with various hues and tones of different colors has been widespread in Brazil for decades. Miscegenation has occurred ever since Brazil was a Portuguese colony, and in the words of historian Alida C. Metcalf, it was "very much a part of the biological story of Brazil in the first half of the sixteenth century. Mixed-race and bicultural children became an integral part of the Portuguese settlements."[59] Furthermore, since 1908 hundreds of thousands of Japanese immigrants and their descendants have added to the already diverse Brazilian population—today Brazil is home to the largest Japanese community outside Japan.

Brazilian populations today reflect a mosaic of skin colors, genotypes, and phenotypes, making the country one of the most genetically diverse societies in the world—in many cases, this makes it difficult, if not impossible to distinguish who is "black" and who is "white" by using U.S.-based standards.[60] In fact, over sixty years ago anthropologists such as Charles Wagley and Marvin Harris highlighted the remarkable levels of racial heterogeneity within population groups in Brazil.[61]

Of course, populations in Brazil were not uniform simply because they were from Europe, in the same way that slave populations brought from Africa were certainly not monolithic. Likewise, geographical monikers that commonly and intuitively inform basic understandings of race and the traditional black/white divide—such as "African" and "European"—should not be interpreted in oversimplified and monolithic terms as they too often are in academic and political discussions. This is especially important because most of the world is neither simply "black" nor "white" but perhaps somewhere in between.

However, the U.S. binary racial optics currently used to discuss racialized politics has evolved in such dominating and insular ways that it is currently deployed as if it were able to make universal interpretations across the world. That is, most existing discussions of race and racism in the United States have become all but synonymous with African American "blackness."[62] Yet "whiteness" and "blackness" are political, social, and ideological terms that should be navigated and interpreted cautiously. They connote different things and meanings at different places and points in time, especially in Brazil and in the United States.

Given these considerations, I examine the topic of race here as it blurs into the narratives of nineteenth-century ideologies and religion—and as it gets disseminated later by political, religious, and scientific elites at the time—all of which eventually intersect with the Confederado migration story.

A Theoretical Backdrop

The term "push/pull factors," traditionally used to describe migration processes, can be traced to terminology used by the late-nineteenth-century geographer Ernst Georg Ravenstein, who formulated the well-known "laws of migration" theory.[63] Push factors refer to causes that drive migrants away from their place of origin; pull factors, conversely, refer to forces that attract migrants to their destinations. Ravenstein's work later influenced other migration models, such as neoclassical theory's assertions that as they make rational economic choices to maximize their benefit by migrating, migrants will search for the best place to reside in.[64]

However, more recently Stephen Castles and Mark J. Miller explain that "macro-, meso- and micro-structures are intertwined in the migratory process, and there are no clear dividing lines between them. No single cause is ever sufficient to explain why people decide to leave one country and settle in another."[65] Though based on contemporary studies and potentially open to charges of presentism, this notion is valuable here—albeit applied to a mid-nineteenth-century context. Multiple kinship, agrarian, ideological, religious, commercial, and political forces emerge in the Confederado migration process, in which several push and pull factors intertwine against the backdrop of global capitalism. Given the complexity of these various factors, the Confederado decision-making process should not be reduced to any single reason that explains their migration enterprise in Brazil. Examining Confederado migration therefore involves broad methodologies that reflect interconnections at the micro and macro levels.

Confederados inhabited in-betwixt and in-between dimensions, living in two places at the same time. They were tied to two cultures—U.S. Southern and Brazilian, for example—transitioned between them, and maintained complex connections between the U.S. South, the United States, and Brazil. As Judith MacKnight Jones explains, the Confederados "came to live in two worlds at the same time, serving as a binding element between them."[66]

Confederados also brought their own distinctive cultural traits of the time to Brazil. It is also important to understand the vernacular used by politicians, Protestant leaders (such as Reverends Dunn, Fletcher, and Kidder), and scientists of the day (such as Louis Agassiz, Matthew F.

Maury, and Arthur de Gobineau) to forge and disseminate a worldview of human hierarchies that informed much of the "culture of the times."[67]

Place Matters

We should also look at the concept of place more carefully. In *Topophilia* (1974), geographer Yi-Fu Tuan explains how place is shaped by human activity and meaning, giving it emotional value. The concept of place is imbued with symbolic and human emotional attachments—the location at the cemetery at Campo takes on a powerful symbolic meaning as a site of pious pilgrimage and reunions for Confederado descendants, creating a sense of place. In this way, over time, place is produced, shaped, and transformed by Confederado immigrants, who insert their own syncretic cultural meanings and imprints into Brazil.

Moreover, as geographer Tim Creswell points out, "places are neither totally material nor completely mental; they are combinations of the material and mental and cannot be reduced to either." Creswell clarifies: "A church, for instance, is a place. It is neither just a particular material artifact, nor just a set of religious ideas; it is always both." Applying the abovementioned notions of place to this migration story proves fruitful, as this book shows. However, understanding and interpreting the symbolic meanings at different places and times in any migration process requires carefully navigating a sea of multiple temporal and cultural complexes. This is because "places are duplicitous in that they cannot be reduced to the concrete or the 'merely ideological;' rather they display an uneasy and fluid tension between them."[68] Interpretations of place therefore offer ample, wide-reaching views on the lingering relationships and tensions between an immigrant's places of origin (the U.S. South) and destination (Brazil).

The making of place also emerges from the process of the geographical imagination. In this case, "imagining" often elicits ideas about place(s) that are built upon sociocultural constructions. That is, imagining can bring strong emotional sentimentalism into perceptions commonly held in popular culture. For example, the imagining of the romanticized and glorified antebellum U.S. South in *Gone with the Wind* (a

Metro-Goldwyn-Mayer classic film released in 1939, itself an adaptation of Margaret Mitchell's novel of the same title) is but one of many examples found in popular culture that has portrayed and eulogized archetypical and imagined U.S. Southern communities, calcifying them in a world of "cavaliers" and "cotton fields" and rendering them as "no more than a dream to be remembered ... A Civilization gone with the wind."[69]

D. W. Griffith's *Birth of a Nation*, released in 1915, offers another example of the geographical imagination's strong role in the racist construction of nationhood. The film had widely popularized myths by reimagining the U.S. South, tapping into new kinds of racialized fears and anxieties through the criminalization of U.S. black populations. Consequently, the film also helped to popularize the reemergence of the Ku Klux Klan and its justification: the need to restore order because of the perceived threat and fear of black populations.[70]

Moreover, Benedict Anderson articulates in *Imagined Communities* (1983) that nations, as political communities, are "imagined"—most individuals of any nation will never meet every other individual from that same nation (as they would in a community). John Kirtland Wright observes, speaking on the geographical imagination in his presidential address to the Association of American Geographers in 1947, "The entire earth appears as an immense patchwork of miniature *terrae incognitae*. Even if an area were to be minutely mapped and studied by an army of microgeographers, much about its geography would always remain unknown, and, hence, if there is no *terra incognita* today in an absolute sense, so also no *terra* absolutely *cognita*."[71] These theoretical underpinnings of place—and by implication, the interactions of adaptation, changes, or transformations of and within place—are essential elements to understanding the multifaceted dimensions of the migration process. I have therefore framed the focus of this project in the tradition of geographical inquiry, using multi- and interdisciplinary approaches.

Confederado Contributions

The examination of contributions made by immigrants is an integral component of most migration studies. Here, I intend to situate the contributions of Confederados within the broader literature of Brazilian and migration studies. However, this examination should be approached carefully, and several clarifications need to be made at the outset. First, Confederados did not introduce cotton to Brazil, although this is a common misconception. Wild cotton (*Gossypium mustelinum*) is native to Brazil and already had been cultivated and used for centuries by Indigenous populations in Brazil. Furthermore, Brazil had been the largest exporter of cotton to Europe from the mid-eighteenth century up to the early nineteenth century—long before the arrival of Confederados in Brazil.

Second, William Hutchinson Norris was not the "founder" of Americana or Santa Bárbara—again, a claim often made. Norris was one of the first Confederado "settlers" in Santa Bárbara, which was already a small rural village at the time of his arrival.

Third, Americana is a separate political entity from Santa Bárbara, though the two are frequently mistaken for each other. The Confederado cemetery and grounds at Campo are in Santa Bárbara, not Americana. Yet Americana (or Villa Americana) tends to receive popular attention; perhaps because of its namesake, it is commonly viewed as the "city founded by Americans." However, before Americana gained its name, it was just a railway station, Villa da Estação de Santa Bárbara, about six miles from the village of Santa Bárbara. It was only much later in 1924 that it became an official municipality, known as Villa dos Americanos (Village of the Americans)—so named by locals because of the numerous American families that lived in the area. Moreover, it was only in 1938 that its official name changed to "Americana." Today Santa Bárbara and Americana are neighboring municipalities.

Fourth, past publications have tended to disproportionately glorify the arrival of Confederados in Brazil with a romanticized sentimentalism, particularly in the eyes of Confederado descendants. This has greatly mythologized a few Confederado contributions to Brazil, resulting in claims that turn out to be either misleading or untrue.

Another common predicament in the literature available is the tendency to view U.S. Southern migration to Brazil in isolation: as an isolated event divorced from broader global events and commercial, political, and sociocultural contexts, or one separated from other migration patterns that were also occurring at the same time. For example, U.S. Southern immigration to Brazil was miniscule compared to the massive influx of immigrants to Brazil from other countries—for example, Italy, Portugal, and Germany—who were flocking to the same regions in the interior of São Paulo or the southern provinces. These immigrants also brought with them to Brazil their agricultural and technological expertise. The synergies and confluences that merged with other immigrants living in proximity, in conjunction with the Confederados, help to explain the diffusion of various agricultural and domestic items at that time in Brazil. Therefore, other immigrants to Brazil, along with Confederados, collectively helped to popularize and disseminate the use of domestic items as well as agricultural implements and methods, particularly in the southeast and south regions of Brazil.

For example, Krähenbühl, a local manufacturer started by a Swiss immigrant, accelerated the spread of wagon use, and the spread of the steel-tipped plow is attributed to a manufacturing company started by John Domm, a Dutchman who had lived in Texas and come to Santa Bárbara with the Confederados.[72] However, many sources available commonly credit these advents to Confederados alone without references to European immigrants in the region, who played a role in not only the manufacturing of these items but also their diffusion. Once Confederados had established themselves in Brazil, they evidently played an important role in promoting and disseminating the use of agricultural implements and domestic items (especially in the vicinity of Santa Bárbara); nonetheless, they did not *introduce* these to Brazil.

Other misleading claims made in past publications, such as the claim that Confederados introduced kerosene lamps, sewing machines, and common plows to Brazil, need to be rectified here. As early as 1854 (more than a decade before the arrival of Confederados in Brazil) Brazilian newspapers such as *Jornal do commercio* and *O commercio* (both in Rio de Janeiro) had been publishing frequent advertisements for kerosene lamps, sewing machines, and plows, including cotton gins (*machinas de descaroçar algodão*; Eagle cotton gin)—these were advertised as "North American items" (*generos norte-americanos*).⁷³ In addition, in 1856 José da Maia gained a patented license in Rio de Janeiro to manufacture and sell his own cotton gin as well as to import foreign-made cotton gins.⁷⁴ Kerosene lamps, sewing machines, and plows were already known items commercially available in Brazil before Confederados arrived in that country.

Moving on, I aim to provide a brief and objective overview of Confederado contributions to Brazil, albeit without unwittingly or capriciously glorifying them by trumpeting all their achievements.

In terms of their agricultural contributions, the dissemination of the "Georgia watermelon" and pecans (*noz pecã*) in Santa Bárbara have been attributed to Confederados.⁷⁵ Joe Whittaker ("Uncle Joe") is said to have brought the first seeds of the "Georgia rattlesnake Watermelon" (*cascavel da Geórgia*) to Brazil in the 1870s.⁷⁶ By 1909 Santa Bárbara was responsible for half of the state of São Paulo's watermelon production.⁷⁷ Today these fruits are known as Santa Bárbara watermelons (*melancias de Santa Bárbara*).⁷⁸

In 1869 the newspaper *Correio Paulistano* reported on the new thriving agricultural Confederado settlement in Santa Bárbara, and *O diário do Rio de Janeiro* reprinted the report, speaking "very favorably of the tobacco produced by the Confederates settled near Santa Bárbara, S. Paulo, and pronounce[d] the cigars made by them to be equal to those of Bahia." Local agriculturalists would eventually flock to Santa Bárbara and neighboring towns to learn agricultural technologies and methods disseminated and taught by Confederados and their descendants. For example, the Escola de Agricultura de Piracicaba (Agricultural School of Piracicaba) held demonstrations of their agricultural knowledge, and the Instituto Agrícola de Campinas (Agricultural Institute of Campinas) maintained close ties to Santa Bárbara agriculturalists.⁷⁹ These agricultural technologies and methods, taught by Confederados and their descendants, mostly remained concentrated within the interior of São Paulo. For example, a dispatch in *O diário de S. Paulo* in 1872 deliberated the lag in agriculture throughout Brazil and highlighted how Santa Bárbara had been flourishing because of agriculture and the impact of *norte-americanos* (a reference to the Confederado settlement there).⁸⁰

Confederados also brought new crops such as sweet potatoes and newly introduced pig breeds to Brazil.[81] Settlers in Santa Bárbara initially grew mostly corn, cotton, tobacco, and sugarcane, and eventually many of the second generation became successful medical doctors and dentists. The first dentists and medical professionals in Santa Bárbara were Confederado descendants and were often advertised as *dentista Americanos* (American dentists).[82]

Some cultural facets in the interior of São Paulo (Oeste Paulista) can be traced to Confederado influence. The marked spoken Portuguese accent of the interior Paulista region is likely to have been influenced by the Confederados—take, for example, the inflection of the *r* in *porta* (door) or *maior* (greater), also known as the *r caipira* (countrified *r*).[83] In her study on American–Brazilian English (and the language spoken by Confederados and their descendants), Regina Del Negri Medeiros states, "Lexical interference is of two kinds. First, a Portuguese word that is similar in form to its English equivalent may be substituted for it, for example, *simplesmente* for *simply*. Second, Brazilian Portuguese words for things newly encountered by the Confederate immigrants or for things perceived as characteristically Brazilian were freely borrowed: farinha 'a kind of flour,' triste 'sad,' alegria 'happiness,' caboclo 'mestizo,' roça 'countryside,' camarada 'fellow,' fazenda 'ranch.'"[84]

Two Confederado contributions (perhaps among the most salient) to Brazil were the introduction and development of multiple "American schools" and the proliferation of Protestantism. On this note, Confederado women merit special attention. They were instrumental in introducing U.S. pedagogical methods to Brazil as well as preserving a written record of their trajectories to Brazil. Moreover, Confederado women also spread the importance of literary value and education, common principles in the Presbyterian and Methodist traditions; they became educators and directors at schools such as the Colégio Americano in Campinas, Colégio Piracicabano in Piracicaba, and Colégio Bennett in Rio, all still operating today. These American schools in Brazil introduced innovative U.S. pedagogical methods.

The American Methodists founded their first school in Brazil in 1881:

the Colégio Piracicabano, an extension of the Newman sister's school (founded in 1879). One of the first students at this school was Pedro Morais Barros, a nephew of Prudente de Morais, former President of Brazil (1894–98), and Governor of the state of São Paulo (1889–90).[85] The former Brazilian president's niece, Ana Maria Morais (daughter of Manoel Morais de Barros) was also a student there—at a time when school enrollment for female pupils was extremely rare in Brazil.[86] In addition, the children of Prudente de Morais and his wife, Adelaide Benvinda da Silva Gordo de Morais Barros, daughter of a prominent landowning family from São Paulo, also attended the Colégio Piracicabano. This school thrived largely due to the efforts of its director, Martha Hite Watts of Kentucky, a missionary and educator who went on to open other U.S. Methodist schools in Brazil such as the Colégio Americano in Petrópolis (Rio) and Colégio Izabela Hendrix in Belo Horizonte (Minas Gerais). The Methodist Church in Brazil "was destined to take its place as one of the prominent evangelical churches in the country."[87] The Confederados were the first organized immigrant group to establish Protestant churches rooted in Brazil (see chapter 5).

The legacy of the Confederados continued in the twentieth century through Brazilian popular music. For example, one of Brazil's most popular singers in the 1920s and 1930s, Elsie Houston, was the great-grandniece of Sam Houston (senator for the state of Texas in 1845 and Texas governor in 1859). Moreover, Brazil's legendary rock icon Rita Lee (Rita Lee Jones, vocalist from the renowned 1960s Brazilian band Os Mutantes) is the daughter of Confederado descendant Charles Fenley Jones. Her uncle Leonard Yancey Jones (named after William Lowndes Yancey, one of the leaders of the U.S. Southern secession movement) founded the Public Radio of São Paulo. Rita Lee Jones is the great-granddaughter of Robert Cicero Norris, the son of William Hutchinson Norris and Mary Black.[88]

Today the region of Santa Bárbara is nestled in São Paulo's polycentric urbanized area (also known as a conurbation). The thriving textile and agroindustrial cluster formed by Santa Bárbara, Piracicaba, Tietê, Sorocaba, Rio Claro, Limeira, Sumaré, Americana, Nova Odessa, and

Capivari (in the interior of the state of São Paulo) emerged as a result of Confederado settlements, elite Brazilian agriculturalists and their interrelated family clans, and European immigrants, which collectively helped give rise to an evolving, prosperous region. These cities form a conurbation known as the Expanded Metropolitan Complex, or Macrometropolis (Complexo Metropolitano Expandido / Macrometrópole), an urbanized corridor spanning the port of Santos on the southeastern Atlantic coast and the greater São Paulo metropolitan area, straddled by São José dos Campos to the east and Sorocaba to its northwest. Forging farther into the interior, one reaches Jundiaí and Campinas and Piracicaba lies to the northwest. Altogether, this area has become one of the most populated agglomerations in the world today.

Geographical Backdrop

It is also important to consider, at least briefly, the significance of Brazil's diverse physical geography and the nation's immense territory. Soil types, climates, and topographies vary tremendously in each region in Brazil, considerations that help to explain, at least partially, the success or failure of certain crop cultivations in different Confederado settlements. Brazil's territory is slightly larger than that of the continental United States; measured from the country's territorial extremities, Brazil's east–west axis extends about 2,689 miles and its north–south axis about 2,684 miles; both axes are virtually equidistant.

Brazil, as well as the rest of the South American continent, lies slightly to the southeast of the North American continent. For example, the city of São Paulo is about 621 miles closer to Miami, Florida (4,016 miles), than it is to Mexico City, Mexico (4,562 miles). Brazil is also closer to Africa than it is to a few of its South American neighbors. For example, the easternmost point of Brazil is closer to Guinea-Bissau (on the west coast of Africa) than it is to the westernmost coast of Peru. Most of Brazil is characterized by tropical, semihumid, or subtropical climates. The northeast region's climates range from equatorial to semiarid (in the dry interior *caatinga* region) and tropical (central and southern Bahia). The temperate southernmost regions of Brazil experience frost in the winter at times, but—very rarely—light snow only occurs in its southernmost extremities.[89] Each of Brazil's five regions (north, south, southeast, northeast, and center west) are subject to a wide and extreme array of differences in climate, vegetation, fauna, and soil type. The regional contexts of each of the five major Confederado settlements are located in the following four regions: São Paulo and Espírito Santo in the southeast, Paraná in the south, and Pará in the north (discussed in chapter 2).

For example, Santarém—tucked away in the northern region and located just slightly south of the Equator line—is engulfed by the humidity of the colossal Amazon rainforest. This was where Maj. Lansford W. Hastings established his Confederado settlement, 500 miles away from the closest cities of Manaus (to the east) and Belém (to the west). While average annual temperatures remain at about 82 degrees Fahrenheit, humidity levels run at an average of 80 or 90 percent. The Santarém settlement was worlds away from the rolling hillsides of the Santa Bárbara Confederado settlement in the interior of western São Paulo. Santa Bárbara is just 86 miles away from the city of São Paulo and 31 miles from Campinas. At about 1,968 feet above sea level, with annual average temperatures of about 72 degrees Fahrenheit, the area virtually sits on the Tropic of Capricorn. The elevation in Americana and Santa Bárbara is only about 1,867 feet above sea level, and the land is characterized by sedimentary and igneous rock, which produces fertile soil, in sharp contrast to the soil types, geomorphology, and vegetation of the other Confederado settlement sites.[90]

The Confederado clusters that emerged in Linhares (in the province of Espírito Santo), Cananéia, and Iguape (in the province of São Paulo) were located in regions characterized by coastal, lowland areas, generally with poor soils for cotton and agriculture (with the exception of rice and tobacco cultivation). Altogether, these geographical factors add to the sociopolitical and ideological dimensions discussed later in this book, and they deserve brief consideration here so we can understand the success, challenges, or ultimate demise of each Confederado settlement.

Chapter Overview

Chapter 1 of this book examines the importance of Baltimore, Baltimorean entrepreneurs, and the latter's trade and kinship relationships with Brazil and Brazilians. Chapter 2 examines the move to and within Brazil, the settlements, and immigration agents who were active stakeholders in the migration project. Chapter 3 focuses on the agricultural, economic, and labor circumstances and contexts in Brazil. The end of the U.S. Civil War was the catalyst for the decision-making process to move to Brazil. Conversely, Brazil was interested in welcoming Southern immigrants to bolster its agricultural base. Chapter 4 underlines the importance of selected scientists and writers who disseminated ideologies of the time—here, the dimension of race is explored cautiously. Chapter 5 highlights the importance of the proselytization of Protestantism in Brazil, the town of Santa Bárbara, and the Confederado cemetery at Campo. I have also included a discussion on the surmising Freemason influence and its connection to this migration story, as evident in the photographs of tombstones at Campo.

So, why Brazil? How did Brazilian immigration policies play a role in attracting Southerners? How were Baltimoreans involved? How did trade relationships between Brazil and the United States at the time promote the migration enterprise? In what ways were networks, institutions, individuals, and communities involved? What were the concerns voiced in the U.S. press about the U.S. Southern exodus? The following chapters address these questions.

1

The Baltimore Connection

On March 25, 2018, Baltimore celebrated the passage of 150 years since the arrival of its first German immigrants. In 1868, the same year several thousand U.S. Southerners arrived in Brazil, 141 German passengers aboard the SS *Baltimore* arrived in Baltimore, marking the first of another 1.2 million immigrants who arrived between 1868 and 1914 at Locust Point, the "Ellis Island" of Baltimore. The Baltimore and Ohio (B&O) Railroad and the North German Lloyd Co. partnered to consolidate this migration flow in order "to build the immigration pier and connect it to its railway system. Lloyd Co. would send ships of immigrants to Baltimore at least monthly."[1] Among those consolidations was an association with James Birckhead, the largest Baltimorean shipping merchant in Brazil during the 1820s and 1830s and the son of Solomon Birckhead, who had helped found the Union Bank of Maryland and the B&O Railroad.[2]

Here important interconnections forged into a systematic coordination between Baltimorean railway and shipping companies and Baltimorean mercantile families. Together, they situated themselves in optimal political and financial positions by bringing more laborers to build new industrial projects, such as the building of railroads and ships, effectively turning immigration into a viably profitable enterprise. It was a schematized conglomerate with various stakeholders at hand. As we shall see, similar schemes developed in Brazil with the Confederado migration, with comparably connected stakeholders.

Despite the existence of the Protestant "English Cemetery" in Gamboa, Rio de Janeiro, an increased concern for the lack of burial grounds for U.S. citizens living in Rio emerged in the mid-nineteenth century. This concern developed because at that time, only Catholics could be buried in Brazilian public cemeteries. The *New York Times* reported in 1860 that Robert Clinton Wright had maintained a close relationship with the Brazilian government and with Dom Pedro II, as the U.S. Consulate in Rio had organized the "National Benevolent Society" to help fund the purchase of a burying place and relieve fellow U.S.-born citizens "by money and otherwise."[3] Maj. Andrew Ellison Jr. (chief engineer of the Dom Pedro Segundo Railroad) nominated Robert Clinton Wright as temporary chairman.[4] Ostensibly, Wright must have anticipated an immigration influx and laid the groundwork for future large-scale American immigration to Brazil. This endeavor shows the type of political power that the Wright family members held in Rio. These networks, as we shall see later, supported and facilitated the mobility of U.S. Southerners within Brazil.

Baltimorean entrepreneurs were already well-established in Brazil by the end of the U.S. Civil War through the kinship, social, and commercial ties they had created with Brazilian politicians and elite families since the 1820s. The Wright family members of the firm Maxwell, Wright & Co. resided and worked in two countries at the same time, working for a firm that was both Brazilian and American. Furthermore, Baltimoreans had invested capital into Brazilian-owned companies while playing vital roles within the Atlantic mercantile world.[5] They also provided the key Brazilian contacts and trade knowledge necessary to sustain a migration of such a large scale. That is, the milieu of Confederate migration to Brazil did not occur in a vacuum; as John Majewski and Todd W. Wahlstrom point out, "the antebellum and postbellum South were enmeshed in the nineteenth century global economy."[6] In addition, the salience of trade and commerce between the two countries provided an ideal backdrop for U.S. Southern agriculturalists who became attracted to the economics of agrarian prospects in Brazil. An examination of mobile U.S. Southern families in the nineteenth century can be constructed through the lens of agrarian capitalism. To understand why and how Baltimore developed strong and reciprocal relationships with Brazil, a description of the commercial backdrop that existed then is needed.

When Baltimoreans Arrived in Rio

As early as the 1820s the first U.S. imports had flooded Brazilian markets. In 1823 Maxwell, Wright and Co. published a pamphlet reporting that sixty-two U.S. commercial vessels had arrived at the port of Rio de Janeiro, and by 1829 that figure had increased to 125 vessels. By 1839, the number of U.S. vessel arrivals had increased to 151.[7] Typical exports from Baltimore to Brazil included breadstuffs, tea, whale oil, lumber, and salts; typical imports to Baltimore consisted of coffee, sugar, and hides. In addition, the list of goods suitable for market in Rio also included silks, linen, cotton, hardware, beef, pork, hams, wheat, cheese, codfish, peppers, cloves, cinnamon, and, especially, wheat flour (Gallego, Rutherford, and Haxall-Crenshaw brands). On January 13, 1838, a shipment to Rio consigned by Maxwell, Wright & Co. consisted of two hundred barrels of "Super flour"; seventy-eight bags of coffee (160 pounds each) were then exported back to Baltimore.[8] Rio de Janeiro was Brazil's capital city and the largest city in South America at that time. By the 1840s and throughout the 1850s, with a growing urban population, Rio had become the world's major importer of U.S. wheat flour from Baltimore (91 percent of imported flour was supplied by Maryland and Virginia mills during the 1850s).[9]

The demand for imported flour from Baltimore increased as the population of Rio grew. Rio's population increased almost fivefold in a period of fifty years, from 451,648 in 1823 (Brazil's total population that year was estimated at 3,960,866) to 2,030,735 in 1872 (Brazil's total population that year was 9,930,478).[10]

On the other hand, Baltimore was a city long associated with maritime trade. As David Schley explains, "as early as the 1750s wheat farmers from northern and western Maryland sent their produce to Baltimore for shipment to markets in Europe and the West Indies."[11] Baltimore was also recognized for its advantageous proximity to the wheat regions and milling industries of Maryland and Virginia, as well as its well-known nineteenth-century "Baltimore clippers" (fast schooner-rigged vessels that sailed closer to the wind, which also allowed them to escape privateers).[12] In the words of Francis F. Beirne, "the clipper was 'streamlined' to cut through the water much as a present-day automobile is streamlined to reduce air resistance."[13] The first Baltimore clippers appeared at a time when vessels were in demand to run the British Blockade during the War of 1812, and the speed of the world-renowned Baltimore-built vessels contributed to Baltimore's growth in international trade, particularly with Brazil.[14]

Baltimore's location offered several commercial advantages: "(1) Its proximity to the wheat region of Western Virginia; (2) its extensive milling industry; (3) its proximity to the foreign markets; (4) the famous 'Baltimore clipper;' and (5) its spirit of enterprise."[15] Situated near six streams close to the city, Baltimore offered a notable supply of motive waterpower, and by 1825, there were sixty mills within twenty miles of Baltimore.[16] By 1844 Baltimore millers had established the new Patapsco Extra brand of flour, which became the standard in Brazil.[17] Throughout the 1840s, except for 1844 and 1847, Baltimore exported more wheat flour to Brazil than any other port in the United States.[18] New Orleans flour was unacceptable for the Brazilian market.[19]

As far back as 1838 John M. Baker—former U.S. consul to Brazil, writing under the auspices of the U.S. Office of Democratic Review, Washington DC—had already described how the flour trade reflected the bulk of exports to Brazil while U.S. vessels returned with coffee, thus confirming the vital commercial reciprocity between Rio and Baltimore.[20] Over half a century later in 1892 the Merchants and Manufacturers Association in Baltimore published a book in Portuguese, *A reciprocidade commercial: Baltimore e Brazil* (The commercial reciprocity: Baltimore and Brazil), which likewise focused on the strong and ongoing commercial reciprocity between Baltimore and Brazil; the book was evidently published for Brazilian readers. Baltimore had been promoted as a vital port city with a "friendly population," commercial advantages, and superior manufacturing goods (a commercial reciprocity with Brazil that had been established for more than sixty years by that time). As Dauril Alden explains, manioc flour made in Brazil "was commonly disdained by the elites as fit only for slaves and other common folk."[21] Consequently, Maryland wheat flour was in high demand in Brazil, and no flour was superior to the flour produced by Maryland mills and exported via Baltimore ports.

Furthermore, the distance between Baltimore and Rio was forty-eight hours closer by sailing vessel than New York was to Rio, which provided commercial trade advantages (and steamers were more expensive than sailing vessels).[22] The duration of an average trip on a sailing vessel from Baltimore to Rio was eventually cut by half, from seventy to eighty days to an average of between thirty-five to forty days.[23] With his new navigational ocean current charts, Matthew Fontaine Maury (see chapter 4) took credit for the reduction in this trip's duration. Maury's obituary read, "By following Maury's directions, a barque early in 1848 on its trip made the voyage in 35 days and returned in 40 days"—"Maury was able to write that by 1851 he had more than one thousand ships in all the oceans observing for him."[24]

Rio had also become a well-known port to Americans by the mid-1800s. At that time thousands of Americans from the eastern part of the country who went to California during the Gold Rush (1848–49) would have traveled the fifteen-thousand-mile trip southward, around Cape Horn. This voyage had been transformed into a busy navigational passage far more traveled then than it is today—there was no railroad system connecting the east and west coasts of the United States at the time. As a result, the population of California swelled from fourteen thousand in 1849 to a quarter of a million in 1852. The average voyage around the Cape was 180 days, although many ships made it in 110 days.[25] Nonetheless, it was the fastest and safest way to travel from one coast to the other before the Panama Canal was built and before the extension of U.S. railway systems connected the east and west coasts. Passengers from the United States traveling to California would have stopped in Rio on the way. North Americans who had ported in Rio at that time frequently described their surprise or shock as they took notice of the number of African slaves and miscegenated people observed walking around in that city (several of those Americans were from northeastern cities, and many were unfamiliar with the institution of slavery and miscegenated populations).[26]

Trade and Commerce in Rio

With the transference of the Portuguese royal family to Brazil in 1808 due to the Napoleonic wars, demand for foreign goods increased. Subsequently, reciprocal trade between Baltimore and Rio increased. In 1827 flour from Baltimore represented 71 percent of total U.S. exports to Brazil, increasing slightly in 1858 to 75 percent.[27] Furthermore, with the *carta regia* in 1808, the Prince Regent at that time, Dom João VI, had opened the ports of Brazil to world commerce. Beforehand, foreign commerce and any foreign interaction on Brazilian territory were prohibited, a strict policy compared to Japan's and China's at the time.[28]

Several publications between the late 1820s and the late nineteenth century promoted and described this dynamic and profitable commercial relationship between Baltimore and Rio.[29] Among the top coffee importers from Brazil, for example, Maxwell, Wright & Co. was by far importing the most coffee from Brazil between 1845 and 1847 (followed by the firms James Birckhead, Phipps Irmãos, and Coleman Hutton & Co.).[30] On this list is the aforementioned James Birckhead, a Baltimorean closely associated with members of Maxwell, Wright & Co. By 1834, coffee imports accounted for more than ninety percent of the total imports from Rio to Baltimore.[31]

Most firms that operated internationally during that time had their headquarters in one place and one or several branches elsewhere. This structure is reflected in the names of those entities, which varied slightly from one to the other. The Phipps companies are a good example, with headquarters in Liverpool ("Phipps & Co."), a branch in Rio ("Phipps Brothers & Co.," "Phipps, Brothers & Co," or "Phipps Irmãos"), and another in New York and New Orleans ("J. L. Phipps & Co."). For example, "when communications from J. L. Phipps & Co. and from Phipps & Co. are sent to Phipps Brothers & Co. in the same telegram, the communication from J. L. Phipps & Co. will be completed before that from Phipps & Co. is begun."[32] Another example is Coleman, Hutton, and Co., also the "English House" of Coleman and Co. of Rio de Janeiro.

In contrast, Maxwell, Wright & Co. had coequal branches that used the same name in Baltimore and Rio rather than having a headquarters–branches structure; one could argue that Rio was the de facto headquarters and that "the House [was] never to be left without one American partner at Rio de Janeiro."[33] Yet no provision was made for a Brazilian partner at the Baltimore branch. Note how the reference to "House" is singular instead of "the houses and its branches." Hence, referring to Maxwell, Wright & Co. as an American company raises questions and is problematic—the firm was both American and Brazilian (in modern vernacular, transnationalism exemplified).

Financing Trade

The house of Brown Bros. & Co. held a prominent role as a vital antebellum importer in Baltimore.[34] Brown Bros. & Co. financed Maxwell, Wright & Co. with the latter's importing business, as the former "drew bills under two clean, revolving lines of credit . . . which were fully secured by U.S. government bonds." In this case, "at Rio's main customs warehouse, Maxwell, Wright [& Co.] sold the flour to local brokers for Brazilian mil-reis and used that currency to buy coffee, which they sold in Baltimore to westbound merchants in exchange for either U.S. currency or more bills of exchange." Thus, Maxwell, Wright & Co. "used the credit lines to assist some of their customers in financing shipments to Baltimore and other American ports. Whenever the Browns received reimbursement for a bill drawn under the credits, the line was automatically reopened to the extent of the reimbursement. The lines were renewed every fall for the next calendar year and were subject to renegotiation at that time. Graham handled the account for the firm because the Wright's chief American agent resided in Baltimore."[35] Moreover, through his Baltimorean connections, William H. Graham (son-in-law of Brown Bros. & Co. founder George Brown) was closely associated with members of the Wright family; the Baltimore agency of Brown Bros.

& Co. was therefore able to facilitate the financing of Maxwell, Wright & Co. without any difficulty, through the issuance of letters of credit.[36] For example, "a Baltimore merchant could open a letter of credit . . . purchase merchandise almost anywhere in the world, send his cargo to any major American port for sale, settle his account with any Brown office that was convenient, and, finally, have his drafts accepted and paid in Liverpool."[37] Hence, Maxwell, Wright & Co. were able to not only finance but also establish and expand their global trade and commercial networks, facilitated through their Baltimorean connections and letters of credit issued through Brown, Bros. & Co.

In a publication in 1873, an advertisement for Alexander Brown and Sons (established in 1811 and a forerunner of Brown Bros. & Co.) read: "Bills of exchange on Great Britain and Ireland, commercial and traveling credit issued available in any part of the World. Telegraphic transfers of money made to and from London and Liverpool. Advances made on cotton and other produce."[38] In 1870 George Brown's son, George Stewart Brown, went to Rio to become partner in Wright, Brown & Co., which took over Wright & Co. (a spin-off from Maxwell, Wright & Co.). Ten years later the firm was dissolved after Brown returned to Baltimore to resume a position with Brown, Bros. & Co.[39]

Baltimorean merchant James Birckhead (1792–1870), sometimes referred to as "Diogo," "Gabriel," or "Jaimes" (variations of "James") in Brazilian archival records, was a member of Rio's nine-member committee on international commerce: the Praça do Comércio commission. He owned the most successful U.S. commercial house in Rio in the 1820s. An example of this success: "of the 80 U.S. ships embarking in Rio in 1827, 50 were consigned to Birckhead."[40] While James Birckhead headed the company's operations in Rio, his brother Hugh Birckhead oversaw business at the Baltimore branch. James Birckhead's wife, Elizabeth Hunter Birckhead, was the daughter of William Hunter of Rhode Island, former U.S. Minister to Brazil (1839–45). The Birckhead family eventually returned to the United States by the end of the 1840s. William Henry DeCourcy (W. H. D. C.) Wright was close with the Birckheads and had been in direct communication with James Birckhead through frequent letters while Wright was still U.S. consul in Rio, highlighting the strong personal and commercial connections among Baltimoreans in Rio.[41]

Thus, Baltimorean entrepreneurs emerged as major exporters of flour to Brazil and major importers of Brazilian coffee to the United States. They were inherently inserted in this mid-nineteenth-century Atlantic mercantile trade network. By maintaining close ties with Brazilian social and political elites, they developed the necessary knowledge, political capital, and influence needed to aid U.S. Southerners later in their quest for a new home in Brazil after the U.S. Civil War.

The Impact of Trade and Commerce on Brazilian and U.S. Physical Landscapes

The growth of the U.S. flour export market to Rio dramatically transformed physical landscapes in Maryland. Farmers had replaced tobacco for wheat by that time, and even the most extensive wheat farms on the Eastern Shore had begun to specialize in producing a white wheat brand that did not discolor.[42] This trade relationship between Baltimore and Rio grew to the point that farmers and millers specifically produced their goods to cater to the Rio market.[43] The wheat flour from Maryland mills was particularly desirable by bakers in Rio; as Daniel Rood explains, it "yielded more bread per pound flour since it absorbed more water during baking." Maryland wheat flour contained more gluten, had less water, and would not rot as easily as other northern varieties during the long trip to Brazil and in the humid tropical Brazilian climate.[44]

The large number of Portuguese immigrants living in Rio helped to spread the taste for the "French style" bread made by the French "Rolland baking system," and consumption of flour increased almost threefold in a twenty-year period between the 1830s and 1850s.[45]

In 1831 Maxwell, Wright & Co. dispatched a report in the *American and Commercial Daily Advertiser* stating that ships from Norfolk, Virginia, and Baltimore, Maryland, had arrived in Rio with forty thousand barrels of flour—about six months' supply for Rio bakers.[46] Ten years later Rio consumed between a hundred thousand to two hundred thousand barrels of flour annually.[47]

However, wheat flour was highly perishable; G. Terry Sharrer points out that "of all the major commodities that entered into the Atlantic trade during the early nineteenth century, wheat flour was the most perishable."[48] As a result, the merchant millers of Maryland formed a unique enterprise to troubleshoot this problem. They engaged in selling as well as manufacturing flour, and used a special handling process when drying flour that allowed the flour to last from eight months to a year in tropical climates.[49] This drying process was introduced by Nathan Tyson around 1830, to keep flour merchantable up to eight months. Sharrer explains that manufacturers and merchant millers "could provide the full extent of special handling necessary for trading flour to the most distant markets." Hence, "between 1783 and 1830 the merchant-millers perhaps more than any others provided the necessary elements for Baltimore's growth."[50]

The Patapsco brand was a high-quality wheat flour, known for U.S. domestic "family use," and the strong grade flour, such as the so-called "Rio" brands (e.g., Mount Vernon), was used for foreign trade and better known for its duration on long voyages.[51] For example, an advertisement that ran in 1873 for W. M. E. Woodyear and Co. Merchant Millers read, "'Mount Vernon' Extra Flour High Grade. Suitable for shipping to the Tropics."[52]

The first known flourmill, in the United States—Patapsco—was completed in 1774 in Ellicott City, Maryland (the first mill operated by steam in the country was the Phoenix Mill in 1776).[53] In 1799 Baltimore had 50 merchant mills within an eighteen-mile radius of the city. By 1860 there were 424 flourmills in Maryland.[54] As Sharrer points out, Maryland-owned firms such as the Ellicott Company "owned several mills near Baltimore and in Virginia, operated wagon and shipping lines, maintained warehouses and wharves at Baltimore harbor, and carried on an export business within [their] own network of commercial connections."[55] Moreover, the Ellicotts, a Quaker family and part of the Quaker entrepreneurs of Maryland—such as the McKims and Tysons, who sought to bring railroads to their mills or docks[56]—were "investors and directors of Baltimore's banks, insurance companies, shipping lines, and railroads."⁵⁷ The Tysons and Ellicotts joined forces, becoming a powerful Maryland family clan. Nathan Tyson married Martha Ellicott in 1815, and their son James Ellicott Tyson became a ship owner and well-known exporter of flour. Ellicott City, Maryland, is named after the family. Their business model, in which no distinction is made between entrepreneur, manufacturer, wholesaler, and retailer, was typical of 1850s Baltimore.⁵⁸

Flour milling in Baltimore helped with the city's growing economic development, as "flour milling was what preceded and conditioned the growth of Baltimore's economy for the generations that followed the Civil War."⁵⁹ Therefore, physical landscapes in Maryland were shaped by cultural mores of the times, with the increasing demand from urban bread consumers in Rio. Conversely, new Brazilian coffee plantations in the provinces of Rio de Janeiro and São Paulo were being shaped by the high demand for the new and growing American taste for coffee, as Americans became the largest consumers of coffee in the world.⁶⁰

In addition to the reciprocal flour–coffee trade between Baltimore and Rio, early railway construction and the expansion of railway networks were crucial for the transportation of goods to and from shipping ports—an important geographical framework. As David Schley explains, "the railroad's mission was to reinforce Baltimore's 'natural advantage' over Philadelphia and New York City: the city's position on the Chesapeake Bay made it the westernmost seaboard outlet for Ohio Valley merchants."⁶¹ Furthermore, "the Susquehanna River Valley and the drainage of the Ohio River Valley funneled agricultural products to Baltimore's harbor."⁶² Notably, Robert Clinton Wright (of Maxwell, Wright & Co.)—an important figure in Brazil and later discussed in this chapter—would become president of the Baltimore & Susquehanna Railroad in 1853.⁶³ The B&O and Susquehanna railways were completed in 1829, and the first line to reach Ellicott City mills in 1831 accounted for the transportation of a fourth of Baltimore's flour.⁶⁴

Although it was not until the 1820s that Brazil began to expand its coffee production into an export-oriented commodity, by 1860 coffee exports to the United States had increased from 200,000 sacks to 1.8

million sacks.⁶⁵ From 1822 to 1873 coffee exports from Brazil grew at an annual rate of 5.3 percent.⁶⁶ In addition, between 1838 and 1850 Baltimore became the world's largest flour market and was unsurpassed as the largest exporter of flour to Brazil and the rest of South America.⁶⁷ Three companies—Maxwell, Wright & Co.; Phipps Brothers & Co.; Roston Dutton & Co.—supplied 60 percent of U.S. wheat flour exports to Brazil; they became the three largest importers of Brazilian coffee during that period.⁶⁸

The Wright Family

The Wrights were often recognized as a Baltimorean family as much as a Brazilian or South American one. For example, in the dedication in her book *Colonial Families and Their Descendants* (1900), Mary Bourke Emory wrote, "This book is affectionately and respectfully dedicated to the memory of the Wright family of Maryland and South America."⁶⁹ Moreover, here are a few examples of the positions that Wright family members held in Brazil: William Henry DeCourcy Wright (cofounder, with Joseph Maxwell, of Maxwell, Wright & Co.) served as U.S. consul in Rio from 1825 to 1831 and later as U.S. chargé d'affaires ad interim. His nephew Robert Clinton Wright was secretary of legation and chargé d'affaires (1870–71) in Santos, and William T. Wright was secretary of legation (1857–58) and later U.S. consul in Santos.⁷⁰ In addition, several prominent Wright family members in Maryland and Brazil married their first or distant cousins, as most prominent Maryland families did at that time, and many were related to one another by blood, marriage, or both.⁷¹

Many of the Wright family members were either raised or born in Brazil. For example, Robert Clinton Wright's son, Judge Daniel Giraud Wright (1840–1922), was born in Rio. He moved back to Baltimore at the age of two and enlisted in the Confederate army at twenty-one, serving with Robert E. Lee and Stonewall Jackson as well as under John Singleton Mosby's "Mosby Raiders." After being captured and leaving a Union prison, he returned to Baltimore; soon after he became a lawyer and was admitted to the Bar in 1867. By 1888 he had been elected to associate justice, and in 1896 he became one of the charter members of the Maryland State Bar.[72] In an interview with the *Baltimore Sun* in 1889, Judge Wright recalled the significance of the coffee trade between Brazil and Baltimore, which had been going on for more than half a century by then. He cited other fellow Baltimorean businessmen who were involved with the coffee import and flour export trade in Brazil—such as Hugh Jenkins, Thomas Pierce, William Whitridge, and John M. Bandel— who were "famous in the catalogue of enterprising businessmen." He explained how Maxwell, Wright & Co. "was one of the pioneer houses in the coffee trade, and that the firm had made Baltimore and New Orleans principal markets of this country."[73] Thus, Judge Wright's background embodied the complexity of a nineteenth century "transnational" figure: a Brazil-born Confederate soldier, Baltimorean lawyer, and court judge.

The history of the Wright family in Maryland can be traced to 1673, when Nathaniel Wright migrated from England to Maryland and his son, Solomon Wright, became a prominent Maryland judge and married Mary (Tidmarsh DeCourcy) from the DeCourcy's of Maryland, another prominent family. The Courcey family derives its name from their demesne of that name in France—"Courcy" or "Coursey"—and when Henry Coursey moved to Maryland in 1649, the spelling of the name continued until 1760, when it changed to "DeCourcy."[74] Among the Wright family members, either by marriage or blood, there are prominent Maryland judges, lawyers, businessmen, and politicians, including two governors of Maryland.

Solomon Wright was a member of the Maryland Convention of 1771– 76 and member of the Assembly (1771–74); he was appointed judge of the provincial court and later judge of the first court of appeals until his death. His son Robert Wright (1752–1826), born at the Wrights' family house—"Blakeford" in Queen Anne County, Maryland—was a lawyer; he was elected U.S. senator in 1801 and later became the thirteenth governor of Maryland for three consecutive terms (1806–9). He had served as a private in Capt. James Kent's Company of Queen Anne "Minute Men" against Lord Drummond's Tories of the Eastern Shore of Virginia in 1776. By 1820 Robert Wright had been elected district judge of the circuit comprising Queen Anne, Kent, and Talbot Counties, Maryland.[75]

Robert Wright married Sarah DeCourcy; their youngest son, William Henry DeCourcy Wright, is the first important link between the Wright family and the "Baltimorean connection" in Brazil identified here.

W. H. D. C. Wright was also born in Blakeford on September 9, 1795. He married Eliza Lea Warner of Delaware (widow of Samuel Turbutt Wright, her cousin), and their children were Clintonia, Gustavia (who died in Rio), Gustavus, Caroline Louisa, Victoria Louisa, and Ella Lee. Clintonia married twice: first Capt. William May and second former governor of Maryland (1848–51) Phillip Francis Thomas.[76]

In 1825 U.S. President John Quincy Adams appointed W. H. D. C. Wright as U.S. consul at Rio. However, it was not long before the U.S. government tried to offer him other positions, steering him toward leaving Rio. In 1829 then U.S. Secretary of State Martin Van Buren urged Wright to take a position as consul in Stockholm or Copenhagen, which he declined. There had been several complaints by Brazilian officials accusing Wright of having a "troublesome disposition."[77] Wright complained of an underlying hostility toward him on the part of Brazilian government officials, and he claimed to the late Brazilian chargé d'affaires in DC, José Silvestre Rebello, that he had proof that Van Buren had read his personal letters without his permission. Wright described Rebello with animosity, stating that he was his "inveterate enemy."[78]

On May 24, 1831, Wright was officially discharged as U.S. consul at Rio.[79] John Martin Baker succeeded Wright in the office of U.S. consul. On November 3, 1831, Wright received a harsh letter from the Hon. Edward Livingstone, U.S. Secretary of State, informing him that Brazil had annulled his commission as U.S. consul in Rio, stating, "It gives me great concern to inform you . . . upon pressing solicitation of the Brazilian government . . . to annul your commission as Consul."[80] Wright had been working at the same time for Maxwell, Wright & Co., although he was only admitted as an official partner to the firm a decade later in 1843.

Wright wrote a letter to Joseph (José) Maxwell Sr. on January 18, 1832, explaining the circumstances of his removal as U.S. consul. According to Wright, there had been confusion regarding forty-one barrels of flour aboard one of the firm's brigs in Rio, which had been allegedly deemed "contraband" by the Brazilian Guarda Marinha (Naval Guard).[81]

On October 1, 1831, Wright wrote to Hon. Edward J. Chambers "to ask [his] friendship and the exercise of [his] influence in an application for the consulate of the U.S. at this place." Wright requested that his nephew, Robert Clinton Wright, replace Mr. Baker, the new U.S. consul. Robert had already been living in Brazil since 1826 and was fluent in Portuguese and French. W. H. D. C. Wright claimed, "the utter incapacity of Mr. Baker for the office is a subject of general remarks among our naval officers, ship masters and other Americans where business leads them into intercourse with him."[82] Furthermore, he asserted that Mr. Baker and his family "were Catholics," and therefore that they were friends with his archenemy, Rebello—who also boarded at Baker's house. Together Rebello and Baker, he claimed, had come to overpower the U.S. consulate in Rio.

It remains unknown how exactly William Henry DeCourcy Wright formed a binational Brazilian–American firm (Maxwell, Wright & Co) with Joseph Maxwell, one that became among the nineteenth century's most successful and largest coffee houses in the world. It is likely that Wright and Maxwell had met while Wright was still U.S. consul at Rio (1829–31). The firm's first address in downtown Rio was at the street from "behind the hospice" (*rua detrás do hospício*; Rua Buenos Aires today), where Joseph Maxwell had had his first business in the 1820s. By 1830 the firm had moved to Rua da Praia; it then moved to Rua do Peixe in 1842 and finally to its last-known registered commercial location at Rua do Mercado in 1850.[83]

W. H. D. C. Wright became partner at Maxwell, Wright & Co. in 1843 to replace the temporarily retiring partner Robert Clinton Wright (his nephew). W. H. D. C. Wright was one of six partners in the firm, together with Joseph Maxwell Sr. (of Gibraltar), Joseph Maxwell Jr. (likely born in Brazil), George Rudge (from England), William Francis Jones (from England), and John Skinner Wright (from Maryland). Robert Clinton Wright rejoined the firm in 1849.[84]

The Wright family members clearly made a concerted effort to maintain their political clout in Brazil throughout most of the nineteenth century, and such vignettes illustrate their political connections through the office of U.S. consul, even as they continued their close commercial association with the flour and coffee trade (through Maxwell, Wright & Co.). This political and commercial entrée evidently gave them easy access to vital information that enabled their success in their business enterprises in Brazil.

The influence of this firm's family members in Brazil merits attention here. For example, the well-known commercial warehouse (*trapiche*) in Rio's docks in Gamboa, Trapiche Maxwell, was named after Joseph Maxwell Sr. (also known as "José," cofounder of Maxwell, Wright, and Co.). The house "was built under the supervision of the vigilant and prompt Mr. Joseph Maxwell, of Gilbratar [*sic*], and various members of his family, in connection with Messrs. Wright of Baltimore. Few Americans and Englishmen have gone to Rio without receiving attention from some of the principals or employees of this house."[85]

Furthermore, when Joseph Maxwell Sr. died in 1854, Reverends Fletcher and Kidder reported that at that time, "probably the funeral of no other private citizen in the capital of the empire was ever attended by such a throng as that which followed to the grave the remains of this kind father and respected citizen."[86] Nonetheless, despite Maxwell, Wright & Co.'s known influence and commercial success in Brazil, very little information is available about the firm's early years. Laura Jarnagin has unearthed the most information on this out of anyone who has taken the task of researching the firm so far.[87]

Maxwell was born in Gibraltar to an Anglo-Portuguese family; he arrived in Brazil in 1809 at the age of thirty-seven as a British subject with British connections and skills in spoken Portuguese. He married a Brazilian, Maria Rosa de Sousa, from the prominent Sousa Coutinho family. Maxwell formed a partnership (Maxwell, Silva & Companhia in Rio) with another Englishman, John Rudge, who had arrived in Brazil as a sixteen-year-old.[88] The importance of this type of merger between family and business matters became increasingly salient as intermarriage strengthened and expanded business and kinship networks. For example, Maxwell's fifteen-year-old daughter Maria Amalia married forty-year-old John Rudge (a partner at Maxwell, Wright & Co.) in 1831; John Rudge's cousin, George Rudge—also another partner in the firm—married Joseph Maxwell's other daughter, Sofia.[89]

By the 1870s Maxwell, Wright & Co. had grown a number of spin-offs, "including Joseph M. Wright & Company of Rio and Baltimore (headed by Robert Clinton Wright's son), and Wright & Company of Rio, Baltimore, and New York, where it was known as Wright, Brown & Company."[90]

However, the emotional stress of dealing with business and Brazilian politics together had likely caught up with W. H. D. C. Wright. He returned to Baltimore and was committed in 1854 to the MacLean Asylum in Sommerville, Massachusetts (also known as the McLean Asylum for the Insane). We do not know exactly why he was committed—it is likely that he had been suffering from what is known in today's vernacular as "deep depression" and that he may have had suffered a nervous breakdown of some sort. Robert C. Wright wrote several letters to his uncle while he was institutionalized for at least eight months (Robert's letters were typically unemotional and straightforward, about business as usual). Conversely, letters by W. H. D. C. Wright's wife were emotional and affectionate, with news about their children at Blakeford. She described how she "loved him dearly" and how he had been a "good husband and father" to his children, and she exhorted him to do the best he could by getting treatment during his remaining time at the institution "for his own health-sake."[91]

W. H. D. C. Wright died not too long afterward in Baltimore in 1864, aged sixty-nine, just a year before the end of U.S. Civil War and a year before U.S. Southern immigration to Brazil began to increase. His obituary in the *Baltimore Sun* announced his passing: "Died. On Friday morning, 25th instant, William H. DeCourcy Wright, in the 69th year of his age. The friends of the family are invited to attend his funeral from his late residence, No. 109 N. Charles Street."[92] The location functioned as a rectory for years after, and today 109 N. Charles Street is the location of an African restaurant. W. H. D. C. Wright is buried among other Wright family members at Greenmount Cemetery on North Avenue, Baltimore.

Here, the story moves to another Wright family member who developed important connections and who possessed notable political clout among Brazilian politicians in the mid-nineteenth century, including with Brazil's emperor. W. H. D. C. Wright's nephew, Robert Clinton Wright (not to be confused with Judge Robert Wright, his great-uncle) was perhaps one of the most shrewd partners of Maxwell, Wright & Co. He married his cousin, Anna Selina Anderson, and had ten children with her.

Robert Clinton Wright directly helped the U.S. Southern migration enterprise to Brazil. For example, in a letter addressed to the *New York Journal of Commerce* and to the *Philadelphia Ledger* on May 23, 1855, Rev. Fletcher described how Robert Clinton Wright had facilitated his trip to Brazil: "Messrs. Corner & Sons of Baltimore, generously place[d] their bark at my disposal for a free passage . . . Robert C. Wright, Esq., of that city . . . did every thing in their power to facilitate the enterprise, and to them more than to others I am indebted for the successful consummation of my desired object."[93]

Living between Brazil and Baltimore, Robert C. Wright returned to Baltimore to become the president of the Susquehenna & Ohio Railroad; he then ran for mayor of Baltimore in 1856 but was defeated by Thomas Swann, who at that time served as the director and president of the B&O Railroad.[94]

By 1871 Robert Clinton Wright, at the time chargé d'affaires to Brazil, continued to facilitate the mobility of Americans within Brazil. For example, he personally organized and secured the first interview with Dom Pedro II with a special correspondent from the *New York Herald*.[95] He died in 1879, a decade before Brazil became a federal republic. If Robert Clinton Wright had been alive after 1889, one can only ponder how his astuteness and close ties with Brazilian Republicans would have influenced business and policy.

The third Wright family member to become politically and personally involved in Brazil, and who directly supported U.S. Southern immigration, was William Turbutt Wright. He started work as a young clerk at Maxwell, Wright & Co. in Rio, and at twenty-eight he returned to Baltimore for a short time before heading to Santos, where he married Carlota Marquês Lisboa, from a prominent São Paulo family. The Wrights would come to own a farm (*fazenda*) in the interior—Itatiba—near Campinas and not too far from the Confederado settlement in Santa Bárbara.[96]

In reports written by U.S. Southerners in their search for Brazilian lands, William Turbutt Wright is often referred to as "William T. Wright from Santos" or "William T. Wright from Baltimore." He was the great-great-grandson of Nathaniel Turbutt Wright and great-great-grandson of Thomas Hynson Wright.

William T. Wright directly helped U.S. Southerners by furnishing them with key Brazilian contacts who ensured their prospected lands and helped them settle in Brazil. In addition, William married into a prominent Brazilian family, which further strengthened his political influence among the Brazilian elite and politicians alike. For instance, Dr. Gaston wrote, "I was furnished with a letter by Mr. Wright to an uncle of his wife, Senhor João Bernadino V'ra Barboza, at São Pedro, in this province. He has lands to dispose of himself, and will be able to refer me to others having large estates that may be for sale."[97] Carlota Marquês Lisboa's uncle was the eminent plantation owner, *sargento-mór* João Bernadino Vieira Barbosa (versions of his name provided by Gaston, such as "Barboza"—spelled with a *z*—were common at the time).

The Humbirds of Maryland

Jacob Humbird of Cumberland, Maryland, was another figure in this narrative with strong Maryland roots, connections to Baltimore, and sympathies with U.S. Southern emigration to Brazil. Although Jacob Humbird was born in Westmoreland County, Pennsylvania, in 1811, he married Elinor McKee in 1835 and moved to Cumberland, Maryland, in 1837.[98]

On May 11, 1866, inspecting suitable lands for Southern immigrants, Rev. Dunn reported in an official report written to the Brazilian Minister of Agriculture that Jacob Humbird was among U.S. Southerners (including Dr. R. M. Davis of Virginia, and Capt. W. F. Shippey of Florida) aboard a schooner leaving Rio de Janeiro on their way to inspect Cananéa: "Mr. Humbird, who is an eminently practical, go-ahead man, was so much pleased and so well convinced that our labors will result successfully, that he invested largely in the choice of the Ribeira and Juquiá rivers, paying the cash, and giving these *sitios* [ranches] into my charge, with instructions to turn them over, at cost, to our people."[99] Here, it is clear that Jacob Humbird, who was "paying in cash," held a critical political role, especially so by financing the migration project. Humbird became an important contact in Brazil who personally knew key figures within the Brazilian political elite as well as in Baltimore; he would become a powerful ally and intermediary in the process of relocating U.S. Southerners to Brazil.

For example, at the request of Jacob Humbird, an article was written by an Englishman, John James Aubertin (superintendent of the São Paulo Railroad Co. Ltda.) and reprinted in the *Anglo-Brazilian Times* on February 8, 1866. This article was intended to specifically promote the immigration of U.S. Southerners to Brazil, and it targeted readers in Baltimore: "In our constant anxiety to promote the grand movement, now going on, to lay before our readers." Aubertin begins the article by addressing it to Jacob Humbird, "In order that [Humbird] might send it for publication to Baltimore, and thus to a certain extent make the public in the Southern States, even more acquainted with certain facts." He continued to describe the possibilities for U.S. Southerners in Brazil, including the potential for cultivation of cotton: "[Humbird's] coming would expedite the road-making, and lastly what thousands of hard-working Germans would come to you from aboard; really hard-workers, ready and anxious to learn to employ themselves." This strongly suggests that the Brazilian government and immigration societies had considered hiring German immigrants to replace the black slave labor working for U.S. Southern immigrants. Aubertin then concludes, "This whole Province, in proper hands may, in short time be made a garden of Coffee, Cotton, Corn, and Sugar."[100] Humbird was clearly interested in spreading the idea of immigration to Brazil through newspaper outlets in Baltimore.

Humbird went to Brazil on January 1, 1859, to bid for a railway engineering contract that was secured in 1860 (the Dom Pedro Segundo Railway through the Serra do Mar in Rio); "The Railroad [was] a double track, and the great highway of Brazil. The Tunnel was, at the time of its completion, the greatest work of the kind in the world ... The character of this Railroad and especially the Tunnel, enhanced [Humbird's] reputation among Railroad constructors, and the exceeding importance of the Road to Brazil, made his success highly gratifying to the Emperor and the Government."[101]

After his contract in Brazil ended Jacob Humbird returned to Maryland, and in 1867 he joined D. A. Baldwin of New York to build the West Wisconsin Railroad (between Chicago and St. Paul). In 1872 he started with the construction of the North Wisconsin Railroad (between Hudson to Bayfield, Lake Hudson), again with Baldwin, but Baldwin died before its completion. Humbird then joined forces with his own brother John Alexander Humbird to build the railroad between Waynesboro and Shippensburg, Pennsylvania, which was completed in 1891 and later connected to the Western Maryland Railroad; Humbird would become the mayor of Cumberland in 1866, 1867, 1868, and 1875.[102] Jacob Humbird died in Cumberland, Maryland, in 1893 at the age of eighty-two. He had been associated with his son John Alexander in various lumber enterprises in Brazil, the western United States, and Canada.[103]

Connections between U.S. Southerners and Baltimorean entrepreneurs illustrate how trade and investment, agroeconomic, and sociopolitical interests helped to fuel U.S. Southern immigration to Brazil. Baltimorean entrepreneurs were major stakeholders in this case. By encouraging Southerners to migrate to Brazil, Baltimorean mercantile companies were also positioning themselves to optimize their economic opportunities in a global market they already knew well.

Freemasonry and the Baltimore Connection

Freemasonry membership ostensibly played an important role in establishing network connections between Rio, Baltimore, and U.S. Southerners. Baltimorean Freemasons were already well-established in Brazil by the mid-nineteenth century. Among the known Freemasons in this story were immigration agents Charles Nathan, Tavares Bastos, and Joaquim Nabuco; Brazilian political elites such as Dom Pedro II and the Sousa Coutinho family members; and many Confederados such as William H. Norris and Robert C. Norris. These figures were commercially and politically involved with one another, invested in this migration enterprise together. This would give them even more reason to aid, welcome, and encourage other U.S. Southerners (particularly Freemasons) to find new homes in Brazil.

The origins of Freemasonry (or Masonry) are largely unknown and are said to have emerged in Scotland, stemming from the societies of stonemasons who built castles and cathedrals during the late fourteenth and early fifteenth centuries. Commonly perceived as a "secretive" organization and shrouded in speculative accounts of ancient knowledge and powerful world networks, Freemasonry has been greatly mythologized in popular culture. The first Grand Lodge (local organizations of Masons are called "lodges") was formed in England in 1717.[104] Today, there are around 13,200 lodges in the United States, and Freemasons make no secret of their membership by wearing rings, lapel pins, and tie clasps with Masonic emblems (the Square and Compasses). It is also well-known that many of the U.S. "Founding Fathers," including George Washington, Benjamin Franklin, Paul Revere, Joseph Warren, and John Hancock, were Freemasons; the Freemasons also played an important part in the Revolutionary War, the Constitutional Convention, and the debates surrounding the ratification of the Bill of Rights.[105]

At the Stephen J. Ponzillo Jr. Memorial Library & Museum of the Grand Lodge of A. F. & A. M. of Maryland (Maryland Masonic Museum), located in Baltimore, William Henry DeCourcy Wright is listed as a member of Cassia Lodge No. 45 in Baltimore (chartered in 1811).[106] Cassia Lodge was one of the most prestigious lodges at the time, with members of the Ridgely family at Hampton House among its membership. Wright is recorded as being initiated as a member on January 3, 1825, and as "demitting" (requesting to withdraw his membership from the lodge) on November 1, 1825. Usually members demit in order to transfer their membership from one lodge to another lodge, as plural membership was not permitted at the time. This strongly suggests that Wright was transferring his membership to a Masonic lodge in Rio, where he lived and served as U.S. consul in Rio from 1825 to 1831. After Wright left his position as U.S. consul, he was readmitted as a partner to Maxwell, Wright & Co. in 1843, and he went back to the Baltimore branch office located on 109 Charles Street, Baltimore; he later returned to the Rio branch office in 1845.[107]

Notably, Charles Nathan (an important immigration agent discussed in chapter 2) was a member of St. John Lodge No. 703, an English-speaking lodge in Rio that operated under the jurisdiction of the United Grand Lodge of England.[108] Recently, the Cassia Lodge No. 45, the same lodge in which Wright had been a member, merged on December 1, 2006, with both the St. John's Lodge No. 34 of Baltimore (chartered 1802), and the Amicable Lodge No. 25 (chartered June 21, 1797) to become the Amicable–St. John's Lodge No. 25 on December 1, 2006—Maryland's third-oldest Freemason Lodge.[109]

The connection between Baltimorean and Brazilian Freemasons likely evolved into an important network that strengthened the ties between U.S. Southerners and Baltimorean entrepreneurs in Brazil, and there is some evidence that suggests this relationship existed. For example, an old apron (dated circa 1820s), given as a gift to the Grand Lodge of Maryland to Capt. William Forbes, a Baltimorean Mason who visited a Freemason lodge in Rio in 1873, can be seen on display at the Stephen J. Ponzillo Jr. Memorial Library & Museum of the Grand Lodge of A. F. & A. M. of Maryland, Maryland Masonic Museum.[110] This is a Masonic Past Masters Apron from Rio de Janeiro, Brazil. The main panel of this apron has a templelike structure roofed with a square encompassed by a wreath and flanked by two columns (King Solomon's Temple) and supporting flowers (a French influence). The sun and moon also appear in gold bullion sequence. Therefore, connections between Masonic lodges in Rio and Baltimore suggest that there were important links between the two lodges, given their influential members and the ongoing commercial ties between the two cities.

In addition, Jarnagin was able to ascertain that Col. William H. Norris, who settled in Santa Barbára, shared a distant common ancestor with W.

H. D. C. Wright.[111] Altogether, these multilayered dimensions point to the strong "Baltimorean connection" with Brazil and show how these linkages would ostensibly facilitate the mobility of Confederados to and within Brazil.

Conclusion on Baltimoreans in Brazil

A few conclusions can be made, then, about Baltimore, Baltimoreans, and their connections with this Confederado story. First, Baltimoreans W. H. D. C. Wright, Robert Clinton Wright, and James Birckhead initiated and developed commercial and trade reciprocities between Baltimore and Brazil. Maxwell, Wright & Co. and the Wright family members married into Brazilian elite families and held important positions as U.S. consuls (e.g., William H. D. C. Wright and Robert C. Wright). These people were all deeply involved with political and commercial enterprises in Rio, with direct ties to Emperor Dom Pedro II. Baltimoreans thus developed and strengthened sociopolitical networks in Brazil during the first half of the nineteenth century and were intricately involved in the growth of agricultural and commercial ties and interests between Baltimore and Rio.

Second, Jacob Humbird and William T. Wright were sympathetic to the U.S. Southern immigration enterprise to Brazil, offering the endeavor necessary financial and political clout, encouragement, and advice, especially as Confederados researched suitable lands to settle in Brazil.

Finally, it is important to acknowledge the significance of Baltimore as a "border-state" location. That is, Baltimore enjoyed commercial connections with both the U.S. North and U.S. South, was located south of the Mason-Dixon Line and shared a close proximity to "U.S. Southern culture," and was simultaneously in close proximity to the nation's capital in Washington DC and its geostrategic position.

Moreover, Baltimore's role during the U.S. Civil War delineated the war's beginning and end. It is a commonly held view that Baltimore was the city where the U.S. Civil War began on April 19, 1861. When members of the Massachusetts militia were walking to Washington DC, they were attacked by Baltimorean Confederate sympathizers on Pratt Street, resulting in twenty fatalities (including six Union soldiers)—this is often regarded as the first instance of bloodshed that resulted in casualties during the U.S. Civil War, also known as the "Pratt Street Riot."[112] At the tail end of the Civil War, John Wilkes Booth (1838–65)—the theater actor and Confederate sympathizer notorious for shooting and killing Abraham Lincoln on April 14, 1865, was from Baltimore. Booth is buried at the Booth family plot in Greenmount Cemetery, Baltimore (curiously, at the same cemetery in which William H. D. C. Wright is buried). Together, these two events place Baltimore at the start and the end of the U.S. Civil War. Although Maryland was not part of the Confederacy, many of its citizens were Confederate sympathizers—particularly those who were plantation slaveowners—and many Baltimoreans, including members of the Wright family, had enlisted and fought for the Confederate Army.

In summary, trade, family, and political networks developed with the presence of Baltimoreans in Brazil, as they laid the groundwork for galvanizing and aiding the mobility of U.S. Southern immigrants.

On February 2, 1866, a correspondent for the *New York Herald* arrived in Rio from Baltimore on the steamship *Havana*. He describes his first observations of the city of Rio de Janeiro: "The bay forming the extensive harbor of Rio is one of the most magnificent that the eye can light on. On nearly all sides it is encompassed by lofty mountains, while it is filled with beautiful islands. Opposite the city are several landing places, while a trip to Botafogo, overlooked by the lofty mountain called the Corcovado, is a delightful excursion. On your way the high peak of the Sugar Loaf frowns grimly on you, seemingly daring you to scale its inaccessible sides and to arrive at the summit." The same correspondent continues, describing downtown Rio: "The Rua Direita, the principal street of Rio, smells as bad as Roosevelt street in New York, and that is saying a great deal." He also describes a marketplace in Rio: "You can always obtain monkeys and vegetables, fruit and snakes, parrots and fish—the latter in great variety, though not in much abundance—game and sweetmeats, etc.; and such a variety of jargon as would have rather astonished the builders of Babel themselves."[113] These descriptions of the sights, sounds, and smells of Rio are likely to have overlapped with the experiences of most U.S. Southerners when they first arrived at that city, explored further in the next chapter.

2

Moving to Brazil

Now that the "Baltimorean Connection" has been established and discussed, this chapter focuses on the movement of Confederados to and within Brazil. Vignettes taken from various sources are used here to show how politicians, communities, networks, and institutions were directly involved in facilitating land acquisitions once immigrants had arrived in Brazil. The U.S. press strongly opposed the migration project and viewed Brazil and Brazilians in a negative light. However, this opposition developed in sharp contrast to the overwhelmingly positive Brazilian public opinion on U.S. Southern immigration.

At the end of the U.S. Civil War, many Confederates also sought out new homes in other countries—for example, in Canada, England, Egypt, Honduras, British Honduras, and Mexico. L. E. Elliott described her visit to a settlement in British Honduras (today the country of Belize) where, at that time, U.S. Southern immigrants had been "growing sugarcane and prospering."[1] However, all those settlements eventually failed and dissolved.[2] Thousands of U.S. Southerners sought new homes in large U.S. cities, searching for jobs in urban environments. In the case of Mexico, the vast majority who migrated there returned to the United States or left for Venezuela, Brazil, or Jamaica because of the hostility of Mexicans toward foreigners at that time.[3] The execution of Austrian-born Emperor Maximillian of Mexico (placed in power by the French) by Benito Juárez's Mexican Republican forces in 1867 put an end to the larger exodus of U.S. Southerners to Mexico.

Brazil was the only country in the western hemisphere that retained a long-lasting native-born emperor. Dom Pedro II was born in Brazil in 1825, and his empire lasted from 1831 to 1889 (unlike Emperor Maximillian of Mexico, a cousin of Dom Pedro II, who was Austrian-born and whose empire lasted only four years).[4]

Dom Pedro II's empire was an unofficial ally of the Confederacy, allowing U.S. Southern ships on Brazilian shores to secure supplies and refusing Union demands to treat them as "pirates."[5] Brazilian policies had ignored diplomatic protests from Washington demanding the forcible removal by a U.S. warship of the Confederate cruiser *Sumter* at a port in Maranhão on September 6, 1861. Two years later, in a fiery exchange of diplomatic correspondence between the two countries, U.S. Ambassador Gen. James Watson Webb called on Brazilian Minister of Foreign Affairs, Miguel Calmon du Pin e Almeida, the Marquês de Abrantes, on May 21, 1863, about two other Confederate steamers—the *Alabama* and the *Georgia*—that were ported in Brazil, drawing attention "to a gross breach of neutrality perpetrated and now being perpetrated . . . at the ports of Pernambuco and Bahia." The two steamers had been receiving "hospitalities," provisions, and repairs. Gen. Webb finalized his letter by stating that "a grosser breach of neutrality has never come to the knowledge of the undersigned."[6] These actions contributed to a growing animosity between the United States and Brazil, and they furthered Brazilian sympathies for the Confederacy.[7]

Moreover, Dom Pedro II, a Freemason, was fluent in seven languages; he "was a scholar by instinct, and did his best to advance Brazil by the encouragement of railroad building, invitation to foreign capital, and the throwing open of wide spaces of southern land to good class immigrants."[8] The favorable political, agricultural, and economic inducements to Brazil offered important pull factors that encouraged U.S. Southern emigration to Brazil, such as various Imperial government subsidies that could include transportation costs, temporary food provisions and boarding costs, and land ownership. Thus, U.S. Southerners were openly sought out and welcomed by Brazil's emperor.[9]

Circumstances in the U.S. South

By the end of the U.S. Civil War, socioeconomic circumstances in the postbellum U.S. South were grim, churches and schools had closed, and "Confederate currency, bonds, and mortgages were worthless by May 1865."[10] Furthermore, "every bank was insolvent. Homes, farms and plantations were destroyed. Entire towns and cities were reduced to rubble."[11] By the 1870s South Carolina had lost about fifty thousand of its white population, and about 15 percent of the white population in Alabama had left the state.[12] *Debow's Review* estimates that by 1867, about twenty thousand Southerners had migrated to New York,[13] and "wreck and ruin, desolation and starvation covered the land from Virginia to Texas."[14] As John Lowe put it, "the age of Southern Reconstruction can easily be read through the lens of displacement, exile and loss."[15]

In a letter written to Rev. Dunn, Capt. William Francis (Frank) Shippey, from Kansas, raised in Tennessee and an officer in the Confederate Navy, poignantly highlighted his choice to leave the United States for Brazil. He wrote, "Here the war worn soldier, the bereaved parent, the oppressed patriot, the homeless and despoiled, can find a refuge from the trials which beset them, and a home not haunted by the eternal remembrance of harrowing scenes of sorrow and death."[16]

Several former Confederates who had left for Brazil decided to take on Brazilian citizenship; these include Maj. Frank McMullen and Col. Charles Grandison Gunter, who became leaders of two separate Confederado settlements in Brazil.[17] Though immigrants who purchased lands in Brazil could become Brazilian citizens after two years, they could also, "on application [. . .] to the Legislature [. . .] obtain dispensation from this lapse of time and may be naturalized soon after their arrival . . . after making oath of fidelity to the Constitution and the laws of the Empire."[18] If immigrants arrived in Brazil without a passport, they were allowed to land on Brazilian soil, "unless suspected of being malefactors"; "a certificate from their respective Legation or Consulate will stand substitute for that document in case of need."[19]

One correspondent for the *Chicago Tribune* reported that during a trip through the U.S. South in 1866, he had met on a train a former Confederate who had just returned from Brazil for a visit back home. This former Confederate had recently become a Brazilian citizen, and was returning to help propagate the "Brazil fever." He had come back to inform other fellow Southerners that the U.S. South had found the "happy land of Canaan in the Empire of Brazil." Moreover, he was "proud to say that he was a Brazilian; that he had taken the oath of allegiance to Dom Pedro."[20]

The Search for Lands

Soon after the Confederate surrender at Appomattox, Virginia, in 1865, Dr. Hugh A. Shaw and Maj. Robert Meriwether were mandated as agents of the Southern Emigration Society of Edgefield, South Carolina, to look for Brazilian lands suitable for U.S. Southern settlements. This society was created specifically to promote and facilitate immigration to Brazil.[21] The Southern Colonization Society was established at the Edgefield Court House, South Carolina, on August 21, 1865. It was just one of the many immigration societies that were created throughout the U.S. South; soon, "there was not a single state south of the Potomac and Ohio rivers that did not have its society for the promotion of emigration."[22]

Maj. Meriwether and Dr. Shaw left Augusta, Georgia, on October 18, 1865; once they arrived in Rio de Janeiro, they met other U.S. Southerners who had arrived earlier on the same mission. One of them was Dr. Gaston, who introduced them to Brazil's Minister of Agriculture, Antônio Paula e Sousa—who, in turn, offered them "every facility desired in the prosecution of our investigations, furnishing transportation, a guide and interpreter, and in most cases food and lodging."[23]

Dr. James McFadden Gaston (1824–1903), a former Confederate surgeon and physician from Columbia, South Carolina, joined the Edgefield group. Together with Maj. Meriwether and Dr. Shaw, they searched for suitable Brazilian lands to settle. They went first to the port of Santos, then by rail to the city of São Paulo (the capital of the province), where they packed their mules and supplies and headed into the interior, about two hundred miles west to Araraquara, but decided that the lands near Botucatu, Lençóis, and the valley of Tietê were more suitable. However, they predicted transportation problems, as they were at least a hundred miles from the closest railway. Finally, they decided that properties around the Campinas region (just about twenty-four miles from Santa Bárbara) were better suited.[24]

Again, the aiding influence of Baltimoreans in Brazil on U.S. Southerners is clear. Dr. Gaston had received help and advice from Baltimorean William T. Wright (from the Wright family of Maxwell, Wright & Co.), who at that time was residing in Santos with his children and Brazilian wife. Dr. Gaston described Wright's wife and, on several occasions, Wright's invitations to participate in local social gatherings and dining events.[25] He recalled, "Mr. Wright tells me that he has received some account of the lands and water facilities at a small town upon the coast, called Concliçao [Conceição], which makes him suppose that it might be a matter of interest for me to visit it."[26] He wrote, "When I return to Santos, he thinks that he can accompany me to see this place, and advises me not to make any definite arrangement elsewhere, until I examine that locality."[27]

Furthermore, Dr. Gaston remarked, Wright "has been a modern advocate of our cause during the struggle, and sympathizes with us in our misfortune . . . my visit to the family of Mr. Wright was marked by such kind consideration, as to make me feel like I was again amongst friends."[28] Wright had introduced Gaston to key Brazilian social and political elites with the specific intent to help U.S. Southern emigration; with the help of Wright's introductions, Dr. Gaston and his fellow Southerners were aided and encouraged in their pursuit to migrate to Brazil. Finally, Dr. Gaston concluded that Brazil was the ideal home for U.S. Southerners, stating emphatically, "There is a dignity and a hospitality among these people that correspond in many respects to the lofty and generous bearing which characterize the Southern gentlemen in former times. We find people in Brazil capable of appreciating the

Southern character, and ready to extend a cordial greeting to all who come. I HAVE SOUGHT AND FOUND THEM A HOME."²⁹

The determinations in Maj. Meriwether and Dr. Shaw's report, published in *Debow's Review* in 1867, were favorable toward Brazil, its geography, and its people—albeit with a few challenges. For one, an immigrant could not reach "one or two of the highest offices in the State, and may not, if he be a Protestant, erect a cross upon his church." The latter challenge was eventually solved: since Protestants could not bury their dead in Catholic cemeteries in Brazil, settlers in Santa Bárbara began to bury their dead on a private farm, building their own Protestant church (Campo) on that same farm. Meriwether and Shaw concluded in their report that while transportation and agricultural implements presented additional challenges, they believed these would be solved with the Brazilian government's promise to construct new roads and railroads; the immigrants themselves would bring their own agricultural implements.³⁰

Transportation from New York to Rio at that time took about twenty-six days by a small steamer and cost two hundred dollars in gold; second class cost a hundred dollars, and "children at breast [traveled] without cost; from twelve to fourteen half price; under twelve one-third." The cost of traveling from Rio to Santos was twenty dollars.³¹ The total cost of the trip was partially subsidized over time by the Brazilian government. In a statement on August 13, 1866, Joaquim Maria Nascentes de Azambuja (the "Counsellor of Azambuja"), from the Brazilian legation, New York, explained:

> Minors under six years of age shall have free passage; from six to twelve inclusive shall pay one half. Agriculture implements for the use of immigrants as also their respective baggage shall be taken free of freight . . . the tickets will be issued by a special Agent to be appointed by the aforesaid company with the approval of the Imperial Government . . . to issue the passports and certificates for the delivery of the tickets, you have to attend to the references the emigrants must point out as caution of their morality and precendents [*sic*]. I am directed

by the Imperial Government to give you some instructions in regard to persons who may be disposed to emigrate to Brazil.

Free passages will be allowed on board of the Steamers of the United States and Brazil mail Steamship Company to all agricultural laborers, single or married men . . . To participate in this liberality the intending emigrants have to buy public lands, measured and divided by order of the Government . . . These lands will be engaged until the repayment of the value thereof and of the amount preceeding [*sic*] from the advanced passages.[32]

Clearly, the various inducements offered by the Brazilian government show how Brazil eagerly promoted and encouraged the migration of U.S. Southerners to Brazil. Considering the widespread ruin across the U.S. South, U.S. Southerners were enthusiastic to seize the inducements and opportunities offered by Brazilian immigration agents. They understood the advantages of relocating to Brazil, with its agricultural base and low prices for land. In addition, "like the antebellum South, Brazil was governed by a rural aristocracy [that] had as the main support of its power and prestige the vast *latifundia*—the cotton, sugar and coffee farms."[33] Conversely, if these Southerners had stayed in the United States, they would have feared "the imminent possibility of criminal action for treason."[34]

The *Baltimore Sun* ran continued coverage about the Edgefield search group; they reported, "The committee also found plenty of land near river Tietê called 'Terra Roccha', which means 'land of inexpressible richness and fertility . . . Fifty bushels of corn to the acre, and two to three thousand pounds of cotton can be raised; sugar and coffee in perfection." The term "terra rocha" (*terra roxa*) in Portuguese literally means "purple land," a reference to the distinct color of the land and its fertile soil (the soil is not really purple; it is more a reddish, orange-brown color). The report concludes, "There can, however, be no doubt that the liberal and enlightened counsels of the Emperor, and the immense fertility of the soil, will rapidly build up an important and most friendly nation in South America."[35]

Gen. William Wallace Wood from Mississippi (born in Louisiana) would become one of the first immigration agents to represent four Mississippi counties. In 1865 when Wood sailed to Brazil, eleven thousand Southern families had been recruited. By this time, reports of how U.S. immigration agents had been received in Brazil were decidedly positive. The reception Gen. Wood received was typical of that of other U.S. Southerners when they arrived in Rio de Janeiro: "Masses of people extending three blocks waved flags and shouted 'vivas for General Wood.' Bands played 'Dixie' and the Brazilian national anthem."[36]

In late 1865 the *New York Herald* reported several U.S. Southerners who had already arrived in Rio, including agents who represented families wishing to emigrate; "The most conspicuous is General Wood, formerly of the Vicksburg *Whig* . . . Parties have taken up land in the provinces of Paraná in the endeavoring to form a colony of Americans."[37] A year later, Gen. Wood published a pamphlet promoting the possibilities in Brazilian colonies in *Ho! for Brazil*, published in 1866. However, much to the chagrin and embarrassment of Brazilian officials, Gen. Wood had unexpectedly returned to the United States with his entourage by the time his publication came out. The barrage of negative criticism about his migration project in U.S. newspapers prompted Wood to change his mind, despite his enthusiastic publication on U.S. Southern emigration to Brazil. He returned to the United States in 1866 and became a "country attorney" in Adams County, Mississippi.[38]

In 1866 the Imperial Legation of Brazil in the United States printed a statement (signed by B. F. Torreão de Barros on January 24, 1866) with a list of seventy-five Americans who wished to migrate to Brazil. The list, based on letters received at the Brazilian consulate in 1865, included the full name, date, residence, and objective (reason for query) of each letter writer. Each individual name often represented other groups of families—groups that ranged from fifty to two hundred other individuals also interested in migrating to Brazil. The residences of these individuals included Virginia, Mississippi, North Carolina, Missouri, Kentucky, Tennessee, Georgia, Alabama, South Carolina, Maryland, Washington DC, and even Boston, Massachusetts. Most of their questions were about government inducements and agricultural implements and how these would be adequately allocated to immigrants. There was only one letter out of the seventy-five queries on whether slave labor was allowed in Brazil.[39]

Brazil Facilitates the Immigration Project

On July 24, 1865, the *Anglo-Brazilian Times* reported that a party of newly arrived U.S. Southern immigrants had just disembarked in Rio de Janeiro. This group of newcomers was welcomed by the Brazilian government and private land proprietors, and they were "given every encouragement and assistance by the present Minister of Agriculture . . . [who is] determined to do away with all routing and afford every facility to the immigrant for the purchase of land wherever the government has it." They could find local lodging and board at a moderate price at the "Government Boarding House"; "There, and on board the vessel on arrival, they [would] receive all the information they desire from the Government agent appointed for that purpose."[40] The Brazilian government gave them free transportation from Rio to their desired destination ports.

An immigration office was set up (the Agency Office for Colonization), and as soon as they arrived, passengers could obtain information on the lands available for sale. These immigrants were exempt from Brazilian national military service if they chose not to obtain Brazilian citizenship; however, they were subject to the national guard of the municipality. Immigrants were allowed to "acquire and possess all sorts of property and dispose of it in every way" as well as "exercise all branches of trade, commerce and industry by wholesale and retail."[41]

The first contact most U.S. Southerners had with the Brazilian government in Rio was at a former residential house—"beautifully furnished and surrounded by formal gardens"—converted into the Emigrant's Hotel (*hospedaria*), and run by U.S. Southerner Col. Broome.[42] Evidently, the Brazilian government was making a concerted effort to welcome the new settlers as they arrived in Brazil, eagerly accommodating them in the hope that they would stay for the long haul.

As early as June 19, 1865, José C. Galvão, an official agent of the Agency of Colonization—located at 23 Rua dos Ciganos, Rio de Janeiro—placed an advertisement in the *Anglo-Times* newspaper, "Notice to Emigrants: Sale of Lands." The advertisement states that the sale of lands located in the provinces of Rio de Janeiro, Espírito Santo, Minas Gerais, and along the seacoast of the province of São Paulo, were to be left to the disposal of immigrants, and that these lands were suitable for the "growth of coffee, sugar-cane, cotton, tobacco, mandioca [manioc], maize, beans, and rice." The prices of these lands ranged "from 8 to 15 reis the square braça . . . 1 dollar and 40 cents to 7 dollars the acre."[43]

It is clear here that by placing an English-language advertisement in an English-language newspaper in Rio, this agent indicated his eager sales promotion tactics. In this manner, the *Anglo-Brazilian Times* newspaper became a vital source for Confederados, especially newcomers (who could not yet read newspapers written in Portuguese).

The Brazilian government sent immigration agents to New Orleans, Mobile, Savannah, Richmond, and New York City to recruit new settlers. Among those agents was Quintino Bocaiúva, Brazilian Minister of Foreign Affairs, editor of the newspaper *O diário do Rio de Janeiro*, and a Freemason. When Bocaiúva opened the agency in New York City, one thousand potential immigrants signed up to move to Brazil just in the first week.[44]

After the brig *Derby* was shipwrecked in 1867 off the coast of Cuba, Bocaiúva sent "a steamer from New York to transport them, at the cost of the Imperial government, to that city, whence afterwards, to the number of 250, they departed, and arrived in this port by the North America along with other immigrants."[45] The schooner *Talisman* also arrived in 1867, bringing another thirty-five passengers sent by Rev. Dunn. However, Bocaiúva was later criticized in the press by some Brazilians (as we shall see later in this chapter) for his alleged lack of discretion in selecting ideal prospects; many of those who had signed up in New York were not agriculturalists—a supply of labor that Brazil urgently needed.[46]

Between the mid- to late 1860s and the 1880s, three immigration societies were created in Brazil to induce foreign agriculturalists to move to Brazil. These included the International Immigration Society (Sociedade Internacional de Imigração)—formed in 1866 by Tavares Bastos, its members included Charles Nathan and William Scully—which was created specifically to bring European and American immigrants to Brazil. This society was featured in 1866 in a report published by the newspaper *O diário do Rio de Janeiro* under the name "Associação Internacional de Emigração" (International Immigration Association). Listed among its members were George Nathan, Charles (Carlos) Nathan, Tavares Bastos, and Quintino Bocaiúva (the editor of that same newspaper), all well-known stakeholders in this Confederado story and also Freemasons.[47] In 1867 the *Anglo-Brazilian Times* reported that the Imperial Legation of Brazil in Washington had resolved to front the steamer passage cost for "individuals who wished to emigrate to Brazil, upon the conditions of their being agriculturalists of assured morality, of their disposing of some means for their first establishment, and of purchasing public lands on time, which would remained mortgaged until the payment of their value and of the sum expended with their passage."[48]

By mid-1867 the Brazilian government alone had recruited and brought 1,477 American immigrants to Brazil; these immigrants were distributed among several Brazilian provinces. The breakdown of the distribution and whereabouts of those *norte-americanos* were as follows: São Pedro [currently the state of Rio Grande do Sul], 250; São Paulo, 206; Santa Catarina, 203; Pará, 61; Paraná, 13; Pernambuco, 8; Minas Gerais, 6; Bahia, 5; "government housing on the Morro da Senda," 540; "employed in the city of Rio," 40; "absent with the knowledge of Official Agent of Colonization," 91; "engaged with the Baron of Mauá," 37; "went to work on the Pedro II Railway," 15; as well as one who returned to the United States and one other who died.[49]

This wide distribution of immigrants throughout Brazil clearly indicates how Brazil was actively pursuing its long-term U.S. Southern "colonization project" throughout its empire, which ranged as far away as its northern and northeastern regions as well as its southeastern and southernmost regions. At the time Brazilian immigrant settlements were known as *colônias* (colonies).

William Scully

William Scully, the editor and proprietor of the *Anglo-Brazilian Times* in Rio, is often mistakenly identified in the literature as a U.S. Southerner. However, as mentioned earlier, Scully was born and raised in Ireland—according to Irish—Latin American scholar Edmundo Murray, Scully was born in Buolick, South County Tipperary, into a Catholic family. According to Murray, Scully purportedly left for Brazil in the 1850s or early 1860s after the Irish potato famine (1846–49) and became a calligraphy teacher in Rio.[50] Later he married into an English-Anglican family (he purportedly married again to an American woman later) and became a shipping agent for the National Bolivian Navigation Company, which held a majority share in the Madeira–Mamoré Railway Company.

Scully began publishing the *Anglo-Brazilian Times* newspaper on February 7, 1865. Originally, its intended readership was the English-speaking community that lived or worked in Rio (in today's vernacular, the expat community), which included a large American readership. It ran several in-depth editorials and articles on immigration, reporting on detailed accounts and concerns about U.S. Southern immigration and specifically delineating locations for potential U.S. Southern settlements in Brazil. Scully also promoted Irish immigration to Brazil, though that never panned out. The Irish colony of Princípe Dom Pedro in Santa Catarina (1868–69) ultimately failed for unknown reasons, but it was most likely because of lack of roads and transportation as well as widespread diseases.

Scully published the guide *Brazil: Its Provinces and Chief Cities; the Manners and Customs of the People; Agricultural, Commercial and other Statistics, etc.* in 1865, as well as *A New Map of Brazil* in 1866 (drawn and engraved by George Phillip & Son, Liverpool and London). He later died in Pau, France, on February 14, 1885.[51]

Scully also published several editorials and articles in the *Anglo-Brazilian Times* that favored U.S. Southern immigration to Brazil. Scully, along with Charles Nathan (frequently mentioned in Scully's editorials, Nathan was also a founding member of the International Society for Immigration in Rio) and other Brazilian immigration societies and agents, was investing and promoting the settlements to emerge in the same locations, particularly in the provinces of São Paulo, Paraná, and Espírito Santo. Scully's newspaper became an important venue for the dissemination of information in the migration of Confederados, especially once they had arrived in Brazil.

The Settlements

By late 1865 the Brazilian government had set up a process clearly intended to facilitate the mobility of U.S. Southerners to move to and within Brazil. This process involved a negotiation by way of an "immigration agent" or a few individuals who would travel to Brazil searching for adequate lands, secure those land tracts and hold themselves responsible for these lands with the Brazilian government, and thereafter return to the United States to recruit colonists to settle there.

For example, Dr. Gaston described his experience when he met with Brazilian Minister of Agriculture Antônio Paula e Sousa: "I told him that the object of my visit was to look for a home for my own family, and to make an examination of the country, with a view to report the result for the information of other families, whose unfortunate situation in the South induced them to desire a change in residence, and, in like manner with myself, hoped that a desirable location might be found in this country."[52]

In 1865 the *New York Herald* reported, "The Brazilians are aware that Americans are the best emigrants for this country, because they bring with them intelligence and energy to introduce agricultural implements, which are needed to take the place of the decreasing power—slavery."[53]

Dom Pedro II agreed to a private audience with Rev. Dunn in early 1866, in which the latter assured the emperor that with the right inducements and land grants, he and his associates (Maj. Meriwether, Dr. Gaston, Col. McMullen, and Col. Gunter) would secure the move of five hundred thousand individuals to Brazil (this never happened).[54] Here we observe the political influence of religious leaders such as Rev. Dunn and his direct involvement with the emperor. A year later, Rev. Dunn met again with Minister of Agriculture, Antônio Paula e Sousa, who informed

Dunn: "I will furnish you with free transit to any part of the Empire you wish to examine; and with an engineer and interpreter, who will see that your journeyings cost you nothing."[55] Rev. Dunn was decidedly optimistic, as he wrote from New Orleans on January 14, 1867, to Counselor Azambuja of the Brazilian legation in New York: "Everything moves on as well as could be expected. Our emigration will prove a success. My book is stirring the best of our people tremendously. I have received as high as twenty-five letters per day, since my return to this city, asking for informations [sic] and ordering my book on Brazil . . . I will sail from this City about the last of March, with one or two hundred families direct to Iguape . . . The opposition is strong, but the feeling to go is intense."[56] Clearly, Rev. Dunn's book *Brazil, the Home for Southerners*, published in 1866, played an important role in helping to spread the interest of U.S. Southerners in migrating to Brazil. Despite public opposition in the United States, spirits were high.

Col. Charles Grandison Gunter, a planter and lawyer from Alabama originally from North Carolina (also a Freemason, Past Master, Montgomery Lodge No. 11), secured a few thousand acres in the Rio Doce Valley by Lake Juparanã in the municipality of Linhares, province of Espírito Santo (about three hundred miles north of the city of Rio de Janeiro).[57] In its first few years, Gunter's settlement flourished. He appeared cheerful in his communication with family and friends; for example, in a letter published in the *Charleston Mercury*, Col. Gunter wrote, "We are about twenty-five miles from the sea, and have a daily breeze from the Atlantic . . . there are now about twenty families here."[58]

Interestingly, before he left for Brazil, Gunter had contributed to securing a legal act passed by the U.S. legislature of 1847–48, the first of its kind in the country to protect the rights to property of women in marriage.[59] Later in 1889 his son, Basil Manly Gunter, became the U.S. consul in Vitória, in Espírito Santo; his other son, Horace Gunter, became wealthy building railroads in Espírito Santo.[60]

By 1870 reports were spreading that Espírito Santo was capable of yielding the finest quality "Sea Island" cotton and that Gunter's settlement was "planting [sugar]cane extensively, to give immediate employment to newcomers, leaving the culture of cotton until more settlers arrive, and preparations can be made for taking care of it."[61] The report in the *Anglo-Brazilian Times* described the huge potential for further agricultural possibilities, clearly attempting to lure more immigrants there. The report was simply signed by a "H. L." of Rio (this is likely to have been Horace Lane).

In 1866 William H. Norris and Dr. J. E. Cloutier purchased a farm in Santa Bárbara. Norris reported, "We have purchased a Fazenda [farm]. Say to my North-American friends that I think the Province of S. Paulo is the best for cotton planting, and that this is what they desire. Tell them to come and examine the country."[62]

Capt. Silas S. Totten had already formed a partnership by then and erected a steam sawmill adjacent to Cananéia, along the Guarahú, a confluent of the River Jacupiranga. The survey of the lands contracted by Horace Lane from Louisiana, on the margins of the bay of Paranaguá, between the Assunguy and the Serra Negra, had been completed. Maj. Frank McMullen, William Bowen, and Rev. Dunn agreed on lands in Iguape that had been purchased from private landowners in the province of São Paulo; they obtained the concession of other public lands situated along the margins of the São Lourenço and Juquiá rivers.[63]

In a completely different environment, far away from Brazil's political and agrarian hub and about 1,988 miles away from Santa Bárbara, Maj. Lansford W. Hastings went to the northern region of Brazil. He settled 614,000 acres authorized by the Brazilian government, near the Amazonian port of Santarém, between the River Amazonas and the Tapajós and Coruá Rivers in the province of Pará.[64] A dispatch published in 1866 in the *New York Herald* reported that members of the Hastings colony were required to pay a hundred dollars in gold before they departed for Brazil, "finding their own provisions and bedding . . . For terms of membership apply to Major R. Hastings, 100 St. Anthony Street." By 1867 Charles N. Rowly of Natchez, Mississippi; Calvin Hughes of Chapel Hill, Texas; and W. C. Jones, "and other parties in South Carolina, Arkansas, Mississippi, Louisiana . . . lands were likewise guaranteed."[65] By 1867 the major Confederado clusters had begun to gradually emerge.

Land in the rural northeast region of Brazil was also surveyed. Examples include a settlement headed by William Graham in Pernambuco (between Pimenteiras and Água Preta) and another "likewise destined for North Americans, whose pioneers are Ogden Thompson, John McCul, C. S. Gunter and others" in Bahia, in the valleys of the Jequitinhonha and Pardo.[66]

Rev. Dunn had prepared for more settlers to arrive at his settlement; "Rev. Ballard S. Dunn has four or five farms on the lands he purchased, besides a farm called Paco Grande, where [there] is a great hut made for the temporary residence of the immigrants coming. It is advantaged by the proximity of the road which by orders of the Government is making to the foot of the Serra do Mar."[67] However, despite his fiery words of encouragement in his flamboyant book *Brazil, the Home for Southerners*, and without warning, in late 1869 Rev. Dunn abandoned the immigration idea entirely. He returned to the United States, much to the surprise and disappointment of the immigrants he had recruited, now left without their leader. Rev. Dunn had managed to establish a good rapport and entrée with Imperial agencies, yet settlers were left to fend for themselves without Dunn's political leverage with the Empire. After Dunn's return to the United States, the settlement of Iguape gradually dissolved, and rumors circulated among Confederados that Rev. Dunn had absconded with all their funds. It is known that Dunn was eventually "demitted" from the Diocese of Louisiana in 1869 after he returned to the United States, although it is not known exactly why (at that time Dunn was living in New York).[68]

Another settlement, the Rio das Velhas settlement in Minas Gerais, also failed quickly in 1869. The reason for this failure, explained by then president of that province José Maria Correá de Sá e Benevides, is as telling as it is anachronistic. He did not endorse U.S. immigration, because he believed that Americans would not adapt to Brazil and that "the Latin race ought to be preferred as the source of [Brazil's] colonization, and American and Germanic colonization should be availed only if subsidiarily and very cautiously . . . the American foreigner loves liberty, independence and property, and will not subject himself to be a hired servant of the great private proprietors."[69]

Eventually five major Confederado clusters emerged in Brazil. (1) In the Vale do Ribeira area, a cluster emerged along the Iguape River basin, in Cananéia and Iguape on the southeastern coast of the province of São Paulo, headed by Dr. Gaston, Rev. Ballard Dunn, and Frank McMullan. Rev. Dunn settled along the Rio Juquiá, calling his settlement "Lizzieland" after his daughter, Elizabeth. (2) Along the Assunguy River, another emerged on an estuary flowing into the Paranaguá Bay on the coast in the province of Paraná, headed by Col. M. S. Swain, Horace Lane of Louisiana,[70] Dr. John H. Blue, Judge John Guillet, and Guillet's brothers, all from Missouri.[71] (3) In the Santa Bárbara region, in the western interior of the province of São Paulo, a cluster headed by Col. William H. Norris emerged. (4) In the province of Espírito Santo, in Linhares along the Rio Doce by Lake Juparanã, another cluster was headed by Col. Charles Grandison Gunter. (5) Maj. Lansford Warren Hastings, who headed north to the settlement in Santarém, Pará, in the Amazonian region.[72]

The most successful settlement was in Santa Bárbara. When the Norris family arrived in Santa Bárbara, the local population, numbering around two thousand at the time, largely comprised small- to medium-sized agriculturalists who mostly grew corn, beans, and rice, sufficient for subsistence and for furnishing the neighboring Constituição (today, Piracicaba).[73] The subregions of Funil, Bom Retiro, Estação Santa Bárbara (Santa Bárbara Railway Station, the old railway station and today, the city of Americana), and Campo (where the Confederado cemetery is) collectively formed the Santa Bárbara region.

Emigration Becomes a "Contagion"

From New York and Richmond to Savannah, Mobile, and New Orleans, Brazilian immigration agencies established their own "emigration colonization agencies" offering "superior facilities and inducements for making Brazil an attractive home for the settler."[74]

By 1867 the Imperial Agent's Office in New York City was swamped with new applicants who wished to move to Brazil. The office had to turn away at least one hundred applicants:

The Imperial Emigrant Agent is located at No. 2Qh Broadway, New York, (upstairs) who will furnish emigrants with passports and transportation, by signing the above obligation and paying five dollars, either in gold or currency, which money will be refunded to emigrant[s] on producing a receipt given by the agent, after the packet has left the port . . . This money is required to be paid as a guarantee that the emigrant will embark, but should he fail, he forfeits the five dollars. Whilst in his office, we witnessed the refusal of at least one hundred applicants desirous of embarking on the packet.[75]

By now, the *Pulaski Citizen* in Tennessee reported, "Emigration has indeed become a contagion."[76] The "Brazil Fever" was widespread, and it was estimated that every ship leaving the United States for Brazilian ports during the period between 1868 and 1869 carried immigrants. Most served in the Confederate Army; several were plantation owners, lawyers, or medical doctors.[77]

In 1867 Charles Nathan organized a steamer line between Rio, the northern ports of Brazil, and New Orleans, with a Brazilian government contract that supplied passages to immigrants. Diogo "James" Hartley was the contractor for the line of steamers between Rio and Santa Catarina, "The intermediate ports, has also contracted with the Presidency of Sao [São] Paulo for a line on the Ribeira and Iguape, to run between Iguape and Xiririca [today the municipality of Eldorado], and to connect with the fortnightly calls of the steamers on the *Linha Intermediária*, thus serving a region which has already become the home of a considerable number of Americans."[78]

These potential immigrants (especially those recruited in New York City) were a heterogeneous group. Their social classes and occupations varied widely, and they included "generals, colonels, doctors, lawyers, merchants, planters, ministers, teachers, barroom loafers, bounty jumpers, and vagabonds." There were even Irish and English emigres—newly arrived in the United States—who had signed up to leave for Brazil.[79] The party of U.S. immigrants that the New York Packet Company sent by way of the Brazilian government was not well-received in Rio. These immigrants recruited in New York City were not agriculturalists, in sharp contrast to the echelon of agriculturalists (merchant planters) such as the Norrises, Gunters, Halls, and Millers. A correspondent from *Jornal do commercio* (São Paulo) voiced his complaint:

> The North-American emigrants who have come from Rio to Iguape have already given us evident proof of their morality. They practice disorder of every kind, arson, attempts to murder, robberies... Pretty toys Mr. Quintino Bocayuva has sent us from the United States! He gathered up in the streets of New York all the loafers, vagabonds, and thieves from the gutters, and sent them to his country... the Minister of Agriculture should keep them and send Mr. Quintino Bocayuva to found a colony with them, even if it be on top of the Corcovado [A reference to the hill where the statue of the famous "Christ the Redeemer" stands today in Rio].[80]

The assumption here is that those immigrants, deemed "troublemakers," had been recruited despite not being agriculturalists. Hence, some residents of Rio did not buy into the U.S. immigration scheme, as the *Anglo-Brazilian Times* reported in an editorial in 1867: "What a contrast to such loafing intriguers is presented in Mr. C. G. Gunter of Alabama, now the great pioneer of American emigration to the fine region of the River Doce, who up to the present has sought favors from the Government, preferring independently to be himself alone the architect of his own fortunes; and we are happy to learn his energies are likely to see a full measure of success."[81] This report then highlighted "city immigrants" (purportedly the "loafing intriguers") in sharp contrast to U.S. Southern immigrants such as the Gunters.

However, in 1869 a newly introduced English-language newspaper in Rio, the *Brazilian World*, published an editorial in its first edition that went to the extent of comparing the plight of the U.S. Southerners in Brazil to that of the Puritans who had left England for the New World. It stated, "Like the Puritans of the 16th Century who abandoned England, their former home... the Confederates of the south incline to abandon to-day in the same manner and with the same strength of will, the Government that destroyed their political rights and arbitrarily changed their family and every social relation, in a manner of degrading to them as freemen." This same editorial went on to state that the new U.S. immigrants were "not vagabonds" and, much to the contrary, that "besides their financial means, [they] bring intelligence, indefatigable energy, and though last not least in value, the theory and practice of improved Agricultural and Industrial labor. We have more than sufficient proof of what they can do."[82] In general, most Brazilians, especially agrarian families, intellectuals, and politicians, were unquestionably pleased with the ongoing influx of U.S. Southern immigrants.

Nonetheless, U.S. newspapers continued to oppose the migration project. The title of a dispatch published in 1871 in the *New York Times* carried an alarming tone: "The Self-Exiled Southerners: Terrible Sufferings of the Planters who went to Brazil. A Picture of Despair, Depravity and Destitution." The same dispatch reported that it had been six years since "several thousand persons of all classes and degrees [. . .] have left their comparatively comfortable homes in the Free States of America, to exchange them for questionable residences in the wilds of mongrelized Brazil." The language used to describe Brazilian populations (e.g., "mongrelized") reflects the predominant racial ideology of the time. The same report continued, "It is difficult for an Anglo-Saxon to become habituated to the customs and practices of the *effete* Portuguese who here have been engrafted upon a stupid, solid Indian stock."[83] The usage of this type of language, common at that time, also reflected general U.S. sentiment and public perception of Brazil and Brazilians.

In 1877 the *New York Times* summarized a report about emigration to Brazil: "Tobacco-growers from Virginia, cotton-planters from the Carolinas, Georgia, Alabama and Mississippi, and extensive sugar-planters from the famous Red River district of Louisiana and Middle Texas . . . emigrated with their families to the provinces of San [São] Paulo and Espiritu [Espírito] Santo, in lower Brazil. Whole districts of the finest land in the South, from Maryland to Texas, were sacrificed for a mere song. Entire counties were almost depopulated by the great exodus of reputable emigrants and disreputable adventurers, who were alike infected with the fever for Brazilian colonization."[84]

The U.S. press characterized U.S. Southern migration and its migrants to Brazil in a highly negative tone, demonizing the immigration plan altogether. The *Daily Dispatch* of Richmond, Virginia, admonished those who thought about moving to Brazil:

> We leave a land where our own race is in the majority, and where no legislation can extend beyond the conferment of political privileges upon the blacks, for a land in which the African and mixed races largely predominate and in which no social distinction of color prevails. We must have a new language, acquire customs, live amongst jaguars or yellow fever, find no sympathy in our religious ideas, have no adequate means of education for our children, but permit them to grow up ignorant little Brazilians instead of cultivated Virginians. We advise our countrymen to think twice before they make the experiment of emigration to Brazil.[85]

The underlining theme of Brazilian "wilderness" was palpably clear. Note the reference and warning about Brazilian "mixed races" and that "no distinction of color prevails," as well as the concern that potential children of immigrants would "grow up ignorant little Brazilians."

Jefferson Davis also opposed the move, and Gen. Robert E. Lee urged U.S. Southerners not to leave for Brazil, advising all "who could remain; to adhere to their homes and friends; and [that he had] seen no reason to change [his] opinions."[86] Gen. Lee finalized his letter by stating that he was not a Freemason, which strongly suggests that there was an implicit Freemason network involved within the migration process to Brazil.

Despite political and public U.S. opposition, thousands of U.S. Southerners left for Brazil. This enthusiasm "indicate[d] the spirit of gaiety and romance which enveloped South American colonization schemes by the spring of 1866."[87]

The Backdrop of Iguape, Cananéia, and Linhares

Entries of Americans in Cananéia (in the province of São Paulo), found in the Regional Archives of São Paulo, show that Americans Benjamin

Map 1. The major Confederado settlement clusters in Brazil. Map by Paporn Thebpanya.

Ash and Ferdinand Cox (likely Ferdinand Coxe, probably misspelled as "Cox") arrived there as early as 1836. Nearly twenty years later, the same Ferdinand Coxe of Philadelphia would become the U.S. secretary of legation in Rio.[88] It is unknown what kind of business the two Americans were conducting at that time in Cananéia (on the coast of São Paulo). It is likely that knowledge about this area was made available to them because of the Ribeira do Iguape's reputation for high-yield production of rice. This location would eventually become the area for one of the U.S. Southern settlements decades later, as seen later in this chapter.

On October 10, 1865, the *Anglo-Brazilian Times* devoted a special section to the topic of U.S. Southern immigration, highlighting the lands suitable and available for potential immigrant settlements (*colônias*). It outlined in geographic detail the specific locations of lands where Confederados should eventually establish their settlements. This newspaper was written in the English language and was available to newly arrived U.S. Southerners searching for information and geographical pointers—these Southerners could not yet speak or read in Portuguese. Clearly, Scully (the editor), Nathan, Bocaiúva, Bastos, and other members of the International Immigration Society of Rio—all of whom knew each other—were working together toward one goal, and, the *Anglo-Brazilian Times* provided vital information.[89]

While knowledge of these lands would have been new to U.S. Southerners, those locations were already well-known to Brazilian elite families centuries beforehand. That is, Linhares, Cananéia, and Iguape had been Portuguese colonial port towns established centuries earlier in the 1500s. In contrast to U.S. ports, other Brazilian cities and ports such as Santos, Rio de Janeiro, Vitória, Salvador, São Luís, and Recife had already been old towns before "Jamestown, New York, or Boston were dreamed of."[90]

All five major Confederado settlement clusters were familiar to Luso-Brazilian sociopolitical elites. The emperor himself, Dom Pedro II, had visited them all at some point. Linhares, Cananéia, and Iguape had been etched into Brazilian historical annals centuries before the arrival of U.S. Southerners.

The Ribeira de Iguape region, part of a broader hydrographic basin and a coastal estuary area, comprises the conglomerate of Iguape and Cananéia (both in São Paulo) and Paranaguá (in Paraná); known as the Iguape-Cananéia-Paranaguá estuary lagoon complex, they together form the Ribeira Valley (Vale do Ribeira).[91] Lake Juparanã along the River Doce (in the province of Espírito Santo), where one of the settlements had moved to, stems from a Tupi word that means "sea of fresh water"; it is the largest freshwater lake by volume in Brazil.[92]

Both Cananéia and Iguape played significant roles in the development of Brazilian historical geography. For example, the imaginary line designated by the Treaty of Tordesilhas in 1494, which divided Spanish and Portuguese world territories 370 leagues west of the Cape Verde islands, passed through Iguape. In 1503, none other than Amerigo Vespucci—after whom the continent "America" is named—arrived at the harbor of Cananéia for a brief exploratory trip. Furthermore, in 1822, in his three-volume *History of Brazil*, Robert Southey mentions Cananéia and Paranaguá and highlighted its important rice exports (though he never visited Brazil).[93] Last, eminent French geographer Élisée Reclus aptly describes this area as "a perfectly distinct geographical region."[94] He continues:

> It is but thinly settled, and its chief towns are mere villages, such as Apiahy, now forsaken by gold-hunters[;] Xiririca, with unworked quarries of lovely white marble; Iguape and Cananéia two riverside ports, the former near the mouth of the Ribeirão, communicating by a navigable canal with the so-called Mar Pequeno, 'Little Sea,' which extends for over 60 miles along the banks. Cananéia, occupying an island in this flooded depression, is accessible to large river craft at high water. This port marks the spot where Christovão Jacques and Amerigo Vespucci landed in 1503, and from the same place set out the first bandeira of eighty adventures in search of gold.[95]

Thus Iguape developed into a prosperous region, and in 1841, while still an adolescent, Dom Pedro II bestowed to Antônio da Silva Prado the title of Barão de Iguape (Baron of Iguape). The Silva Prados, a prominent Brazilian family, were at the forefront of developing agricultural commerce in the interior of the province of São Paulo, where the Santa Bárbara settlement emerged.[96] With the decline of the Gold Rush of the eighteenth century, Iguape developed its wealth through rice production, yet with increasing infrastructural and political problems, the city's prosperity later deteriorated. Charles Nathan advised Dr. Gaston that he should visit Cananéia and Iguape in 1865 (Gaston described him as "that noble-souled friend of Southerners").[97] Dr. Gaston had been assured by the Brazilian Minister of Agriculture Paula e Souza—among other unfulfilled promises he received—that the Brazilian government would open a wagon road from the port of Cananéia to Xiririca (today the municipality of Eldorado). This would not happen for decades to come.

Linhares, on the other hand, on the coastal province of Espírito Santo (just north of the province of Rio de Janeiro), gained its name in 1860 from Dom Rodrigo de Sousa Coutinho, Conde de Linhares

(Count of Linhares)—again, an honor bestowed by Dom Pedro II, who visited the village that same year. The Sousa Coutinho family, another prominent Brazilian family (also known Freemasons) had long been associated with the Portuguese Crown and had married into the Maxwell family (of Maxwell, Wright & Co.). Rodrigo de Sousa Coutinho had been promoting his own agricultural and technological projects as early as the late eighteenth century and the early nineteenth century in Brazil; he played a vital role in bringing the Portuguese court to Brazil in 1808.[98]

All three places—Linhares, Iguape, and Cananéia—were well-known to Brazilian elites; the Confederados did not just select random, backwater hinterlands to settle. These locations had been researched and promoted under careful advisement of Brazilian immigration societies and promoters (e.g., Nathan, Scully, Bastos). This confirms the collaboration of immigration stakeholders in Brazil to guide migrating U.S. Southerners to places with direct connections to old Brazilian elite families.

However, Linhares, Iguape, and Cananéia are located within a connected ecosystem comprising rivers, estuaries, sand dunes, mangroves, and coastal rainforests. This ecosystem's soil proved to be inadequate for U.S. Southern agriculturalists; moreover, it turned out that the lack of transportation became one of the biggest problems for the settlements. The failure of Linhares on the Rio Doce (a settlement headed by Charles G. Gunter) was attributed to "various causes, and it would be difficult to find two persons who will agree entirely on this subject."[99]

The settlements' problems included the lack of communications with Rio, the failure to successfully recruit other U.S. Southerners to join the settlement, and the lack of care by the Brazilian government for the settlers (quite surprising given the eagerness of the Brazilian Empire to recruit and welcome immigrants). While Col. Gunter's settlement showed signs of prosperity at first, "the immigrants who nearly all settled around the beautiful Lake Juparanã, were charmed with the beauty of the scenery, they believed the soil to be fertile, and all went to to work with brave hearts and willing hands." However, over time, more and more problems emerged with disease and the lack of food and adequate communication, which led to the ultimate abandonment of the settlement. As the *Correio mercantil* dispatch reported in 1867, "only a few families remained, and are yet trying to combat successfully the difficulties by which the area is surrounded . . . there is no hope of the founding a large and prosperous colony on the Doce."[100]

The Demise of the McMullen-Bowen Settlement

The settlement in Iguape, headed by Maj. Frank McMullen and Col. William Bowen—both originally from Texas—rapidly saw its own demise.

McMullen's trip to Brazil was plagued with several mishaps, heavy financial burdens, and other problems even before its departure. On November 6, 1866, McMullen wrote to J. Azambuja from the Brazilian legation in New York, appearing very concerned and anxious about the transportation arrangements to Brazil. He wrote:

> I am disappointed in not being able to take out the amount of machinery and agricultural implements which I hoped to take with me. The amount to be paid here is $6,000 in United States currency, which several of us, by putting means together, have been able to raise. Of course, we rely on the promises of the Brazilian Government, to refund this amount to us, on our landing in the Empire; together with the balance due on the charter, all amounting to $7,500 in United States currency, or its equivalent in gold at 148. Besides this, we feed ourselves and furnish our own fuel. But no other vessel, carrying 150 passengers will ever be chartered at these low figures.
>
> We sail from the port of Galveston about 10th of December, but not later than the 15th. We will clear for Iguape, but just before sailing I will notify Your Excellency, when you please notify the Brazilian Government that the necessary order may meet us at Iguape, and that we may not be disappointed on landing there for I have already suffered so many disappointments that I am half becoming disheartened.[101]

Azambuja replied to McMullen's concerns on November 16, 1866, in a stern tone: "It seems to me very strange that my own signature in the official document I sent to you in triplicate would not be considered as sufficient security for the fulfillment of the concessions made to you . . . by the Government of His Majesty the Emperor of Brazil."[102]

Finally, after waiting for five weeks, McMullen and the 154 settlers he had recruited left for Brazil. From Galveston, Texas, he wrote to Azambuja on January 6, 1867, "our vessel has at last left that city, bound for Galveston, and we are hourly expecting her arrival . . . One hundred and fifty-four persons are here and have been here for more than five weeks on heavy expenses, awaiting the happy moment when they should set sail for our new 'land of promise.'"[103]

Nonetheless, McMullen was clearly very troubled as he finalized his letter to Azambuja: "My troubles of all kinds have weighed heavily on me, and my health is fast failing me. I am hardly able to be up. Pardon me for speaking of my domestic matters."[104] No doubt, this was an ominous sign.

Even after the settlers had arrived in Iguape, they faced continued challenges. In four letters written in late 1867 to the president of the province of São Paulo and Minister of Agriculture José Tavares Bastos, signed by Guilherme "William" Bowen, "Agent of American Settlement, São Lourenço River in the district of Iguape" (known as the "McMullen's and Bowen's Collony"—in the English orthographic spelling of that time, with two *l*'s), Bowen provided the names of eighty-nine individuals and their eighteen families (listed by age and sex) residing in the Iguape settlement then. These family names included Cobb, Beasley, Cook, Gill, Wright, Baxter, Bowen, and Smith. Bowen was enthusiastic when he finished his first letter:

> This will soon be the most prosperous and flourishing part of São Paulo. The new Road I am to build under contract is now underway, and very soon our Collony will have communication with Santos. The virgin forrest [*sic*] that is now giving way to the industry and entering energy of American agriculturalists, will within one year blossom with ease, and begin to send its fruits with the national Treasury as the reward of numerous indulgencies and favors grant[ed] to our people by the Imperial Government. I pledge my word that under my management this Collony will gradually improve. Praying your

Excellency's good health and the prosperity of the Empire. I remain your most humble servant. Guilherme Bowen, Agent American Settlement, Sao Lourenço River. November 9th, 1867.[105]

However, Frank McMullen died of tuberculosis in 1867 in Iguape, and despite his initial optimistic tone, Bowen later stated that the provisions promised to the settlers were not adequate. Serious internal problems arose after a new leader was appointed to replace McMullen: George Scarborough Barnsley, a medical doctor of Woodlands Plantation, Cass County, Georgia, and former Confederate soldier and assistant surgeon in the Eighth Georgia Regiment. Bowen described increasing disapproval with the new leadership:

> Some have left the settlement on account of the scarcity of provisions and also on account of efforts making by one G. S. Barnsley at Iguape to get into his possession the affairs of the Collony. This man, Barnsley[,] together with the uncle of my former partner (Mr. F. McMullen), James Dyer is making [*sic*] by lies and false statements . . . very soon they will all be published to the World, in the Journals of Brazil and also the U.S.A by one of the Collonists.[106]

In his third letter to the president of the province, Bowen's clear concern with the lack of adequate provisions highlighted the major problems among the settlers and how the conditions had changed drastically:

> The attention of your Excellency is called to the suffering condition of our people at present, the Imperial Government and your Excellency has kindly sent money to Iguape, to the Delegado [mayor] of that place, with orders to buy provisions of the people here, and it has been done, but such provisions bought as they could not use carne seca [dried meat] spoilt, farinha [manioc flour] so badly spoilt that notwithstanding they were without breadstuffs many did not even draw it others drew it for their pigs. . . . no sugar or coffee was such sent, the fashao [*feijão*, beans] was tolerably good. Your Excellency will understand that these people are not paupers but were unmercifully

robbed by those who brought them out from the U.S.A. having paid out over twenty thousand Dollars.[107]

The settlers saw this new leadership as a detriment to the community. Bowen wrote, "To the management of our affairs will be against the will and interest of the people of this settlement, and will be the means of breaking up the Collony, which is now promising, and in which we wish to live?" Bowen continued in his letter, "If said G. S. Barnsley is put at the head of affairs here. There is not a man in the Collony who will submit to him."[108]

These letters show the initial optimism of William Bowen and provide important insights into the shift from a blossoming Confederate colony to general dissatisfaction and the colony's ultimate demise—a result of famine, mismanagement, infighting, and lack of provisions. William Bowen eventually left for the Santa Bárbara settlement, where he died in 1891 at the age of seventy-two; he was buried at the cemetery at Campo.

Hastings's Settlement in Santarém

Tucked away in the Amazon, Maj. Lansford W. Hastings's settlement in Santarém was isolated from the rest of Brazil. The distance between Santarém and Rio de Janeiro is about 2,249 miles, and overland transportation through central Brazil at that time was virtually impossible. Transportation between Rio and Santarém meant a slow and long trip by boat around the lengthy Brazilian coast. In addition, malaria, dysentery, disease, heat, lack of provisions, and inadequate soil for agriculture would all eventually prove major problems.

Maj. Lansford Warren Hastings (1819–70), a lawyer, veteran of the Mexican–American War, and a Confederate veteran of the U.S. Civil War, originally from Knox County, Ohio, had already devised other migration schemes before his decision to focus on Brazil. In 1842, almost a decade and a half before his settlement project in Santarém, Hastings led the "first planned overland wagon migration to Oregon . . . and led the first emigrants over the Salt Desert Cutoff that subsequently bore his name."[109] Shortly thereafter in 1845 he published *The Emigrants Guide to Oregon and California.* He is often portrayed among historians as a "swindler," a "villain," or the "Baron Munchausen of travelers."[110] After Hastings failed in his pursuit of the presidency and the governorship of California, the U.S. Civil War began; he decided to join the Confederacy and came up with a proposal to capture California, Arizona, and New Mexico for the U.S. South, though he soon dropped that idea. At the end of U.S. Civil War, he had become convinced to move to Brazil, and he quickly secured a land grant in Santarém. His wrote *The Emigrant's Guide to Brazil*, published in 1867—a rare book with only a few copies in existence today—which influenced interest in emigration to Brazil.[111]

After his second consecutive return trip from the U.S. South to recruit more settlers to migrate to Santarém, Hastings left for Brazil for the last time on an iron steamer, the *Red Gauntlet*, which ran into mechanical problems along the way to Pará and made a stop at the Caribbean island of Saint Thomas. It was there, while the ship was docked, that Hastings likely contracted yellow fever and died in 1870, never fulfilling his Amazonian settlement enterprise.[112] Nonetheless, the emigrants onboard continued their journey to Pará.

Soon reports in the U.S. press described the settlers who remained in Santarém, stranded without a leader, plagued by starvation, disease, malaria, and lack of provisions. The plight of the Hastings settlement came to the attention of U.S. President Ulysses Grant. Henry Blow, ambassador and minister to Brazil (1869–71), had received orders from President Grant to allow warships to transport more than four hundred U.S. Southerners residing throughout Brazil (not only those who remained in Santarém) who were pleading to return and needed assistance.[113] Many of the settlers complained that the Brazilian government had not followed through with its promises and inducements, and others admitted that they had made an unwise decision to move to Brazil.

Between 1869 and 1871 the U.S. Navy sent the *Kansas*, the *Quinneberg*, and the *Portsmouth* to transport U.S. Southerners back to the United States. Brazilian senator and later foreign minister Barão de Cotegipe agreed with Ambassador Blow that the transportation of U.S. Southerners (of those U.S. settlers who had been recruited by Brazilian agents) back to the United States would be made at Brazil's expense, beginning in early 1870. However, there was not enough space on the ships for all those who requested transportation, and by 1872 U.S. Secretary Hamilton Fish had informed the new Minister to Brazil, James R. Partridge, that he would not be able to defray any costs associated with the return transportation of those immigrants.[114]

Commander A. P. Cooke from the U.S. Navy Department received final orders for the U.S. corvette *Swatara* to proceed to Pará on special service and offer "free passages . . . to such indigent American citizens and their families. . . . [who were all] brought North and landed at Port Royal, S. C." About 150 individuals were rescued from the Hastings settlement. In 1875 the *New York Herald* reported, "Ten years' experience in those parts has completely disenchanted the colonists; many died, all suffered, and quite a number who were fortunately in funds or who had friends to aid them, gave up the missionary scheme and returned to the United States, happy to find shelter in their native land again. Others, less fortunate being impoverished, could not retrace their steps, and were compelled to remain in Brazil, undergoing distress and all the pangs of penury and want."[115] Hence, by 1875, the Amazonian settlement that Hastings had imagined developing—an idea touted by Matthew F. Maury decades earlier—had ultimately dissolved, with only about fifty Confederados remaining in the area by the end of 1875. Half a century later, just about a dozen descendants remained in Santarém (mostly descendants of the Riker family).[116]

The distances between each of the Confederado settlements also made it too difficult to maintain any kind of political or social unity, and communication in Brazil was slow and unreliable.

By 1875 these problems, including internal conflicts, had emerged in other settlements also, and several hundred U.S. Southerners wanted to return to the United States. All but the Santa Bárbara settlement disintegrated within a few years. Problems included the different modes of labor, the challenges with the language barrier, customs, laws, bad soil, weeds, mildew, insects, disease, internal mismanagement, and broken promises of the inducements that had been made by the Brazilian government. For example, the railroad that was supposed to be built by the Brazilian government at the Ribeira do Iguape area, where transportation of crops was not possible, was never completed—another inconsistency seen throughout this story given Brazil's commitment to welcoming immigrants and Confederados. The Brazilian government evidently did not follow through with its promises. Therefore, many of those displaced settlers began to head toward the Santa Bárbara settlement as soon as they heard about how that colony was prospering. Of the thousands who migrated to Brazil, it is likely that two-thirds returned to the United States.

Dr. Christopher P. Ezell, his wife, and his five children were one of those families that opted to return to the United States. In a dispatch from 1888, the *Baltimore Sun* referred to the Confederados as "refugees": "Dr. Ezell is a part of thirty-three refugees who left New Orleans twenty-one years ago to seek their fortunes in Brazil." Dr. Ezell had prospered relatively well in Santa Bárbara; however, for "some unaccountable cause the crops degenerated and low prices prevailed." His wife, Mrs. Ezell, was the daughter of Col. Robert Broadnax of Alabama (who had returned to the United States from Brazil fourteen years earlier). Dr. Ezell also commented on the end of slavery in Brazil: "Referring to the emancipation of slaves on May 13, Dr. Ezell said it is considered by the Brazilians to [be] a benefit to the country. The government intends to colonize them, and he thought their future is bright." Ezell stated, "[Italian] immigrants are pouring into the country . . . the influx is enormous." Dr. Ezell also mentioned, "Col. Wm. H. Norris of Alabama, founder of the colony, and now a very old man; Captain A. W. Currie and Orville Whittaker, of Louisiana; James Miller and Green Ferguson, of South Carolina; John Domm, of Texas" had all remained in the Santa Bárbara settlement. The report concluded, "He will remain in Baltimore for a few days, and then seek a permanent home in some of the rising cities of the new South. While glad to return to America, Dr. Ezell says he has no cause to regret having gone to the Brazils."[117]

Ultimately, the mass return to the United States may be perceived as a general failure in the U.S. Southern immigration plan, except for Santa

Bárbara. However, the act of leaving the United States voluntarily was a logical move driven by world capitalist and agrarian motivations given the political and economic despondency widespread throughout the U.S. South—which resulted in the largest migration of white populations out of the United States. Moreover, the success of Santa Bárbara can be largely attributed to the leadership of William H. Norris, its location and fertile soil, its settlers, and the way in which community members eventually intermarried with other local and immigrant groups of the region over time. Here, the fact that Confederado descendants eventually became fully "Brazilian" (fluent in the local language, culture, and customs, etc.) was perhaps the best sign of their success in the Confederado immigrant venture. By virtue of embracing the Brazilian national and emblematic metaphor of cultural hybridity, they were able to better adapt, adopt, change, and integrate into Brazilian society while maintaining sociocultural elements that eventually evolved into syncretic symbolisms—with inconsistent interpretations—of the Confederacy and Lost Cause ideologies.

By the mid- to late nineteenth century, trade with Brazil had increased substantially. This commercial relationship would continue to grow in the next four decades after the U.S. Civil War ended, creating a viable working space for individuals who were at once immigration agents and stakeholders. They would incorporate and optimize the immigration enterprise with their own financial interests. Charles Nathan was one of those individuals.

Charles Nathan

One immigration agent and accountant, Charles Nathan (1826–1910), was a chief immigration promoter and a key figure in this Confederado story. He was the personification of a transnational figure: Nathan, known as "Carlos" in Brazil, was Jewish and a Freemason, purportedly born in Rio de Janeiro of English parents who had migrated to Rio in the 1820s, yet also a resident of both New Orleans and Rio.[118] Nathan's name appears in various sources, as he had established important business associations and connections that were vital to facilitating migration processes.

Nathan was instrumental in promoting U.S. Southern immigration to Brazil, and he was one of the most well-known immigration agents of the time. For example, Dr. Gaston explained how Nathan was responsible for the transportation of U.S. Southerners:

> With a view to promote in a more enlarged sphere the emigration of our people, a proposition has been submitted to the Brazilian government by Mr. Nathan, in which arrangements will be made by him for the transportation of persons from the Southern States to Brazil, with the privilege to the emigrants of paying the passage-money in three instalments at the end of the third, fourth, and fifth years, and without interest. He assumes the responsibility of guaranteeing to the government the payment of these passage bills which it is to receive, giving him bonds for the amount, with the allowance of a certain amount for each emigrant that is thus brought from the United States to Brazil.[119]

Besides being an immigration promoter and a Freemason, Nathan was a public accountant (*contador público*) in Rio, and he had written and published a book in Rio (in Portuguese) in 1864, *Exposição que faz o contador público ao commercio do Rio de Janeiro* (Exposition of what makes a public accountant within the commerce of Rio de Janeiro), in which he explained selected case studies that involved detailed accounting practices by firms in Rio (including one case involving Maxwell, Wright & Co.).[120] Nathan regularly placed advertisements for his own businesses in Brazilian newspapers and in the *Anglo-Brazilian Times*. For example, the following advertisement appeared frequently between 1865 to 1869: "Charles Nathan. General Accountant. Average Stater and Liquidator of Bankrupt states, etc. Rua de S. Pedro 72."[121]

Nathan, who was fluent in Portuguese, savvy in Brazilian business and accounting practices, and familiar with various Brazilian laws and customs, was evidently the right person any immigrant group might want vouching for them after their arrival in Brazil.

However, Rev. Ballard S. Dunn disliked Charles Nathan with a passion. Dunn refers to a "Mr. Shylock" throughout his publication—*Brazil,* the Home for Southerners—but never reveals exactly who Shylock was. However, this is highly likely to be a derogatory reference directed at Charles Nathan. He wrote, "Mr. Shylock, who combines in himself many avocations, being real estate broker, house-to-let agent, boarding house runner, with various other profitable employments, soon fits him out with a house."[122] He continued with the barrage: "Mr. Shylock is now paid for the rent of the house, upon which he receives a commission, of course. . . . why do you Mr. Shylock, and you Mr. Go-between remain in this doomed and doubly accursed country? You were not born here . . . Mr. Shylock, who claims to be a British subject."[123] It is unclear why Rev. Dunn's virulent anti-Semitic remarks were directed toward Nathan— assuming this was indeed a reference to Charles Nathan or perhaps a reference to one of his brothers. Charles had two older brothers, Lewis and Henry, who were born in London but moved to Rio with their parents in the 1820s. Perhaps the dispatch published in the *Baton Rouge Tri-Weekly Gazette & Comet* on November 5, 1867, which reported that two separate groups of U.S. Southern immigrants organized by Charles Nathan and Rev. Dunn were to depart New Orleans for Rio, might shed some light on Rev. Dunn's blistering remarks.[124] It is likely that Nathan and Dunn were at competitive odds with each other, given that both of them were simultaneously organizing the trips of two groups of U.S. Southerners moving to Brazil from New Orleans.

A series of vicious letters printed on June 29, 1867, in the newspaper *Correio mercantil* (Rio de Janeiro) reflected Rev. Dunn's foul temper, at least in writing, as he fired personal insults, ad hominem arguments, ad nauseam explicitly directed at Charles Nathan. On the same page in this newspaper, Dunn responded to a disgruntled passenger who accused the reverend of swindling him of his passage money to Brazil. Nathan replied to Dunn politely, and these back-and-forth letters virtually took up half the page of that newspaper issue.[125] Clearly, Rev. Dunn loathed Charles Nathan.

Nathan was also well-known among U.S. and British political figures alike. For example, Sir Richard Francis Burton (1821–90), a controversial British world explorer, diplomat, and writer who was the British consul in Santos in 1865, made mention of him in his popular book *Exploring the Highlands of Brazil*, published in 1869. Burton provided estimates of the number of U.S. Southerners living in Brazil and included a footnote stating that Charles Nathan had furnished him with those figures. Of the 2,070 U.S Southerners living in Brazil in 1868, the majority lived in São Paulo, in the Ribeira district, Campinas, and Capivari (800); others lived in the states of Espírito Santo, on the rivers Doce, Linhares and Guandú (400); Rio de Janeiro, the capital city (200); Paraná, near Curitiba, Morretes and Paranaguá (200); Pará, Santarém (200); Minas Gerais, Rio das Velhas (100); Bahia (100); and Pernambuco (70).[126]

However, the total figures incorrectly added up to 2,700 in Burton's book, when they should have added up to 2,070 instead. Unfortunately, this incorrect figure of 2,700 has been subsequently cited multiple times in secondary sources since Burton's original publication, with the figures credited to Burton instead of Charles Nathan, the original source (e.g., Mark Jefferson's 1928 article "An American Colony in Brazil").

On July 23, 1867, Charles Nathan secured a contract with the Brazilian government, under which he agreed to bring five thousand U.S. Southerners to Brazil within eighteen months. He sailed for Brazil in 1867 on the brig *Tartar* with several hundred immigrants, and it is possible that the others arrived later in waves—whether this happened remains unknown, as it is likely those records are either lost or destroyed.[127] In an account given by Martha Temperance Steagall (1850–1933), wife of Dr. Robert Cicero Norris—who came to Brazil along with other passengers from Texas, Louisiana, Mississippi and Alabama in 1867 on the brig *Tartar* (once called the *Wren*)—she described the brig as an old, "slow, and unsafe blockade runner fashioned into an Emigrant Ship, that had been bought by a man named Carlos Nathan."[128]

By 1868 Charles Nathan had organized transportation and arrangements for hundreds, if not thousands, of U.S. Southerners migrating to Brazil. As the *Gazette and Comet* reported, "A lull has, for some time past been observable in the interest which was so lively manifested the past year or two among the Southern people for emigrating to Brazil and other tropical lands. A fresh impetus seems latterly to have been given to the subject, owing, doubtless partly to the continued depression in political, agricultural and financial affairs in our country, and partly to the increasing inducements held out by parties desiring a change of locality and government, by such well-organized arrangements for transportation as have been effected by Mr. Charles Nathan."[129]

Charles Nathan and his brother Henry Nathan (known as "Henrique" in Brazil), the Birckheads and Humbirds of Maryland, and members of the firm Maxwell, Wright & Co. were close business associates. Furthermore, as Laura Jarnagin aptly states, "the Nathans' proximity to Imperial purse strings furthers our understanding of how Charles became so directly involved in transporting and settling southerners."[130] Brazilian historian Antonio Gutemberg da Silva highlights the influence of the Nathan family in the early years of the Brazilian empire. He refers to a gravesite at the British cemetery in Gamboa in Rio where one of Joseph Nathan's (Charles Nathan's father, known as "José" in Brazil) children was buried, listed simply as "a child of Nathan buried on November 22, 1824."[131] *O diário do Rio de Janeiro* reported on Jews who were buried in this cemetery, including "one of the most traditional Jewish families in Brazil—the Nathans of England, with a fortuitous participation in the history of Brazil's empire, particularly, Joseph Nathan, with numerous activities with the court"—again, a reference to Charles Nathan's father, Joseph.[132] Charles Nathan was listed in this report as an accountant, writer, and songwriter. Furthermore, the Nathans were known as a family of financial brokers, and some of the family's members had presided over the Israelite Union of Brazil in Rio and forged companies such as Nathan Irmãos & Worms and Nathan & Co., both commercial merchant houses.[133] Nathan & Cussen, a company that Joseph Nathan created with Henrique George Cussen, was dissolved in 1828.[134]

When he lived in Rio, Charles Nathan, along with his brother George Nathan, continued to aid U.S. Southerners in their move to Brazil. Both Charles and George married sisters of the Goodman family of New Orleans. The two couples and their respective families lived in Rio in two houses near each other in the neighborhood of Botafogo. Their homes were known to entertain, and temporarily house, many of the first U.S.

Southern immigration leaders, such as Dr. Gaston, Maj. Meriwether, and Col. Gunter. Unlike Rev. Dunn, Dr. Gaston spoke fondly of Charles (Carlos) and his brother George:

> They have been very kindly assisted and looked after by that noble-souled friend of Southerners, Mr. Carlos Nathan. His nets of kindness will relieve the embarrassments of many who have received favored at his hands, and among that number I shall always feel thankful for the gentlemanly courtesy and substantial aid which he has extended to me.[135]

Charles Nathan demonstrated more interest in emigration from the Southern states than any of the former residents of the United States who lived in Rio; indeed, the Nathan brothers were the only men here who were in the South at the opening of the war, they having left to avoid the consequences that seemed inevitable from the enemy's movements.[136]

Clearly, Charles Nathan was directly invested in this migration enterprise and played a pivotal role in aiding and promoting U.S. Southern immigration to Brazil. Nathan eventually returned to the United States to live in New Orleans in the 1870s along with his family. In the U.S. Census of 1880, Charles Nathan, age fifty-four, was listed as a "bookkeeper" born in England (it remains unknown to this author why Nathan chose to self-identify as England-born rather than Brazil-born, if this had indeed been the case). That year, he resided with his family on Carondelet Street 577, New Orleans, with his wife Emma, age thirty-eight, and the census lists six children from five to seventeen years of age in their family: Harry, Alice, Edward, Charles, Joseph, and Virginia.

As late as 1875, with the newly introduced technology of steam transportation and the advent of the telegraph, Nathan was promoting the reciprocal flour and coffee trade with Brazil among St. Louis flour millers.[137]

According to his obituary, Charles Nathan died in 1910 at the age of eighty-four at his residence on 4418 South Rampart Street, New Orleans. His obituary states, "Pioneer Teacher Passes Away. Charles Nathan, who began teaching shorthand in early seventies here, and instructed leading writers, dies at eighty-four." Nathan had undertaken a different occupation upon his return to New Orleans and become a pioneer teacher of shorthand in the Munson system. He taught hundreds of the leading shorthand writers of the city—including all his children—and when he lost his eyesight, his daughter "Miss Virginie took over his shorthand classes."[138]

According to his obituary, Nathan was a public accountant in Rio who then moved to New Orleans in 1861 and married Emma Goodman (daughter of prominent New Orleans merchant Daniel Goodman and Amelia Harris). However, there is no mention in his obituary about his involvement with the U.S. Southern exodus to Brazil, his belonging to a prominent Jewish family that owned a successful broker business in the Brazilian empire, or the Nathan family's residence in Brazil since the 1820s (or that Charles Nathan was a Freemason, for that matter). Although his obituary also states that Nathan was born in London on August 4, 1826, it is well-known that the Nathan family had already been living in Rio at the time of his birth. His parents Joseph Nathan (1790–1876) and Esther Lamert (1791–1860)—as well as his grandparents Moses Nathan (1747–1808) and Amelia (?–1808) were all born in Amsterdam, Netherlands; his mother, Ester Lamert, was allegedly related to novelist Charles Dickens.[139]

The story of the Nathan family's livelihood, set across Rio, New Orleans, London, and Amsterdam, reflects the mobility of families that were simultaneously rooted in different global cities for a long time. After Nathan returned from Rio to live in New Orleans, he promoted Portuguese immigration to Louisiana plantations and advocated for the establishment of a regular steamship line between New Orleans and Brazil, in addition to promoting the flour and coffee trade between St. Louis and Rio.[140]

Clearly, Charles Nathan and his family background describe a figure whose work, residency, religion, and citizenship transcended the confines of formal boundaries and political borders. Nathan is a key figure in this story, one who likely saw the mobility of Confederados with familiar eyes; he was, at the same time, a figure who ostensibly viewed immigration through the lens of nineteenth-century capitalism.

3

The Importance of Agricultural, Social, and Economic Conditions in Brazil

This chapter examines the agricultural, economic, and social conditions during the period in which the migration processes described in this book occurred. Outlining these conditions in Brazil establishes a context that helps one understand why Confederados were sought out and welcomed in Brazil, providing important insights into the pull factors of migration. A brief glimpse into the immigration of other population groups who arrived at that same time also provides a broader context to this narrative. It will become clear how Brazil's agricultural lag and eagerness to import skilled human capital prompted various policies that facilitated the recruitment of immigrants who were sought out for their agricultural expertise (e.g., through inducements). Here, I also point out several common misunderstandings in the literature available about Brazilian domestic knowledge of agricultural implements during the mid-nineteenth century. A short examination of Brazil's extensive territory and the legacy of Portuguese colonialism is important, as these left a dramatic imprint on nineteenth century agriculture and dovetail with the conditions that existed in Brazil when Confederados arrived in that country much later.

A Brief Backdrop of Landownership in Brazil

To understand a few of the important pull factors that attracted U.S. immigrants to Brazil, it is first necessary to consider, at least briefly, the historical backdrop of Brazil and Latin America in general. This is necessary because major political and sociocultural differences existed between the colonial approaches employed by the Portuguese and Spanish empires in the Americas. These differences accounted for the demographic contrasts between Portuguese and Spanish colonies and played vital roles in the implementation of different landownership policies as well as different agricultural, economic, cultural, and political systems—all of which eventually blend into this Confederado story.

Portugal had been under Muslim rule until the mid-thirteenth century; by this time, it had formed Europe's first nation-state and become specifically engaged in looking for natural resources and suitable agricultural lands to exploit commercially. Spain's militaristic "conquest" in the Americas came about as it had just finished its victory over the Moor invasion, something Portugal had accomplished almost a century and a half earlier. Portugal had already begun sugarcane cultivation on the islands of Madeiras and wanted to expand that crop into Brazil. The Portuguese approach in the Madeiras, Azores, Cape Verde, and the Canaries set a precedent for colonizing Brazil; in the words of H. B. Johnson, referring to the aforementioned islands, "it was the Portuguese experience [there] even more than in Africa, that created patterns later employed in the colonization of Brazil."[1] Subsequently, Brazil became a part of Portugal's colonial empire, which extended from Mozambique, Angola, Goa, and Macau to East Timor. Hence, the Spanish military's "conquering" mentality differed from the Portuguese's "colonizing" efforts.[2]

Portugal had focused on its Asian possessions up to the end of the sixteenth century. However, with the founding of the Dutch East India Company, the Portuguese near monopoly of the spice trade had ended by that time. Therefore, Portuguese presence in Asia had become virtually stagnant at that stage; when gold was discovered in Brazil at the end of the seventeenth century, Portugal focused on Brazil, which in turn made the Portuguese elite wealthier. With this new wealth, manufactured imports to Brazil, particularly from Britain, increased at that time.[3] After the Portuguese Court's arrival in Rio in 1808 imports increased significantly. However, by that time Brazil's infrastructure had been seriously neglected, as Portugal placed its focus solely on the Brazilian precious stones boom during the Gold Rush of 1695–1750.[4] Up until the mid-nineteenth century, land ownership and land policy in Brazil developed through convoluted transformations over the course of four centuries.[5]

The Portuguese land laws that were transferred to colonial Brazil left an important legacy in the development of Brazil's land policy structures. Portugal had created the Lei das Sesmarias (Law of redistribution of lands; *sesmarias*), enacted by King Fernando I in 1375, to limit unproductive land ownership. This law limited the amount of land any individual could hold, in order to guarantee that the land would always remain productive; otherwise, the land judged unproductive would be forfeited and given to someone else, a practice that was transplanted to Brazil. However, *sesmarias* did not work in Brazil—it was largely ignored and not enforced, which resulted in huge tracts of lands being held by only a few people. Most of that land was unproductive, and widespread absentee land ownership became a common practice. In 1534, the Portuguese created the system of capitancies (*capitanias*) in Brazil, under which parallel imaginary lines divided twelve, and later a total of fifteen, land tracts along the coastal belt of Brazil into administrative *capitanias*. Some *capitanias* were held by the Crown, and others were held by grantees (*donatários*), who were usually soldiers and bureaucrats; these grantees, in turn, were given the power to grant the practice of *sesmarias* within their own *capitanias*.[6]

In the 1690s the Crown tried again to enforce the size of *sesmarias* in Brazil to limit what a holder could cultivate or ranch; however, those orders were also largely ignored.[7] By the time the Portuguese Crown arrived in Brazil in 1808, land grants that were awarded to favorites of the court had created a great deal of mistrust and resentment among Brazilian political liberals who knew that public domain was being given away. Finally, in 1822 the *sesmaria* system officially ended in Brazil.[8] The agricultural backdrop in the nineteenth century consequently emerged (albeit with regional differences)—as Gilberto Freyre explains, "a sort of medieval landlordism prevailed. Land was owned by Coffee planters in the south, cattle-proprietors in the inland provinces . . . by *senhores de engenhos* (sugar planters) in the northeast. Along the coast and in scattered points of the interior were the 'roçeiros,' [small subsistence agriculturalists] not a few of whom were colored freedmen."[9] The emphasis on social status trumped individualism and industrialism. Although absentee landownership was commonplace, direct supervision was necessary for an effective agricultural operation with the advent of the coffee boom, which peaked in the mid-nineteenth century in the Paraíba Valley region; unlike other Brazilian agricultural plantations, absentee landlordism in large coffee regions was typically not viable.[10]

Despite the decline of the sugar boom at the end of the seventeenth century, sugarcane cultivation in Brazil continued as a monocrop using the slave system (*escravismo*); this was successful on large sugarcane plantations/mills (*engenhos*) in the northeast of Brazil, which thrived on the right combination of rainfall and thick black and dark-red fertile *massapé* soils.[11] The Brazilian *engenho* was both a factory and a farm/plantation at the same time. With a typical twenty-four-hour work cycle, virtually never stopping, the *engenho* employed a diverse labor force ranging from manual workers to skilled labor that included "blacksmiths, carpenters, masons, and technicians."[12] The rural Brazilian *engenho* system predated the archetypal European urban industrial factory/mill, which operated under similar market-driven, export-oriented mindsets.

The sugar boom in Brazil declined in the mid-1600s due to new production in the British, Dutch, and French Caribbean islands with more modern technology; the precious metals boom in Brazil had waned by the mid-eighteenth century. Brazil's next economic booms would come to dominate world markets: cotton and then, coffee. In tandem with the restrictions on transatlantic slave imports, the coffee boom would dramatically affect Brazil's immigration policies.

Cotton Trade and Connections

Economic and agricultural opportunities in Brazil were clearly among the most important pull factors for Confederados. With the Confederados' move to Brazil, optimism about the cotton boom's continuation emerged.[13] Brazil had been Europe's chief supplier of cotton from the mid-eighteenth century up to the early nineteenth century (particularly cotton from Maranhão, Ceará, Bahia, and Pernambuco).[14] Cotton had evidently been on the minds of U.S. Southerners before their migration to Brazil.

Cotton had also been at the forefront of U.S. Navy Lieutenant Matthew Fontaine Maury's projects as far back as the 1850s, when he intended to take over the Amazon and transplant U.S. Southerners with their slaves, thereby replicating the U.S. Southern cotton-plantation economic system, though this never happened (more on Maury and that project in chapter 4). Maury was already familiar with Brazil's high cotton yields. His uncle, James Maury (1746–1840)—the first U.S. consul at Liverpool, England, for almost forty years (1789–1837)—was a major cotton importer from the U.S. South to England.

Intertwined in this narrative is English poet, Robert Southey, who never set foot in Brazil yet published a colossal historical treatise *History of Brazil*, comprising three volumes, published in 1822. He was in direct contact with Portuguese-born Englishman and author Henry Koster (sometimes known as Henrique Costa in Brazil). Koster's publication *Travels in Brazil* (1816) is considered to this day one of the most insightful publications on early nineteenth-century Brazil (Koster dedicated his book to Southey). Both Southey and Koster motivated each other to write their respective publications on Brazil. Their correspondence with each other reveals Koster's experiences in Brazil's northeast, mostly in Pernambuco. Koster had lived there from the age of sixteen (he was sent there because of health reasons), and he died there at the age of twenty-six.[15]

It is known that James Maury (Matthew F. Maury's father) owned a copy of Henry Koster's *Travels in Brazil*, which offered important geographic insights into Brazil at that time. As Matthew F. Maury was close with this uncle, it is likely that he had read the book as well. Henry Koster's father, John Theodore Koster (1750–1828) from Liverpool, was, in turn, a major importer of cotton from Pernambuco and Maranhão. As early as 1802, and at least until 1817, J. T. Koster imported cotton from Brazil to England and Portugal.[16]

Taken together, these individuals and their involvement with the transatlantic cotton trade highlight the importance of the commodity's movement between Brazil, the U.S. South, and Europe, as well as underscores the transnational mindset. This movement predates later mid-nineteenth-century mercantile trading networks as well as family mobilities and genealogies that would also extend between Brazil and the United States. In modern vernacular, both the Kosters (father and son), and Maurys (uncle and nephew) epitomize what we now call "transnational" livelihoods, transcending citizenship and places of residence—their livelihoods were set between the U.S. South, England, Brazil, and Portugal, propelled by Atlantic mercantilism and global capitalism.

These commercial, trade, and kinship networks forged bring us back to the broader implications of nineteenth-century world capitalism—a topic that traverses this Confederado story with members of the firm, Maxwell, Wright & Co, who sustained kinship, political, and trade ties between Rio, Baltimore, Lisbon, and London.

However, by the early nineteenth century cotton exports from Brazil had been surpassed by those from the U.S. South. In the late 1860s cotton in the interior of São Paulo did not flourish to the extent that it had been expected to after the Confederados had settled there—not because of bad soil or unavailability of labor but limited regional demand, poor roads, and inadequate means of transportation. Consequently, U.S. Southern immigrants did not replicate the old Dixie, antebellum, slave-based cotton economic system in Brazil, as Maury had once imagined he would accomplish. Ironically, geographer Christian Brannstrom pointed out that the western region of São Paulo would become in the 1940s "a world-renowned cotton belt, putting the country among the world's top four cotton producers and easily outpacing the rest of Latin America."[17]

In order to understand Brazil's resolute pursuit of bringing more immigrants to work in Brazil and its chronic shortage of human capital, it is important to recognize the impact of the transatlantic slave trade and slavery in that country.

African Slaves in Brazil

George Reid Andrews points out that "slavery was probably the most determinative experience in Brazilian history, profoundly shaping the society, culture, economy, and political system that have emerged in that country."[18] The transatlantic slave trade to Brazil dramatically transformed Brazilian demographics and cultural landscapes. More Africans were brought to Brazil than to any other country in the world.[19] Of all the African slaves brought to the Americas during the transatlantic slave trade period, around 40 percent went to Brazil, 21.8 percent to Spanish colonies, 19.7 percent to English colonies, and 11.6 percent to French colonies.[20] In 1817 more than two-thirds (2,887,500) of the total Brazilian population (3,617,900) was black, and less than one-fourth was white (843,000).[21]

To prevent the concentration of any single group and to avoid rebellions, slaves were brought in waves from different regions in Africa. For example, Sudanese and Bantu slaves were carried to Brazil in four separate waves. The Guinean wave in the sixteenth century consisted of the Wolofs, Mandingos, Songhais, Mossis, Hausis, and Kamite Peuls, followed by Bantu slaves taken from Angola and Congo. In the eighteenth century, the Sudanese arrived from the Mina Coast. In the mid-eighteenth century, slave traders smuggled slaves from the Bay of Benin.[22]

The slave trade began to slow down after the British pressured countries to stop this trade with the Slave Trade Suppression Act. Known in Brazil as Bill Aberdeen of 1845, the act authorized the British to apprehend any ship engaged in transatlantic slave trafficking. In his study, first published in 1958, on the coffee plantation county of Vassouras in Rio de Janeiro, Stanley J. Stein points to the dramatic drop in slave imports after Brazil had abolished slave trafficking from Africa in 1850 with the Brazilian law Lei Eusébio de Queirós.

At the peak of slave imports to Brazil in 1848, a total 60,000 slaves entered that country; however, slave import figures dropped by nearly a third in 1850 to 23,000 slaves, and that number further decreased nearly eightfold to 3,287 slaves in 1851.[23] Consequently, coffee plantation owners maintained their supply of slaves by importing slaves from other Brazilian provinces. In 1852 slave imports to Rio from other Brazilian provinces totaled 4,409, peaking in 1856 at 5,006 slaves. By 1859 those import figures in Rio had dramatically dropped to 963 slaves.[24] However, because of the coffee boom in São Paulo, slave populations increased in that province, from 80,000 in 1866 to 200,000 in 1875.[25] The first Brazilian census in 1872 showed that the largest foreign-born population comprised 183,000 Africans, followed by 121,000 Portuguese, 46,000 Germans, and 6,000 Italians.[26]

Historian Leslie Bethell outlines the reasons for the failure of the Brazilian slave system, a failure precipitated by the prohibition of the transatlantic slave trade in 1850, which directly affected the decrease of slave populations (reliant on the regular influx of slave labor brought in by the slave trade). Bethell explains that due to the slave sex-ratio imbalance (that is, there were far more male to female slaves), slave birth rates remained low, and slave mortality rates remained high as a result of mistreatment, malnutrition, and disease; manumission and rates of escape remained high as well.[27] In a powerful statement illustrating the impact of immigration on Brazil, Bethell maintains, "Italian immigration was both a response to the final collapse of slavery and one of the causes of its final abolition."[28]

The official move to abolish the institution of slavery in Brazil was marked by slow, gradual steps. In 1871 the Law of the Free Womb (Lei do Ventre Livre) stated that any child born of a slave woman was considered free; in 1885 the Law of the Sexagenarian (Lei dos Sexagenários) liberated slaves over the age of sixty; finally, the abolition of slavery in Brazil was made official with the Golden Law (Lei Áurea) on May 13, 1888. Notably, it was only as late as 1880 that the first Brazilian Anti-Slavery Society was formed, headed by Joaquim Nabuco (also a Freemason) and José do Patrocínio (the son of a white priest and a black slave). The Portuguese were the first to initiate and expand the transatlantic slave trade in Africa, and Brazil was the last country in the western hemisphere to abolish the institution of slavery.

Immigration to Brazil as a "Solution"

In the early 1900s travel writer Lillian Elwyn Elliott (writing under the pen name "L. E. Elliott") asked Brazilians during her travels in Brazil, "Where is the future immigrant of Brazil to come from, and to what part of the country is he to go?" She invariably received answers of this nature: "We want white immigrants, and they can settle healthily either in the cool south of Brazil or on the high interior uplands."[29]

As far back as 1817 Dom João VI brought the first Swiss settlers to Brazil.[30] These settlers founded Nova Friburgo (New Freiburg)—"agents of the Brazilian Government recruited no less than five thousand in Bern . . . two thousand sailed from Amsterdam and Rotterdam."[31] The International Society of Immigration of Rio, with its headquarters in Antwerp, sent its recruits to work with Brazilian coffee estates, mainly in the southern and southeastern provinces of Brazil. These immigration recruitments were also undertaken by Theóphilo Ottoni and Manuel Jacinto Nogueira da Gama, the Visconde de Baependi.[32] Later most of the provinces in Southern Brazil became entirely composed of German immigrants, and beginning in 1825 "Germany became for about twenty-five years the very best recruiting ground for Brazil."[33] Between 1838 and 1884 the total number of German immigrants in Brazil swelled to 71,247. By 1891 an estimated quarter of a million of Brazil's inhabitants claimed German ancestry.[34]

In 1870 two-thirds of the total slave population in all of Brazil were found in three provinces: Rio de Janeiro, Minas Gerais, and São Paulo.[35] Gradually, black slaves were replaced by immigrant labor (sharecroppers and indentured laborers), mostly from Italy, Germany, Switzerland, Belgium, Portugal, and Spain.

Between 1871 and 1937 an estimated 67,003 Poles and Ukrainians arrived in southern Brazil. However, between 1890 and 1919 Italians outnumbered immigrants to Brazil of any nationality, with 1,049,927 Italian immigrants entering Brazil, followed by the next seven largest immigrant nationalities during that same period: 733,420 Portuguese, 467,548 Spaniards, 95,610 Russians, 67,015 Austrians, 56,834 Germans,

54,131 Turks, and 28,293 Japanese.[36] In addition, one survey counted 3,575 Americans living in Brazil between 1864 and 1872.[37] Peddlers from Italy, Syria, and Lebanon had also made their way to the Brazilian coffee counties and urban sectors.[38] Curiously, during the mid- and late nineteenth century thousands of European immigrants were brought to Brazilian plantations—mostly in rural regions in the southeast and south, where they often worked alongside slaves—unlike newly arrived immigrants to the United States, who tended to avoid setting up residency in rural areas.[39]

The mid- to late nineteenth century was marked by significant political transformations in Brazil that signaled changes in racial politics. Given the diverse makeup of the Brazilian population, how were dominant Brazilian government policies affected by racial ideologies? How did these ideologies encourage and promote the migration of U.S. Southerners to Brazil?

The Agricultural Backdrop to Brazil

In late 1868 an anonymous author published a long article in the Brazilian newspaper *O diário do Rio de Janeiro* strongly promoting U.S. Southern immigration to Brazil.[40] The author claims that U.S. Southerners—with their inherent "enterprising spirit," "industriousness," and "necessary intelligence," terms in Brazil commonly used at the time to describe immigrants of so-called "European stock"—would be more inclined than any other immigrant group to feel familiar with Brazil's climate and with its crops, such as cotton, rice, sugarcane, and tobacco (*fumo*). These crops are, according to the author, similar to the crops found in the U.S. South.

The author of that article repeatedly lists the reasons why Brazilians should favor U.S. Southern migration to Brazil, stating that the 1,200 U.S. Southern immigrants living in Brazil in 1868 had been able to thrive like no other immigrant group in Brazil. In other words, they were exactly what Brazil needed. According to that author, Brazil needed this new "agricultural class" headed by "ambitious" and "intelligent men" who "prided" themselves in their agricultural enterprise. The same author gives examples of the prosperous conditions that existed in the antebellum U.S. South, citing examples of the "wealth" and "prosperity" that U.S. Southerners had brought to Brazil, particularly in the immigrant settlements of Santa Bárbara and Paraná.[41]

The anonymous author's point was clear: he or she made a strong case that Brazil and U.S. Southerners alike would mutually benefit from immigration and that the future of Brazil lay in these "industrious" agriculturalist U.S. Southern immigrants. It becomes imperative, therefore, to examine the agricultural backdrop in Brazil.

In his study of the roots of Brazil's mid-nineteenth-century export economies, Eugene W. Ridings explains that "insuring the prosperity of agriculture became a chief concern of Brazil's business elite and this strong identification even served as an obstacle to industrial development."[42] The main collective goal of agricultural and immigration societies created in nineteenth-century Brazil was to maintain and strengthen the export economy dependent on agriculture.[43] Therefore, the agrarian milieu before U.S. Southerners arrived in Brazil deserves attention—it was one of the most important pull factors attracting them to that country.

Coffee and Immigration to São Paulo

By the end of the eighteenth century sugarcane plantations had expanded successfully in the Quatrilátero do Açucar (Sugar Quadrilateral) in the western interior of São Paulo, formed by Sorocaba, Mogi Guaçu, and Jundiaí as well as Limeira and Rio Claro (all within about ten or twenty miles from the Confederado settlement of Santa Bárbara, established decades later).

Senator Nicolau Pereira de Campos Vergueiro (1778–1859), a wealthy merchant planter, lawyer, and Portuguese immigrant who arrived in Brazil in 1802, acquired lands in this region, becoming one of the largest sugar-plantation owners in São Paulo. Vergueiro had studied at the University of Coimbra, Portugal, and arrived in Brazil with a law degree. As one of the rare well-educated immigrants of that time, he was treated with distinct deference when he arrived in Brazil. Thereby, he was able to intermarry into a prominent family from São Paulo and eventually came to own extensive agricultural lands with his father-in-law, where he began his plantation projects later. Elite families from the interior of São Paulo became increasingly wealthy with coffee cultivation. Furthermore, intermarriage between cousins as well as between elite agricultural families in the area was common, resulting in the formation of powerful regional family clans. For example, Vergueiro's two sons married the daughters of the Sousa Queirós family in Santa Bárbara.[44] The Sousa Queirós family, along with the Vergueiros, was among the first agriculturalists in Brazil to attempt to replace slave labor with indentured workers from Europe on their large plantations.[45]

Luís António de Sousa Queirós (1746–1819), known as Brigadeiro (Brigadier) Luís António, had like Vergueiro emigrated from Portugal to Brazil as a young man. Likewise, he married into one of the most prominent agricultural families from the interior of São Paulo—his wife was Genebra de Barros Leite, the sister of the Barão de Itú (Baron of Itú) and Barão de Piracicaba (Baron of Piracicaba). One of their sons, Vicente de Sousa Queirós, became the Barão de Limeira (Baron of Limeira), and one of their grandsons, Nicolau de Souza Queirós, married Isabel Dabney de Avelar Brotero (daughter of the prominent Brazilian–Azorian–American Dabny family, the Avelar Broteros).[46]

In the late 1820s, with the new coffee boom emerging, Vergueiro began replacing sugarcane with coffee at the Ibicaba plantation in Limeira; at the same time he began a new program of hiring Swiss, Belgian, Spanish, Portuguese, and German immigrants as indentured workers to work alongside slaves on the plantation.[47] For example, Reverends Fletcher and Kidder observed, "Those whom Senator Vergueiro and his sons have brought to displace the Africans are men of the working-classes from Germany and Switzerland."[48] As early as 1846 Vergueiro created with his son José Vergueiro the firm Vergueiro & Cia. to specifically finance and facilitate the immigration of European workers to work on his plantation, which became known as the "Senator Vergueiro Colony."[49]

In addition to the high demand for coffee and its profitable dividends, there were practical benefits to growing coffee. For example, while sugarcane needed to be replanted every three years or so, coffee groves typically lasted as long as three or four decades.[50] In his study of coffee plantations in Rio Claro (about thirty-two miles from Santa Bárbara), Warren Dean explains that those soils in the province of western São Paulo were the best lands in Brazil for growing coffee, located about fifty-seven miles west and northwest of the city of São Paulo and beyond—"the decomposed gneissic and granitic earth of the region contains nutritive elements in low concentration, but it is deep and very porous." These hills provide good drainage and conditions that are perfect for coffee trees, which send roots down thirty to sixty-five feet into the ground.[51]

This interior region of São Paulo, which Senator Vergueiro cleared and developed with the advent of the coffee boom, became one of the regions to attract many potential settlers who were searching for suitable lands. Rev. Fletcher had visited Vergueiro's plantation in Ibicaba in the 1850s with great interest, remarking on how the rolling hills and landscapes reminded him of Ohio.[52]

More than a decade after Rev. Fletcher's visit to Vergueiro's plantation, U.S. Southerners Dr. James M. Gaston (from South Carolina) and Gen. William W. Wood (from Mississippi), introduced in chapter 2, visited Vergueiro's Ibicaba plantation on several occasions; they were received by his son, José Vergueiro, since his father, Nicolau Vergueiro, had died in 1859. They also visited Vergueiro's other *fazendas* (plantations/farms) in the vicinity of Limeira and Rio Claro. Dr. Gaston was also welcomed by John James Aubertin—an Englishman and the superintendent of São Paulo Railroad Co. Ltda.—and by Antônio Paes de Barros, Barão de Piracicaba (the brother-in-law of Luís António de Sousa Queirós).[53] Interestingly, much later Confederado engineer William Putney Ralston was hired by the brothers Antônio and Augusto de Sousa Queirós to help set up a local textile factory (today located in the city of Americana). By 1884 the factory had been bought out by two brothers from England, Clement and George Willmot, who later named it "Carioba" (a Tupi word for white cloth); Carioba flourished, and today it is considered one of the most successful textile factories in Brazil.[54]

Throughout his search trip, Dr. Gaston had been aided and encouraged by the Vergueiros, who supported U.S. Southern immigration to Brazil (Vergueiro's Ibicaba plantation was spelled "Ybicaba" in Gaston's *Hunting a Home in Brazil*) and are mentioned several times in that same book. The interior western region of São Paulo, for example—the conglomeration of Limeira, Piracicaba, Rio Claro, Campinas, and Santa Bárbara—would soon become the epicenter of the eventual proliferation of American Protestant ministries and missionaries as well as U.S. Presbyterian schools, which expanded as the Santa Bárbara settlement began to flourish.[55]

However, the indentured system the Vergueiros had devised ultimately did not work out, and problems soon began to emerge. Due to the many complaints and the ill-treatment German settlers had purportedly experienced in São Paulo, Prussia prohibited immigration propaganda to Brazil in 1859—a decree only removed in 1896.[56] In 1902 the Italian government also decided to prohibit the recruitment and travel of Italian workers to São Paulo, for the same reason.[57] Thus, the conundrum around replacing the slave labor force continued.

Roberto Saba explains in his doctoral dissertation that a transnational group of activists, diplomats, engineers, entrepreneurs, journalists, merchants, missionaries, planters, and scientists promoted free labor, as they reckoned "these improvements . . . would help Brazilian and American capitalists harness the potential of native-born as well as immigrant free workers to expand production and trade."[58] That is, according to Saba, "free labor meant eliminating slavery while, at the same time, reinforcing proletarianization."[59]

The Agricultural Predicament in Brazil: A Clarification

Horace M. Lane, a businessman, educator, and agriculturalist originally from the state of Maine (not to be confused with Confederado Horace Lane from Louisiana, who went to the Paraná settlement), eventually became the first president of Mackenzie College and director of the Escola Americana, both in São Paulo. Lane also created the firm H. M. Lane & Co., which imported and sold agricultural implements and machines in Rio. As early as 1865 Horace M. Lane had been advertising frequently in the *Anglo-Brazilian Times* newspaper, evidently catering to English-language speakers and to the new and increasing demand for agricultural implements and products among U.S. Southern immigrants. Here is an example of one of the advertisements that ran in that paper in 1866: "H. M. Lane & C. Importers of Agricultural Implements and Machines. Wholesale and Retail. Rua Direita No. 13. Constantly on hand a large assortment of Plows, Harrows, Cultivators, Cotton Sweeps and Scrapers, Hand and Power Grain Mills, Corn Shellers, Hay Cutters, Mandioca Presses, Portable Sugarcane Mills . . . Also on hand: the best publications on Agriculture, Horticulture, and Domestic Economy."[60]

With the items that Lane was advertising and the arrival of thousands of Confederados to Brazil, the demand for those implements by proxy would also increase. U.S. Southerners not only brought their agricultural expertise to Brazil but also now had access to imported agricultural implements in Brazil.

William Van Vleck Lidgerwood, originally from New Jersey, had established a foundry in Campinas (Lidgerwood Mfg. Co. Ltda.). He would later sue the German brothers Bierrenbach from Campinas, who also manufactured coffee hullers (designed by German inventor Johan Conrad Engelberg), and win the case. Lidgerwood claimed that the Germans were infringing on the privilege he had obtained in São Paulo in 1862. Lidgerwood was also a member of the Sociedade Auxiliadora da Indústria Nacional.[61]

Although neither Lane nor Lidgerwood were U.S. Southerners, they were considered *norte-americanos* (Americans). Here they become examples of how U.S. immigrants from both the U.S. South ("Confederacy") and U.S. North ("Union") often fused in this narrative as a single collective category known in Brazil as *norte-americanos*, often making it a difficult task to distinguish the U.S. immigrants who were, in fact, U.S. Southerners from those who were not.[62]

Confederados contributed to the dissemination of new agricultural methods and technologies *in conjunction* with the agricultural knowledge brought by other immigrants in the region. Nonetheless, these implements and agricultural innovations had already been known to Brazilian agriculturalists before the arrival of the Confederados, which some scholars have neglected to acknowledge.

For example, historian Richard Graham claims that nineteenth-century Brazilian agriculturalists had not yet formed any agricultural societies or fairs; he also claims that they rarely read agricultural journals to improve on agricultural methods and that they did not use scrapers, cultivators, harrows, or mechanical seeders until the twentieth century.[63] Furthermore, Graham claims that chemical fertilizer, guano, potash, and lime remained unknown in Brazil at that time.[64] However, these claims are misleading at best.[65]

First, agricultural societies did exist throughout nineteenth-century Brazil.[66] Take, for example, the Sociedade Auxiliadora da Indústria Nacional (Auxiliary Society of National Industry), which was created in 1828; the term *indústria* (industry) here references agriculture and new technological improvements in agriculture.[67] This society published a journal, *O auxiliador da indústria nacional*, from 1828 to 1896. Created by Inácio Alves de Almeida and numbering seventy-five subscribers by 1833, this journal aimed to disseminate new agricultural technology and farming knowledge to Brazilian agriculturalists.[68]

Second, Brazilian agriculturalists used chemicals (*química* or *chimica*) such as lime (*cal*), potash (*potassa*), and guano—items that show up, for example, in various issues published in *O auxiliador da indústria nacional*.[69] Another agricultural society, researched by Laura J. Pang in 1981, was the Sociedade Círculo Agrícola de São João de Cacaria (Agricultural Circle Society of São João de Cacaria); a forerunner of later societies created in the 1870s and 1880s, it was founded in the province of Rio de Janeiro by Antônio Pereira Barreto Pedroso in 1860.[70] Pedroso was educated at the University of Coimbra, Portugal, and had spent time observing agricultural techniques in France. The Marquês de Abrantes (Miguel Calmon du Pin e Almeida)—president of the Sociedade Auxiliadora da Indústria Nacional—and the Sociedade Auxiliadora da Indústria Nacional's secretary and agronomist Frederico Leopoldo César Burlamaque were made honorary members of the Sociedade Círculo Agrícola de São

João de Cacaria. Abrantes authored several publications that deal with agriculture, and Burlamaque published several manuals "ranging from the the use of fertilizers and agricultural machinery to the cultivation of coffee, sugar, cotton, rice and tobacco."[71] Between 1859 and 1860 the Empire also created province-level agricultural institutes intended to further these advancements in agriculture, such as the Instituto Imperial Fluminense da Agricultura, Instituto Baiano da Agricultura, and Instituto Sergipano da Agricultura—the last two were created as a direct response to the devastating drought of 1858–59 in the northeast region.[72]

Third, Brazilian planters were clearly aware of the use of the plow at least as early as the 1850s.[73] A series of articles about the use of the plow in Brazil and how its detrimental effects on Brazilian soils made it not widely used first appeared in *O commercio* (Niterói, Rio de Janeiro) in 1851 and were later repeated in another newspaper, *A aurora Paulista* (1851–52).[74] Several advertisements for the sale of plows appeared between 1850 and 1860 in Brazilian newspapers such as *O diário do Rio de Janeiro*—a decade before the arrival of Confederados.[75]

Yet one of the greatest challenges to the plow's wider usage in Brazil was that imported plows tended to break in Brazilian soils; the best plows for Brazilian soils needed to be imported from Corsica, for example, making them costly and logistically complicated to transport and deliver to farms located in the interior regions.[76] Here, the combination of access, soil composition, different native agricultural methods, and transportation—rather than knowledge itself—played a bigger role in hindering the dissemination of agricultural implements in Brazil.[77]

Hence, despite the existence of farming knowledge, journals, societies, and known methods and techniques in Brazil (including knowledge of the plow and its suboptimal use on Brazilian soils), Brazilian agriculturalists were faced with multiple predicaments, including the problem of transportation—however, they were cognizant of these issues. They were also well-aware of world farming practices and the differences in research methods in northern hemispheres, and they were equally aware of the reasons why most farming technologies and methods developed elsewhere were not applicable or adequate for use in Brazil's hot climate and its different soil types.

Nonetheless, several reports written by the first U.S. Southerners after they had arrived in Brazil to search for suitable lands mention that the plow would provide a quick solution to Brazil's agricultural lag. For example, Rev. Ballard S. Dunn reports, "The planter uses no other implement than the broad hoe."[78] In Rev. Dunn's accounts, he notes the first time the plow had been seen in use at the mouth of the Pariquera-Açu River at a sugar estate: "It was here that I saw a great curiosity in the way of a plow. It is very large, very clumsy, and as nearly as I can judge, after the pattern in use in Europe two centuries ago. I should be sorry to have Brazilians judge of the utility of plows by a trial of this one."[79]

Dr. Gaston of South Carolina also wrote in a 1867 report, "The culture of the land in all parts visited is performed with the hoe exclusively." [80] He continued, "Could anything I may say induce the adoption of plow-culture for the cotton . . . it would serve to enhance greatly the value of this crop, and at the same time lessen the actual amount of labor by those working the lands."[81]

As Dr. Gaston remarked in 1867, "the farmer of the United States is needed here to learn the fazundeiros [*fazendeiros,* or farmers] of Brazil the proper use of the plough, and should any considerable number remove to this country, they will effect quite a revolution in agriculture in a few years."[82] However, the lack of the plow and its poor spread in nineteenth-century Brazil was the result of multiple factors.[83]

Therefore, narratives claiming that Confederados introduced the plow to Brazil, as well as those claiming that Brazilian agricultural societies did not exist and that technologies such as the plow were unknown in Brazil during the nineteenth century, are clearly deceptive.

Overall Social Predicaments in Brazil

Intellectual stifling in Brazil throughout the eighteenth century and during the first quarter of the nineteenth century had been a legacy of the Luso-colonial years dating back to 1707, when the "Portuguese viceroy closed a printing press in Rio and forbade others to open."[84] Access to literacy and knowledge was highly restricted under the Portuguese crown for fear of internal insurrections, and censorship stemmed largely from a concern for national security. It was only in 1808, with the transferal of the Portuguese Crown to Brazil, that a printing press was introduced in Rio and a Royal Gazette published.[85] The Portuguese Crown founded several new institutions in Rio, such as the National Library and the Botanical Garden, and by the end of the first quarter of the nineteenth century, numerous newspapers, pamphlets, and journals were being published throughout Brazil.[86]

In 1823 Brazil was sparsely populated, with a total population of 3,960,866. By 1872 its total population had increased almost threefold to 9,930,478.[87] Yet the country still depended largely on its agriculture-based economy (e.g., sugarcane, coffee, cotton, and tobacco). With this population increase, the city of Rio installed cobblestone walkways (*calçamento com paralelepípedo*), city gaslights, and a new water sewer system by the mid-nineteenth century. However, the rest of Brazil lacked the basic infrastructure and transportation to improve its economy and agriculture.

Moreover, one major predicament contributing to Brazil's lag in nineteenth-century agriculture was the lack of credit. Despite the creation of nationally financed hypothecary banks intended to provide low-interest and long-term credit (all which eventually failed), Brazil's earliest banks between 1838 and 1851 were "reluctant to lend to planters" due to the high risk of planters' unpayable debt.[88] Therefore, Brazil's lag in modernizing its agriculture during the nineteenth century, which hindered its economy, was largely due to several interrelated factors, which ranged from lack of money, poor roads and transportation, and lack of easy farm credit (virtually unavailable in nineteenth-century Brazil) to plain indifference.[89]

Communication and mail were also precarious, as was transportation across the enormous distances within Brazil—the most populous and largest country in Latin America and the only Portuguese-speaking nation in the Western hemisphere. It was not until the last quarter of the nineteenth century, with the advent of a limited railway system concentrated mostly in the southeastern region in the provinces of São Paulo and Rio de Janeiro, that transportation to the main coastal ports began to change and improve. One of the only wide-paved roads that existed at that time in Brazil, reconstructed between 1780 and 1792, was the Caminho do Mar (with an abrupt incline of about three thousand feet to the Serra do Mar), which connected the port of Santos with the city of São Paulo.[90]

Illiteracy in Brazil

Brazil also lacked basic educational infrastructure as well as an appreciation of the value of literacy—fundamental to Anglophone Protestants, as it allowed them to read the Bible without intermediaries. Literacy in Brazil was a privilege limited mostly to the sociopolitical elite and the clergy—that is, to individuals privileged by birth or position—albeit one not universally valued by Brazilian society, which favored social status and wealth over education.

With a total national population approximating ten million, Brazil saw dramatically high illiteracy rates in 1872. That year, about 80 percent of men and nearly 90 percent of women were illiterate. Illiteracy rates for the capital city of Rio that same year were slightly better: about 60 percent of men and 70 percent of women were illiterate; in São Paulo, literacy rates were worse: 68 percent of men and 83 percent of women were illiterate.[91] For a comparative perspective, consider how even some of the Hausa and Yoruba slaves in Brazil, who were Muslim, were literate in Arabic, which allowed them to read religious scripture (many of these slaves had been involved in the Malê Uprising among Muslims in Bahia decades earlier in 1835).[92] Even most U.S. sailors at that time were literate; for example, an estimated 80 to 90 percent of mid-nineteenth-century U.S. sailors were literate.[93]

Almost half a century later in 1920 illiteracy rates for all of Brazil continued to remain remarkably high: 72 percent of men and 81 percent of women were illiterate. That same year, illiteracy rates in Rio were slightly lower: 54 percent of men and 65 percent of women; São Paulo saw similar rates that year, with 56 percent of men and 58 percent of women illiterate.⁹⁴ In contrast, illiteracy rates were dramatically lower in most European countries. For example, in the 1870s illiteracy rates in England were estimated at about 17 percent; in France, 18 percent; Switzerland, 6 percent; and Germany, 2 percent.⁹⁵ However, illiteracy rates for some regions of Spain, rural Russia, and Southern Italy were only slightly lower than Brazil's, and in some cases they were almost comparable to illiteracy rates in Brazil at that time.⁹⁶ The high illiteracy rates among most native Brazilians only made Brazilian elites and agriculturalists even more eager to favor European immigrants or U.S. Southerners, who were seen as minimally literate at least, capable of reading directions and instructions, and—purportedly—able to work more diligently and effectively than the overwhelmingly illiterate native Brazilian population.⁹⁷

However, not all Brazilian agriculturalists belonged to a monolithic illiterate group. It is important to point out that most of the large agriculturalists in the interior of São Paulo and Rio de Janeiro, would have considered U.S. Southern immigrants their peers, since U.S. Southern immigrants were both literate and privileged as well as familiar with agrarian capitalism and global economies. These agriculturalists were from wealthy elite and prominent Brazilian families—for example, the Vergueiros, Sousa Queirós, and Silva Prados, among others—and were at the helm of developing agricultural commerce in the interior of São Paulo.⁹⁸

By welcoming and encouraging U.S. Southerners to migrate to Brazil, Dom Pedro II thought that he could secure the country's urgently needed skilled human capital. However, several Confederados expressed deep concern about the lack of educational prospects and resources their children would encounter in Brazil—specifically, according to Blanche Henry Clark Weaver, the lack of education and schools.

Take, for instance, James Williamson Miller of South Carolina. He had been about to embark for Brazil with his family soon after the U.S. Civil War ended when his wife, Sarah Miller, found it a "foolish scheme, especially as she looked at her children and thought of her ambition that they should all receive a good education. What educational opportunities could possibly be theirs in a backward foreign land?"⁹⁹ Nonetheless, the Miller family left for Brazil despite Sarah's family's opposition, and James sold his land "to his brother Leroy, and after weeks of sewing for relatives . . . the family said good-bye to kinsmen and friends and left for an unknown land and future."[100] After the Millers left South Carolina and settled in Santa Bárbara, Sarah Miller eventually solved the schooling problem by opening a school herself, an English-language-speaking school that was attended by other U.S. Southern children as well as her own. Later, the Miller children would attend the Colégio Internacional in Campinas, run by the U.S. Presbyterian Church, which had established a mission school that was open to Brazilians.[101]

In another example, Phillip Waddell returned from Brazil to live in Virginia, along with his wife and six children. Waddell had left his home in Texas and lived nine years in Brazil; he told the *Public Ledger* in 1877, "The desire to educate [the Waddells'] children properly was a ruling motive in causing the return . . . to the United States."[102]

Many Confederados kept up-to-date with English-language agricultural journals. For example, Confederado descendants "subscribed to several American farm journals and used the latest agricultural methods."[103] A few Confederados and their descendants stayed updated on U.S. news. Richard Pyles, age sixty-five, reported to the *Baltimore Sun* in an interview in 1949: "I was brought up on the *Atlanta Constitution*." Julia Norris Jones (daughter of William H. Norris) recalled, "I remember Uncle Joe Whitaker used to take the *Constitution* . . . Everybody in the community used to pass them around."[104]

The Portuguese's stifling colonial policies left Brazil lagging far behind in railroad infrastructure, agriculture, industry, and technology. This stands in sharp contrast to the U.S. South in the mid-nineteenth century, which was far more industrialized: it had more railroad infrastructure, and several textile factories, shoe manufacturers, flour mills, and iron foundries were scattered throughout the antebellum South.[105]

Transportation Challenges and Railroads

Other Confederado settlements were not as successful as the Santa Bárbara settlement for several reasons. Contributing factors included the settlers' poor understanding of Brazilian soil, poor soil, and inadequate roads. Among the most common complaints was the presence of few regular means of transportation.[106]

Transportation throughout Brazil for most of the nineteenth century consisted of horses, mules, canoes, or oxcarts, and it was often left to the hands of muleteers (*tropeiros*), who were mostly slaves.[107] It was only in 1852 that the Estrada de Ferro Mauá (named after Irineu Evangelista, the Barão de Mauá, a known Freemason and "coffee baron")[108] marked the definite implementation of the first railway system in Rio and in South America.[109] The first railroad system in São Paulo was built later in 1867, linking the port of Santos to the interior in Jundiaí, nearly seventy-two miles long. In contrast to the United States, there were no river–lake networks or canals in the Brazilian hinterlands.[110]

The early Brazilian railroads were limited in certain parts of the southeast regions, where export agriculture was predominant.[111] According to Richard Graham, "although some Brazilian planters invested in railways, the majority refused to contribute even to community road-building programs . . . they knew that fuzziness in land titles strengthened their authority."[112] The "fuzziness" in Brazilian land titles mentioned here came up in the first U.S. Southern search reports. For example, Maj. Meriweather and Dr. Shaw, who were surveying suitable lands, published a special report in *Debow's Review* in 1866 describing their observations: "The lands of Brazil, except in rare instances, have not been surveyed, and no one with whom we have conversed on this subject knows how much land he owns. All guess."[113]

British capital and British engineers were vital to the development and building of a wider Brazilian railway system, and in 1854 "the first of all railways to operate in Brazil was the Emperor's road running from the outskirts of Rio city across level ground to the foot of the Serra do Mar."[114] Starting in 1858 Brazilian railroads were largely financed by the Rothschild House of England. That house issued its first loans to the Bahia and São Francisco Railway Company and the Dom Pedro Segundo Railway Company and, a year later in 1859, to the São Paulo (Brazilian) Railway Company—known as the Ingleza (English)—connecting the port of Santos to Jundiaí, in the province of São Paulo. It was later nationalized in 1946, and today it is known as the Estrada de Ferro Santos–Jundiaí.[115] The first portion of the Estrada de Ferro Dom Pedro II (Dom Pedro Segundo Railroad), later renamed Estrada de Ferro Central do Brasil (after Brazil became a republic in 1889), was built and operated by a British-owned company, the Leopoldina Railway Company.

The second portion of the Estrada de Ferro Dom Pedro II was built by U.S. engineers who had formed a company; its founding members included Milnor Roberts and Jacob Humbird (from the Humbird family of Cumberland, Maryland, discussed in chapter 1). Humbird was mostly in charge of the engineering of the tunnels through the Serra do Mar, which comprised granite rock rising to an elevation range of around 2,600 feet to 3,000 feet from the coast of Rio. A correspondent writing for the *New York Times* described the project in 1860: "It has to traverse a mountainous range some 3,000 feet above the level of the sea, and some of the fillings required are enormous, while the shafts for the tunneling have to be sunk in some places upwards of 450 feet, and these have to be cut through the most solid kind of trap rock."[116]

Overseeing the engineering and construction portion of the new railway infrastructure, Jacob Humbird was also sympathetic to the immigration of U.S. Southerners to Brazil. Rev. Ballard Dunn wrote to Humbird, "To Mr. Jacob Humbird of Maryland, a resident of Brazil, and an active friend of such Southerners, as intended to emigrate to that country."[117]

In his unpublished autobiography, Milnor Roberts of Philadelphia wrote about the contract he had negotiated along with Humbird. Roberts was one of Jacob Humbird's partners in the construction of the second stretch of the Estrada de Ferro Dom Pedro II. In 1857, after Roberts had seen an advertisement requesting proposal bids for the construction of that railway, he called at the consul general of Brazil in New York City. He decided to bid for a contract, which he was awarded, and he quickly put a team of engineers together to form a business partnership. Among the partners were Jacob Humbird from Maryland and, from Virginia, Col. Charles M. Garnett (Chief Engineer) and Maj.

Andrew Ellison (Humbird's principal Assistant). Roberts signed the contract bid on May 1858.[118]

Overall, the railroad construction project took five years by the time "all the work was over and the track laid . . . excepting the Big Tunnel, which had been some time before arranged in a special contract with Mr. Humbird."[119]

Milnor Roberts described meeting with Baltimorean William T. Wright (of Maxwell, Wright & Co., at the time the U.S. consul in Santos), how they became friends, and how they took a trip on mules to the railroad tracks to visit coffee plantations. Roberts wrote of "spending a short time in Santos, where [he] received particular attention from the American Consul, my friend Mr. William T. Wright (formally of Baltimore, and later of Rio de Janeiro)."[120] Here is another clear example of how Baltimoreans in Brazil were facilitating and actively interacting within a network of U.S. Southern immigration sympathizers.

Immigration Efforts

In addition to the Sociedade Círculo Agrícola de São João de Cacaria's concern for the lack of dissemination of farming techniques, both the Marquês de Abrantes and Frederico Burlamaque promoted immigration to Brazil as an alternative to slave-based labor with the impending end of slavery.[121] Here is another example of how elite Brazilian agriculturalists directly and eagerly supported and encouraged immigrant labor.

Antônio Pereira Barreto Pedroso, founder of Sociedade Círculo Agrícola de São João de Cacaria, predicted that slave-based labor would soon come to its demise in Brazil due to low birth rates and high mortality rates among black slaves; instead, "they would have been willing to embrace an alternate, reliable source of labor, if it were available, in order to assure their survival."[122] Given that slavery was about to end, immigration to Brazil became the only solution to fulfill the country's great need for agricultural labor.

The urge to increase immigration to Brazil in order to replace slave labor and provide Brazil's new labor force was commonplace among planters, intellectuals, and politicians in the mid- to late nineteenth century, whether driven by altruistic abolitionist motivations, logistically practical and economic reasons, or ideological motives. Until then, slavery had been, as Eugene Ridings puts it, "an evil absolutely necessary for Brazil's survival."[123]

As early as 1865 William Scully published an editorial in the *Anglo-Brazilian Times* describing the creation of a Brazilian government funding plan for inducing U.S. Southern families to migrate to Brazil and bringing five thousand families in as rapidly as possible. Scully pointed out that this would become an investment to "improve the Empire." He further outlined a plan for the creation of a "Territorial Bank" not only for importing laborers and financing and aiding agricultural interests but also to extend "far beyond the limits assigned to it."[124] The plan was created by Charles Nathan.

The "Territorial Bank" plan Nathan conceived also included a side project to provide free education to black populations by purchasing young Brazilian slaves (between five and fifteen years of age) from Brazilian planters with the aim of, and "under the surveillance of the association in schools, on model farms, and in workshops, educat[ing] them mentally and industrially, giving each one, according to his or her aptitude, a systemic course of instruction, and teaching habits of industry, order, economy and frugality that will fit them to be self-provident and useful members of society. In the meantime supplying, by immigration, free adult labor in the place of the children thus taken from the planter to be educated to usefulness when grown up."[125]

The Territorial Bank and its side plan to educate young Brazilian slaves never panned out. Nonetheless, the various projects in which Charles Nathan was involved are ever-present in this Confederado story.

By 1876 the U.S. Southern exodus had ceased. Yet it was still clear that Dom Pedro II openly favored liberal economic policies and looked up to the United States as a model for economic, political, and social ideals. In that year Dom Pedro II visited the United States, traveling from New York to San Francisco to New Orleans, covering more than nine thousand miles over a period of three months and attending the Centennial Exposition in Philadelphia, June 20–25, 1876.[126] He was still promoting Brazil as a destination for new immigrants. The insights gained as a result from that trip were published in a book, *The Empire of Brazil at the Universal Exhibition of 1876 in Philadelphia*, which promoted Brazil's industries, ports, and trade to foreigners.

The Brazilian government continued to reaffirm its intention to promote and facilitate the immigration process furnished to new immigrants once they arrived on Brazilian soil; "foreigners are received in Brazil with the greatest benevolence; their rights are respected, and, in their civil relations, they are protected by the laws." Furthermore, primary education schools "were as free to [immigrants] and their children, as to Brazilians; and they can, in the same manner, matriculate in public colleges, and in the faculties they may own real property with the same liberty as Brazilian citizens."[127] The tone in this publication was reminiscent of the positive reception U.S. Southern immigrants had received a decade earlier. That is, almost a decade after the Confederados had arrived in Brazil, national policies still continually sought out more immigrants who would suit Brazilian ideological and agroeconomic goals.

The high-density population centers in Brazil had shifted from the northeast region (due to the end of the sugar boom) to Minas Gerais and Goiás (due to the Gold Rush), and then to Rio de Janeiro and São Paulo in the nineteenth century with the coffee boom. For perspective, in 1856 Minas Gerais was the province with the largest total population in all of Brazil (1,300,000), followed by Rio de Janeiro (1,200,000), Bahia (1,100,000), and Pernambuco (950,000). The total population of São Paulo (500,000) at that time ranked fourth, and the province of Espírito Santo had a mere 51,200 inhabitants.[128] With the coffee boom between 1886 and 1900, more than one million Brazilian internal migrants and foreign immigrants moved to the province of São Paulo.[129] Minas Gerais ceased to be the province with the largest total population of the empire and one of the largest slave-holding provinces since the eighteenth century. At that same time, the interior of São Paulo (particularly Ibicaba and plantations in the vicinity of Limeira, Itú, Piracicaba, Pirassununga, and Rio Claro) became a rival coffee producer to Rio's Paraíba Valley, becoming one of the first agricultural areas in Brazil to replace slave labor with a European immigrant work force.

Other Immigrants Arriving in Brazil

According to Lawrence F. Hill, Dom Pedro II was "convinced that the imperial regime of Brazil would be strengthened greatly by accretions to the landholding aristocracy."[130] Thus, the Empire of Brazil "promised land at twenty-two cents an acre, payable twenty per cent annually for five years, free provisions during the period of establishment, free transportation from Rio de Janeiro to the settlement site, and citizenship by the mere taking of an oath."[131] Large debts amounting from the Paraguayan War (1864–70), known as the War of the Triple Alliance (Guerra da Tríplice Aliança), left the Empire of Brazil urgently seeking opportunities and possibilities to increase its economic base to raise Imperial revenues. Furthermore, Dom Pedro's concerns focused on the need to recruit more immigrants to Brazil as "the suppression of African slave traffic at this time increased the need for immigrant labor." Due to the increasing influx of immigrants, the total population in Brazil swelled from about ten million in 1872 to an estimated sixteen million in 1889.[132] Considering the hundreds of thousands of immigrants entering Brazil, it is fitting to frame U.S. Southern immigration within the context of overall immigration to Brazil. For example, 20,144 immigrants of all nationalities arrived in Brazil in 1859. Throughout the 1860s and 1870s immigration of all nationalities steadily increased. In the decades that followed, total immigration increased dramatically, eventually peaking in 1891, with 214,239 immigrants entering Brazil that year.[133]

Three Brazilian immigration societies were created with the specific goal of recruiting agricultural laborers: Associação Auxiliadora de Colonização e Imigração para Província de São Paulo (1871), A Sociedade Central de Imigração (1883–1991), and A Sociedade Promotora de Imigração (1886)—the last of these was formed by agriculturalists in São Paulo and recruited over a hundred and twenty thousand Italian laborers until 1896.[134] Most of the new European immigrants who arrived between the 1850s and the late 1880s typically worked on coffee plantations in the interior of São Paulo and Rio de Janeiro, as well as in southern Brazil.

There are also broader economic and political changes to consider. Beginning in the late 1890s Brazil changed its political and economic structures after Dom Pedro II abdicated his throne in 1889 and Brazil became a federal republic, which coincided with a steady decline in the old agricultural and slave-based plantation economic model. The Brazilian economy then began to shift toward a slow-growing urban base with a new, industrial mode of production, and newly arrived European immigrants in the twentieth century eventually turned to Brazil's growing urban industries as wage laborers.[135]

To summarize, of the thousands of U.S. Southerners who went to Brazil, only a very small proportion of them stayed. Clearly, this move represents a deliberate and audacious political posturing on the part of U.S. Southerners, who could not have imagined what their lives would have been like had they decided to remain in the United States; with Reconstruction underway, they evidently felt strongly alienated and disaffected. As Rev. Ballard S. Dunn asked, "Why should we remain in a country, where we find that there is neither present, nor prospective, and security, for life, liberty and property?"[136]

Jarnagin remarks that U.S. Southern immigrants were making a logical move that hinged on the importance and opportunities "within the agrarian capitalism of the Atlantic world system."[137] This can be clearly seen in Dr. Gaston's outline of his commercial interests, in which he highlights the importance of anticipated trade dividends in the future of Confederate settlements in Brazil: "Should the emigrants from the United States locate in the province of São Paulo, this city . . . will become the centre of trade, and must grow rapidly in all that pertains to business."[138] Commercial interests in agricultural growth in Brazil became one of the strongest motivators for U.S. Southerners migrating to Brazil. In the words of Eric Hobsbawm, "what a growing part of agriculture all over the world had in common was subjection to the industrial world economy."[139]

4

Ideologies of Race, Religion, Politics, and Science

This chapter focuses on the ideologies lurking in the backdrop of the Brazilian migration enterprise. Here I focus on selected individuals, religious leaders, and scientists to show how they contributed to the dissemination of ideologies of the time, influencing Brazilian politicians and intellectuals, and, at the same time, favoring U.S. Southern immigration to Brazil. Moreover, I take a closer look at "race matters" as they relate to nineteenth-century ideologies and, ultimately, to the Confederado story.

At the outset, it is important to understand that the predominant framework that supported the idea of African slavery in the United States was broadly based on the perceived inherent biological inferiority of black populations. Conversely, in Brazil, the predominant notion was based on the idea that slavery was a "necessary evil" to sustain the national economy with. Moreover, the defense of slavery in Brazil did not subscribe to any specifically racist or biological argument, in contrast to the United States; and according to the late Brazilianist Thomas E. Skidmore, "the position of Brazilian supporters of slavery was pragmatic."[1]

Brazilian intellectuals and politicians in the mid-nineteenth century paradoxically upheld that slavery was a backward institution and that precisely because of its existence, Brazil lagged behind most of the rest of the world.[2] Therefore, these considerations are important to keep in mind later, in order to navigate Brazil's shifting stance on mid-nineteenth-century ideologies about race, particularly in comparison to U.S. racial ideologies of the same time.

Why Brazil?

Before the salience and convoluted narratives of race in Brazil are discussed here, it is necessary to understand the significance and the spectrum of push and pull factors involved in the migration of U.S. Southerners to Brazil. First, most towns in the U.S. South lay destroyed after the U.S. Civil War; there was chronic unemployment, lack of money, lack of labor, and a general sense of moral defeat throughout the region. Thousands of U.S. Southerners had moved to the midwest and northeastern regions of the United States, as well as to other countries, including Brazil.[3] Second, the pull factors included several Brazilian government inducements, for example: (1) perceived benevolent monarchy in Brazil, (2) religious tolerance, (3) facility and ease with immigration bureaucracy in Brazil, (4) facilitation through government loans and public lands available for purchase, and (5) promises of improved infrastructure.[4]

However, Gerald Horne proposes that there were only two factors that drove Confederates to leave the United States for Brazil: their "hatred of federal government" and the desire "to continue African slavery."[5] Charles Willis Simmons goes further, reducing the reasons down to one decisive factor: "Racism in the guise of opposition to black equality."[6]

Conversely, historian Claire M. Wolnisty observes that U.S. Southerners who went to Brazil were not engaged in expanding an "Anglo-Saxon slave empire" and "endorsed peaceful emigration efforts through fostering familial loyalties."[7] In addition, according to Blanche Henry Clark Weaver, "ex-Confederates were concerned solely with removing themselves from the unbearable existence under Reconstruction governments."[8] No official color divide existed in Brazil, and the anticipation of the end of Brazilian slavery was well-known to immigrants, but neither factor impeded U.S. Southerners migrating to Brazil. Reducing the decision-making process of migration to a singular factor neglects other overarching and interrelated sociopolitical, commercial, agrarian, and economic considerations—the push and pull factors mentioned above.

Slave ownership in early and mid-nineteenth-century Brazil was widespread, and, according to Leslie Bethell, even "a considerable proportion of the free population, half of itself being black or mulato, owned at least one or two slaves."[9] Other foreigners besides U.S. Southerners who lived or worked in Brazil at the time owned slaves. For example, "the English mining-company, whose stockholders are in Great Britain, but whose fields of operations in S.[São] João del Rey in Brazil, own about eight hundred slaves, and hire one thousand more. French and Germans also purchase[d] slaves."[10]

There is also evidence that a few Confederados had owned Brazilian slaves. Alcides Fernando Gussi points out in his research of the town registry in Santa Bárbara that with about five hundred Confederado family members living there at the time, forty-nine *norte-americanos* were listed as the owners of a total of sixty-six slaves among all of the settlers in that colony between the years of 1866 and 1880.[11]

Robert Cicero Norris (son of William H. Norris), for example, owned two slaves: Manuel and Olímpia, who both took on Norris's surname upon his death in 1913.[12] Hervey Hall, who migrated from Georgia to the Santa Bárbara settlement in 1867, was among those who also owned slaves in Brazil. Yet in a letter Hall sent for publication in the *Georgia Sun and Times* in 1867, he warned his fellow compatriots, "A man has not the means to buy a place with the labor on it, as we did, he had better depend upon his own labor."[13]

Out of the thousands of U.S. Southern immigrants who went to Brazil, the few who acquired slaves did not retain them for long. As Laura Jarnagin points out, "migrants were advised to work with their own hands if they had less than $5,000 to bring to the effort."[14] Moreover, Claire Wolnisty comments on how U.S. Southern immigrants to Brazil did not follow their expansionistic filibustering predecessors in the U.S. South; Southern immigrants to Brazil "promoted escapism and individual enterprise in Brazil instead of advocating the creation of an Anglo-Saxon slave empire in the West and Latin America."[15] This sociopolitical and economic mindset of the Confederados in Brazil was similar to that of U.S. Southerners who went to Mexico at that same time. Nevertheless,

Todd W. Wahlstrom claims differently, maintaining that the existence of the institution of slavery was likely a strong pull factor for those who went to Brazil.[16]

Notably, since the signing of a Brazilian statute in 1831 Brazil had prohibited blacks "from the United States—or from any portion of the world" from entering the country.[17] This was unlike the case in Mexico, where many U.S. Southerners took their former slaves with them.[18] This Brazilian law would have prevented Confederados from bringing former slaves to Brazil if they had intended to bring them. As Dr. Gaston stated, "Negroes are not admitted into Brazil from other countries."[19] Counselor J. M. N. Azambuja from the Brazilian legation in New York replied to a inquiry made by a Mississippi farmer who wanted to migrate to Brazil: "You can apply to Mr. Quintino de Souza Bocayuva, the Agent of emigration in this city, Broadway n. 26, who can proportion passages for you, and your family . . . You cannot take with you negroes; their entry in Brazil is forbidden by our laws."[20]

Confederate immigrants knew about this law before moving to Brazil, and they were aware that slavery would soon end in Brazil. As Dr. Gaston highlighted in 1867, "Slavery may be destined to cease in Brazil at some future day, by gradual emancipation."[21]

Furthermore, although the institution of slavery was still legal, slave trafficking from Africa was outlawed in 1850 by a Brazilian law known as Lei Eusébio de Queirós; the price for a slave in Brazil rose significantly after, increasing fourfold in the following seven years. *Debow's Review* reported in 1858 that before 1830 "the value of a slave was but $66, whereas from 1830 to 1850, growing out of the difficulties of imports, it was $220. In 1853 the value was $605, and in 1857 it has reached, we are informed, on the average, over $800."[22] Newly arrived immigrants from a war-torn U.S. South would have needed substantial financial capital to afford the high prices of slaves, had they intended to purchase them in the first place. In this case, Confederados would have been effectively thwarted in their effort to replicate the U.S. Southern slave-driven cotton-based agricultural system at a large scale, had they envisioned doing so.

A critical and careful approach is necessary here. Thousands of other U.S. Southerners also left for other countries—including Mexico, even though slavery had been abolished in that country since 1824. Confederates also left for Canada and England, where slavery was illegal. If Confederate immigrants were solely interested in continuing slavery, as some scholars have asserted, why would thousands of U.S. Southerners have flocked to countries where slavery was illegal? Here, multiple motivations in the decision-making process become salient considerations.

Moreover, Brazilian government agencies had planned to bring German immigrant laborers rather than local black slaves to work for U.S. Southerners in their settlement farms: "Thousands of hard-working Germans would come to you [U.S. Southerners] from abroad."[23]

It is important to consider that U.S. Southern immigrants were well-aware that Brazil's population consisted of a sizeable number of black and miscegenated populations (one of the largest in the world), many of whom were government officials, journalists, politicians, and law enforcement officers—occupations that would have been unimaginable in the strictly racialized antebellum U.S. South.[24] Therefore, if U.S. Southern immigrants were indeed "recalcitrant," "retrograde," "unforgiving rebels," and "Negrophobic," as one scholar has claimed, it would seem highly unlikely that that they would have chosen to settle in Brazil.[25]

I want to make it clear here, of course, that I am not capriciously minimizing the abhorrence of slavery or trying to exculpate those few Confederados who were slave owners. By offering insights into the inconsistencies and paradoxes weaved throughout this Confederado story, I am making a point to understand the complex, multiple, and interrelated push/pull factors of migration.[26] This "inconsistency" is a common theme here, one that Lawrence F. Hill has also highlighted in his study of the Confederados.[27]

Evidently, knowledge of the lack of official racial and segregation laws in Brazil did not deter U.S. Southerners from moving there. Therefore, it is also important to look at the ideologies that emerged during Reconstruction in the United States.

Reconstruction and Race

Clearly, race was an important facet in the livelihoods of Americans throughout the United States, and not only in the U.S. South. Moreover, race was and is inherently tied to social-class construction.[28] Racial politics in the U.S. South would only become increasingly more violent, magnified, and highly politicized, especially throughout the twentieth century.[29]

During the Reconstruction Era, a new type of relationship between whites and blacks emerged in the U.S. South. Freed blacks were now a threat to the establishment of white supremacy. Therefore, new postbellum policies not only subjugated blacks but also, after Emancipation, criminalized blacks through new "Black Codes" for offenses such as being unemployed or the crime of "vagrancy," for example. After Reconstruction, the concept of "whiteness" would take a turn; in the words of Grace Elizabeth Hale, "some southerners created a common whiteness to solve the problems of the post-Civil War era and built their collectivity on not just a convention or a policy but on segregation as a culture."[30] Black prisoners became a disproportionate majority among most U.S. prison populations, imprisoned for minor offenses—or for none at all—inside notorious prison labor camps such as Mississippi State Penitentiary (also known as "Parchman Farm")—a legacy that continues to this day.[31] With newly created prison labor camps and convict leasing, the oppression of black populations continues from slavery through Jim Crow and then through felon disenfranchisement. After Emancipation, blacks were no longer considered "capital," and there was no incentive to even minimally care for the well-being and health of black prisoners in this new postbellum racialized environment.[32]

After the U.S. Civil War, cotton exports in the U.S. South increased almost ninefold between 1865 and 1900—largely driven by the U.S. railroad boom. The wealth generated by the cotton boom had spiked with the new postbellum sharecropping economic system. It exacerbated the chasm between white supremacy and black disenfranchisement and poverty. At the same time, Lost Cause ideologies spurred new emotions about the old Confederacy; consequently, violent racial politics erupted throughout the postbellum U.S. South.[33] That is, the postbellum construct of "whiteness" described here produced a new kind of virulent racism. Nevertheless, as they had already moved to Brazil when this new environment emerged, Confederados and their descendants did not experience the new postbellum political and sociocultural climates of the United States, and they most likely did not view them through the same lens as those who had remained in the postbellum U.S. South. Once Confederados had settled and established themselves in Brazil, intermarriage with local Brazilians became common (take Brazilians with African, Indigenous, Portuguese, and Italian ancestries, for example). Furthermore, Brazilian law did not legally segregate blacks and nonwhites in Brazil. In summary, Confederados and their descendants did not adhere to the new cultural, political, or social changes that transformed the U.S. South during the Reconstruction period. In fact, they ostensibly followed the Brazilian-based hybrid construction of race.

A few observations between the U.S. and Brazilian stances on race can be made. During most of the nineteenth century, for instance, white Americans had little to no knowledge of U.S. black writers and artists, in sharp contrast to Brazilians, who recognized "writers and artists of African descent such as Tobias Barreto, Machado de Assis, André Rebouças, and Aleijadinho."[34]

Furthermore, a significant proportion of black populations and free persons of color already lived among the general population of Brazil, including prominent political and elite figures such as João Maurício Wanderley, Barão de Cotegipe, Brazil's Prime Minister; Luís da Gama, a lawyer and abolitionist; José do Patrocínio, an abolitionist, orator, and journalist at the newspaper *A cidade do Rio*; Machado de Assis, eminent Brazilian novelist and founder of the Brazilian Academy of Letters; and André Rebouças, a prominent engineer during Dom Pedro II's empire.[35] For example, in 1857 Reverends Kidder and Fletcher observed, "Some of the most intelligent men that [we] met with in Brazil—men educated in Paris and Coimbra—were of African descent, whose ancestors were slaves. Thus, if a man has freedom, money, and merit, no matter how black may be his skin, no place in society is refused him." They continued, "the largest and most successful printing-establishment in Rio—that of Sr. F. Paul[a] Brito—is owned and directed by a mulato. In the colleges, the medical, law, and theological schools, there is no distinction of color"[36] (Francisco de Paula Brito began publishing in 1833 the first Brazilian newspaper dedicated to black readership in Brazil, *O homen de côr*—The man of color).

In addition, Kidder and Fletcher's publication explicitly notes the lack of any official color divide in Brazil, which was widely known in the United States before Confederados migrated to Brazil. Therefore, claims made by scholars that U.S. Southerners went to Brazil for the sole purpose of continuing slavery and "in opposition to black equality" turn out to be misleading and overly simplistic arguments.

Concepts of Blackness and Whiteness

Evidently, before Confederados moved to Brazil, U.S. Southerners had seen the world through a highly racialized experience in the antebellum U.S. South, which helps to explain why some of the language in the documentation and letters from that time period is patently racist in today's vernacular. However, research has shown that Confederado descendants in Santa Bárbara today do not hold racist values for the most part, Cyrus B. Dawsey and James M. Dawsey assert, these descendants are not "die-hard Old South apologists or advocates of antiquated values such as racial segregation."[37] During their well-known annual Confederado family reunions (Festa Confederada), which take place at Campo, attendees at the event include descendants who had intermarried with other Brazilians—in a country where miscegenation is not considered taboo.

Notably, on August 13, 2017, João Leopoldo F. Padoveze, the president of the Fraternidade Descendência Americana (Fraternity of American Descendants)—the organization created by Confederado descendants that oversees the Confederate cemetery and grounds at Campo—wrote a special editorial in the organization's public-facing website. Padoveze vehemently condemned and opposed the violence and racial hatred that took place during the demonstrations in Charlottesville, Virginia, in August 2017 (in which one person was killed). He also went on to clearly state that the Fraternidade Descendência Americana repudiated and opposed any type of discrimination by race, religion, gender, or age. On behalf of the organization, he profoundly lamented what had happened in Charlottesville as a "sad event," claiming that U.S. "extreme right-wing racists" do not represent the same ideals that Confederados hold, especially since interracial marriage had been accepted by this community for generations.[38] This editorial conveys a telling account of Confederado descendants' explicit stance against contemporary U.S. racism. Note here that the organization is named as a fraternity of "American descendants" and not one of the descendants of "U.S. Southerners." However, Brazilian black resistant groups—for example, União de Negros pela Igualdade (UNEGRO)—led a protest in 2019 against the use of Confederate symbols at Campo, using U.S.-inspired slogans from the Black Lives Matter movement. The new scholarly literature points to emerging protests in Brazil structured on U.S. interpretations of Confederate symbolisms.[39]

The backdrop of race in Brazil warrants further consideration here. The traditional interpretation of race in Brazil, albeit often confusing, differs noticeably from the historical U.S. conception of race. That is, "blackness" in Brazil was not based on strict legal ancestry norms as it was in the United States (e.g., the "one-drop rule," under which individuals with any black ancestry would be legally black). In Brazil, physical appearance has ostensibly eclipsed ancestry and race.[40] Furthermore, the terminology used in official surveys and Brazilian Censuses today is based on an elastic continuum comprising arbitrarily selected and subjective color (not race) categories (e.g., *branco, preto, amarelo, pardo*—loosely translated as white, black, yellow, and brown, respectively). The Brazilian Census category "Indigenous" (*Indígena*)—used to identify Amerindian populations—was only included in the 1991 Census. For example, in Brazil the term *pardo* (brown) does not necessarily mean "half-black"; rather, it refers to a wide array of "color" variations ranging from "dark-brunette" to "half-Indian." Moreover, the term *branco* (white) does not necessarily connote the same meaning as "white" in the United States (a person who self-identifies as "white" in Brazil may be a "light-skin" *pardo*, for instance). Since occupation and social class in Brazil play intrinsic roles in the perception of an individual's "whiteness," one's level of affluence correlates to the interpretation of one's color.[41] Unlike the U.S. Anglo-Saxon idea of "whiteness," emphasis was and is placed on physical appearance (e.g., phenotypes) and social class rather than on ancestry or race (e.g., genotypes).[42] Therefore, the construction of "whiteness" in Brazil was (and still is) contested, though it differed sharply from the conceptualization of "whiteness" as seen through the strictly binary U.S. racial optics of black/white.

U.S. versus Brazilian Concerns with Race

Concerns with race matters emerged as a central argument against immigration to Brazil in most U.S. newspapers. For example, in 1865 the *Daily Dispatch* in Richmond reprimanded the migration plan and vehemently opposed migration to a country where no distinction of color existed: "We are at a loss to understand how any southern man can think of emigrating to Brazil. We are not even threatened with a state of things as offensive to the white race of this whole country as already exists in the Brazilian Empire. We leave a land where our own race is in the majority, and where no legislation can extend beyond the conferment of political privileges upon the blacks, for a land in which the African and mixed races largely predominate, and in which no social distinction of color prevails."[43]

Using rhetoric similar to that in most other U.S. newspapers at that time, the report above clearly describes the lack of color divide in Brazil as a "problem" and outlines the concern about how "African and mixed races largely predominate." The Brazilian constitution recognized "neither directly nor indirectly, color as a basis of civil rights; hence, once free, the black man or mulato, if he possess energy and talent, can rise to a social position from which his race in North America is debarred."[44] However, despite the existence of these laws, realistically, limitations were imposed directly or indirectly upon blacks and free nonwhites, depending on each respective Brazilian region and province as well as on the skin color of each individual (ranging from "light skin" to "dark skin").[45]

Some scholars have claimed that an economically based concept of "racialized labor" evolved in Brazil, which led to a social form of discrimination, one not specifically racialized or distinctly motivated by racial politics alone. In this case, free blacks and nonwhites merged into the white labor force. However, coerced labor was associated with "blackness." In this sense, a form of "racialized labor migration" correlated "whiteness" with "industriousness."[46]

However, this elastic conceptualization of color (*côr*) in Brazil is not without challenges and has its own set of serious predicaments. Therein lies the paradox: despite the lack of any official color divide, as well as the flexibility of color self-identification in Brazilian surveys, a direct and interlinked correlation between skin color and social class remains inherent in Brazilian society to this day. That is, the whiter the color of one's skin, the more likely one is able to become upwardly mobile (economically and socially); conversely, the darker one's skin color, the more likely one will remain in poverty.[47] Additionally, over the past fifty years Brazilian censuses have illustrated that race has been an independent variable that affects key life chances, such as education, mobility, and income.[48] Scholars have long grappled with such glaring statistics in the face of Brazil's world image as a "racial paradise." Given the stark nature of past and recent statistics and studies, there was and is nothing "paradisiacal" about Brazil for blacks past or present.

Remarkably, the Brazilian ideological stance for white preference, especially for individuals with blue eyes and blond hair, still holds true in Brazil today. For example, the *Wall Street Journal* reported on March 22, 2018, that the extraordinary demand for U.S. "Caucasian" sperm donors with blond hair and blue eyes has recently skyrocketed in Brazil, where "the preference for white donors reflects a persistent preoccupation with race in a country where social class and skin-color correlate with glaring accuracy."[49] The influence and legacy of mid-nineteenth-century pseudoscientific racial constructions may likely have led Brazilians to convince themselves that they were inadequately placed within an "imagined" human racial hierarchy.[50]

Brazilian nation building had occurred under the premise that Brazil could only effectively progress forward into modernity with the influx of white European and American immigrants (to replace the declining slave labor force), commonly described at the time as "industrious" and "intelligent." As Jeffrey Lesser points out, in Brazil "immigration *was* the construction of national identity."[51]

Repatriation to Africa

While the large-scale migration of populations out of the United States—occurring in the thousands—was extremely rare and an anomaly, it was not unique. The idea of removing black populations to another country had already been set into motion in the United States long before the Civil War. In total, the United States financed, organized, and removed an estimated fifteen thousand freed African blacks who volunteered to move to West Africa—and who were part of a "colonization" project to remove blacks from the country.[52] The American Society for Colonizing the Free People of Color in the United States, also known as the American Colonization Society, was founded in 1816. This society purchased land in 1821, which later became known as Liberia (becoming an independent Republic in 1847).[53] The Maryland Colonization Society, a state society, focused its efforts on resettling freed blacks from the U.S. state of Maryland to the short-lived U.S. outpost named "Maryland" in West Africa, today the country of Liberia. This society was one of the primary financial sponsors of the "Monrovia settlement" (named after U.S. President James Monroe). Most blacks were not "buying into the scheme."[54] Supported by state and federal funds, the repatriation societies also counted on eminent members at the time, such as Francis Scott Key, Henry Clay, John Marshall, and Andrew Jackson.[55]

The idea of repatriating blacks to Africa also took place in Brazil. Much less known, however, was the migration of nearly six thousand freed Brazilian black slaves to West Africa, which occurred voluntarily and without funding from any official repatriation project. These emancipated slaves paid for their own manumission (*alforria*), transportation, and expenses to resettle in Africa. In 1861 about 130 repatriated Brazilian families lived in Lagos, Nigeria. By 1878 nearly six thousand repatriated Brazilian blacks lived in West Africa.[56] The late President of Togo Sylvanus Olympio (1958–63) was one of the descendants of those Brazilian freed slaves who had left for West Africa.[57]

The notion that blacks would be better suited to tropical climates was a likely guise for the ultimate removal of an "unwanted" population group, whether the reasons fell under humanitarian, political, economic, or purely racist pretenses. Proposals advocating for the repatriation of former slaves (to, for example, Liberia, Honduras, Haiti, Costa Rica, and Brazil) had been made by U.S. President Abraham Lincoln, particularly in the early years of his presidency. Although Lincoln is better known for his Emancipation Proclamation, a speech of his reported by the *New York Tribune* in 1862 reveals another side to his racial politics. He began his speech by stating: "You and we are different races. We have between us a broader difference than exists between almost any other two races."[58] Lincoln continued, "Whether it is right or wrong I need not discuss, but this physical difference is a great disadvantage to us both, as I think your race suffer[s] greatly, many of them by living among us, while ours suffer[s] from your presence. In a word we suffer on each side."[59] Just a day before he signed the Emancipation Proclamation that freed slaves, Lincoln signed a contract using federal funds to remove five thousand blacks from the United States to Haiti.[60]

Recently Brazilian historian Maria Clara Sales Carneiro Sampaio has uncovered letters that reveal how General James W. Webb—U.S. ambassador in Rio, (1861–69)—and William H. Seward, secretary of state under the Lincoln administration, had already begun colonization negotiations with the Brazilian government. They proposed setting up a new binational firm to colonize the Amazon with blacks from the United States—in line with Matthew Fontaine Maury's outline for taking over the Amazon almost a decade earlier (discussed later in this chapter). In her study, Sampaio analyzes letters sent from Brazilian Foreign Minister Marquês de Abrantes to General James W. Webb. When Webb asked if deportation of ten thousand to fifteen thousand blacks to Brazil without price would be possible, Brazil said, "No." Abrantes staunchly cited the Brazilian law of November 7, 1831, under which blacks from anywhere were not allowed and would be immediately deported if they arrived on Brazilian soil.[61]

Therefore, discussions about removing blacks from the United States had been in motion as far back as the U.S. Early Republic period.[62] Nonetheless, these contentions offer a glimpse into the ambiguous stance of Lincoln's perceptions on race and slavery and the context of large-scale migration processes out of the United States. In addition, these narratives about repatriation projects reflect how deterministic views affected racial policies in both Brazil and the United States, as well as how they reflect U.S. perceptions of Brazil as a nation at that time.

Maury: The Interest in the Brazilian Amazon

Matthew Fontaine Maury, commander of the Confederate States Navy during the Civil War and founder of the new science of oceanography, was also known as the "Pathfinder of the Seas." He is best known for his work on a "general model of atmospheric circulation depicting the equatorial doldrum belt, the trade winds, the mid-latitude and polar calms, and the Westerlies." However, along with other U.S. scientists of his day, such as Arnold Guyot and Louis Agassiz, he presented his theories in the context of "natural law guided by Providence."[63] Maury published extensively under the pen name "Inca," producing new oceanic charts of ocean currents and winds, and his work has been translated into eight languages.[64]

Maury had envisioned taking over the Brazilian Amazon in a covert operation of preemption. He wanted to create a U.S. territory for slaveholding and deporting black slaves from the United States. Maury had planned to transplant and recreate U.S. Southern agroeconomic hegemony in Brazil; he expected U.S. Southerners to move to the Amazon and to transform it into a U.S. territory—effectively turning it into an extension of the Mississippi Valley. Brazil feared an imminent U.S.-led intervention and a potential annexation of the Amazon to the United

States, threats that Maury's publications outline; however, these never came to fruition. As a result, Brazil's government was outraged by his bold insinuation, a sentiment that Reverends Fletcher and Kidder tried to appease: "Brazil certainly has the right, and the sole right, to control the rivers within her own borders, no matter if they do rise in other states."[65]

Maury believed that "the policy of commerce, not the policy of conquest, is the policy of the United States" He stated, "The country that is drained by the Amazon, if reclaimed from the savage, the wild beast, and the reptile, and reduced to cultivation now, would be capable of supporting with its produce the population of the whole world."[66] In Maury's view, the Amazon could serve as a "safety valve" for the United States by allowing U.S. Southern slaveowners to resettle and continuing to reproduce the offspring of slaves there.

Maury was ultimately guided by policies that were inherently tied to the institution of slavery. Emancipation of U.S. slaves would come at too great a cost economically and socially—Maury feared racial conflict, believing that U.S. Southern plantation owners should all eventually move to the Amazon Valley, where the supply of black slaves would be furnished internally.[67] In addition to paying "lip service to the policy of commerce," as Hilgard O'Reilly Sternberg puts it, Maury was perpetuating common myths that linger to this day: that the Amazon could become the breadbasket of the world, and that local Amazonians were "imbecile[s]" and like children, incapable of making decisions for themselves and making significant contributions to humanity.[68]

As Amazonian experts Susanna Hecht and Alexander Cockburn explain, "Amazon soils are mainly poor and[,] without quantities of fertilizer and insecticides, cannot deliver high yields under monocultural systems."[69] Further, Maury understood the Amazon to be a regional "commercial blank"—a vast, wasted empty space, a "wilderness" sparsely inhabited by Indians who were detached from the modern world and global or local trade.[70] In this way, Maury failed to consider the two or three million Indians who inhabited the Amazon at that time. He also missed the "trading networks of the upper Xingu, or the salt routes that extended from the Atlantic to the Andes, or the connections between

Central America and the Amazon via the Orinico to the Casiquaiare to the Rio Negro." Furthermore, Hecht and Cockburn conclude, "the patronizing eye sees nothing of this . . . making it easier to envisage forest clearance as the only rational form of development."[71]

After the end of the U.S. Civil War, Maury began to urge U.S. Southerners to move to Mexico (where he resided then) instead of Brazil. He had been prompted by several inducements to go to Mexico. For example, Emperor Maximillian had made him the director of the Imperial Observatory of Mexico and, thereafter, the Imperial Commissioner of Immigration. In 1866 Maury wrote a letter from Mexico to his sons, reporting, "The Mexican plan is spreading over the South. We are going to have happy homes, a fine country, and a bright future here. Let those who lack gall or who having it, have steeped it in honey, stay. I seek to plant my posterity here."[72]

However, Maury's enthusiasm for Mexico quickly waned—he stayed in Mexico for only eight months.[73] In another letter written later that year to his son-in-law, Maj. Spotswood Wellford Corbin, Maury explained why he was not returning to Mexico: "I probably should not return to Mexico. I have as you know decided not to go back there in the face of bad faith to me, bad treatment of our people and bad turns that everything has taken."[74] He ended up leaving for Europe before finally returning to Virginia.

Maury had evidently been wrong about his visions about the Amazon becoming an extension of the Mississippi and Mexico becoming a global economic powerhouse; as John Majewski and Todd W. Wahlstrom explain, "Maury's economic geography ultimately offered a misguided pathway to a modern South."[75]

Maury died in Virginia in 1873, and today a monument stands in Maury's honor on "Monument Avenue" in Richmond, Virginia—alongside the monuments of Robert E. Lee, J. E. B. Stuart, Jefferson Davis, and Thomas "Stonewall." In the words of Whitfield J. Bell Jr., "the publicity which Maury and the southern expansionists gave Brazil was doubtless one of the influences which led several thousand self-exiled Confederates to emigrate to that country at the close of the American Civil War."[76]

The Impact of Racialized and Political Ideologies

Dom Pedro II was absorbed with new technological advancements in science, and he encouraged future scientific explorations and research in Brazil. Nonetheless, the Brazilian government prohibited foreign vessels from navigating the Amazon, though—albeit remaining hesitant and suspicious of U.S.-affiliated Amazonian explorations—they granted permission to U.S. Navy Lieutenant William Lewis Herndon and Passed Midshipman Lardner Gibbon to look at potential commercial interests in the Amazon. Herndon and Gibbon's reports were published in *Exploration of the Valley of the Amazon* (1853–54). This was the first U.S. Navy exploration of the Brazilian Amazon, and the publication that ensued was instrumental in generating U.S. political, scientific, and commercial interest in the Amazon.[77]

Maury had handpicked Herndon (his brother-in-law and cousin) and furnished him with specific details and instructions for his Amazonian exploration, which Herndon would conduct with Lardner Gibbon. These instructions and the Amazon proposal were outlined in a letter sent to U.S. Secretary of the Navy William Ballard Preston on March 29, 1850.[78]

Maury's interest in the Amazon was not merely scientific—it was also commercial, ideological, and political. That is, the idea of "Manifest Destiny" played "a significant role in the domestic policy of the United States"—and this had been kept secret from the Brazilian government.[79] Maury had been meticulously calculating with his directions, and he had categorically told Herndon not to let the Brazilian government know about all his goals or intentions. Additionally, Maury informed Herndon that he would supply Herndon with instruments necessary for exploration, effective research, and navigation, including a "pocket chronometer, a sextant, an art[ificial] horizon, a few thermometers, a pocket compass … steel barometers for elevations and meteorological observations."[80]

Maury was strongly influenced by the deterministic ideas of a prominent Swiss-born scientist of that time, Arnold Guyot (a close friend of Louis Agassiz, his Swiss compatriot). In Maury's letter to Herndon in 1850, he included long quotes taken directly from Guyot's publications.

Arnold Guyot (1807–84), professor of geology and physical geography at Princeton University, was like Agassiz a polygenist and an environmental determinist—one who denied Darwinian evolution. Considered the "father of geomorphology," Guyot's influence on Maury was evidently clear. In his letter to Herndon, Maury asked, "The question is then, who shall people the great valley of this mighty Amazon. Shall it be people with an imbecile and an indolent people or by a go ahead race that has energy and enterprise equal to subdue the forest and develop and bring forth the vast resources that lie hidden there?"[81] Note in this excerpt Maury's deterministic mentality and his perception that Brazilians were "imbecile" and "indolent," and how, by transplanting U.S. Southerners to the Amazon, the future growth of "white" populations in Brazil ("a go ahead race that has energy and enterprise"), would then signal the emergence of "development."

Maury then wrote, "My friend Guyot of Neufchatel in speaking of the duties of the North and the destinies of the Southern Hemisphere makes some remarks in a charming course of lectures called 'Earth and Man' with which I have [been] so struck that I quote them for you."[82] Here, "Manifest Destiny" in the Southern hemisphere was seen as the rightful duty of North Americans to fulfill—clearly, a narrative framed within the vernacular of Guyot's determinism.[83]

Herndon died not too long after his Amazonian exploration. In 1857 he was traveling back from Panama on the SS *Central America*, which he was commanding, when the ship ran into a storm and sank, killing over four hundred passengers. Herndon went down with the ship. Today a twenty-one-foot-tall monument stands in Herndon's honor at the U.S. Naval Academy in Annapolis, Maryland.[84]

Herndon's publication about the Amazon had also impressed a young Samuel Clemens, who was enthralled with tales about the coca leaf and possibilities of making it rich with its commercialization. In 1857 Clemens made plans to embark for Pará, Brazil, and made it all the way by steamer to New Orleans while searching for a passage to Brazil. However, when Clemens realized there were no ships heading for the Amazon, he decided to travel along the Mississippi River instead—thus began the stories of Mark Twain.[85]

Gobineau

Another public figure who influenced Brazilian intellectuals and politicians on the need to bring white immigrants to Brazil was Count Joseph Arthur de Gobineau (1816–82), a French writer and diplomat known as the "father of scientific racism." He had been appointed French Minister to Brazil (tantamount to the contemporary position of an ambassador) from 1869 to 1870—a period that overlapped with the U.S. Southern move to Brazil. He quickly became a close friend of Dom Pedro II.

While Gobineau lived in Rio, "soon it became the accepted thing for the Comte [Count] to visit Dom Pedro once or twice a week for the sake of enjoyment the two had in each other's company."[86] The meetings between the two took place at the lavish tropical Imperial Palaces in Petrópolis or São Cristóvão—virtual imitations of the palaces of Versailles and Vienna—a far cry from the rest of Rio.

However, Dom Pedro II did not share all of Gobineau's ideas on staunch racial hierarchies, because "the emperor believed in the good of all humanity."[87] Dom Pedro II embraced this sentiment, perhaps because this was a common view shared by Freemasons. However, Dom Pedro II agreed with Gobineau about the importance of bringing white immigrants to Brazil. This was the argument made for the inducement to bring German immigrants to Petrópolis (a hillside city west of the city of Rio), which Dom Pedro facilitated.[88]

Gobineau believed that Brazilian populations were genetically "degenerate" because of the miscegenation between Europeans, Amerindians, and black Africans. Therefore, Gobineau concluded that in order to improve this perceived genetic "degeneracy," Brazil's government needed to encourage more whites to migrate to Brazil in order to replace blacks and free men of color. In an article published in 1874 in the French newspaper *Le correspondent* titled "L'émigration au Brésil" (Emigration to Brazil), Gobineau maintained that the total Brazilian population would become extinct in less than two hundred years because of Brazil's "mixed-race" population makeup. In this case, Brazil needed to replace its "degenerate" population with "desirable" immigrants.[89] This view would fan the anxiety of Brazilian politicians and intellectuals about their world self-image and ultimately promote more white immigrants to move to Brazil (for example, several late-nineteenth-century Brazilian intellectuals, including Sílvio Romero, Nina Rodrigues, and Oliveira Vianna were influenced by Gobineau's ideas).

Gobineau vehemently opposed the Luso-colonial norms that encouraged miscegenation and sexual intercourse between European, African, and Amerindian populations. Despite Gobineau's abhorrence of the general Brazilian population, he thought that the emperor was the only Brazilian worthy of his friendship; Dom Pedro II had blond hair and blue eyes, and according to Gobineau, this was an indication the Emperor was intellectually and morally "superior," unlike the rest of the Brazilians.[90]

Gobineau is best known for his *Essai sur l'inégalité des races humaines* (Essay on the inequality of the human races), published in 1853, in which he made claims about the existence of inherent differences within human races and that white populations were naturally "superior."[91]

During his stay in Brazil, Gobineau was involved in a couple of violent incidents that ultimately resulted in his removal from his diplomatic position in Brazil. The same year he arrived in Brazil, Gobineau was involved in a physical altercation with Dom Pedro II's medical doctor, Dr. Vicente Cândido Figueira de Sabóia, at the exit of a theatre in Rio, after Gobineau apparently bumped and knocked Sabóia's wife to the ground.[92] A day after that scuffle, Gobineau called on Sabóia and challenged him to a duel, which never happened. Gobineau was finally ousted from his post to Brazil after a bloody street fight with a senator's son in Rio, who was insulted by Gobineau's commentaries on Brazilian populations and had confronted him. After this fight, Gobineau was asked to return to France upon the emperor's own recommendation.[93]

Despite his removal from office, Gobineau would personally accompany the emperor in Europe on a trip to Greece, Turkey, and Italy, and he continued his correspondence and friendship with the emperor for eleven years until Gobineau's death in 1882. The bulk of the letters exchanged (from 1870 to 1882) between the emperor and Gobineau were translated from French to Portuguese and published in 1938. These letters reflect the exchanges and the interest in similar ideas the two shared as well as point to the close friendship they developed. Dom Pedro II was likely to have been directly influenced by Gobineau's ideas, evidently favoring U.S. immigration to Brazil.[94]

Gobineau gained popularity and recognition after his death in Italy in 1882, not in his native France but in Germany. Writer Ludwig Schemann (who eventually became Gobineau's biographer) introduced Gobineau's work to German composer Richard Wagner, a friend of Gobineau's for a brief time. Subsequently Gobineau's work was popularized in Nazi Germany and even read by Adolf Hitler. Brazilian scholar Ricardo Alexandre Santos Sousa, who studied Gobineau's influence in Brazil, claims that if Gobineau had lived to witness World War II, he would have been wiser to change his staunch racial posturing after knowing the consequences of his work—all of which led to tyranny and violence.[95]

In his now classic study *Casa-grande e senzala*, first published in 1933 and translated into English in 1946 as *The Masters and the Slaves*, Gilberto Freyre vehemently opposes the rhetoric of Brazilian "degeneracy" proposed by Gobineau. Freyre argues that Gobineau's biological determinism was condescending toward Brazilians, and that Brazilian hybridity, stemming from a multiracial plasticity, should be a cause for national celebration rather than embarrassment. According to Freyre, Brazil's collective national uniqueness and hybridity was shaped by the fusion of Portuguese, Indian, and African populations in Brazil—ostensibly a distinguishing characteristic that Confederados and their descendants mirror today.

The Influence of Agassiz and Environmental Determinism

Louis Agassiz was another important figure who influenced environmental determinist ideologies in Brazil at that time and who strongly favored U.S. Southern immigration to Brazil. He had visited Brazil twice, was friends with Brazilian elites—for example, Dom Pedro II and Tavares Bastos—and was closely associated with Rev. James C. Fletcher.

Born in Switzerland, professor of zoology and geology at Harvard University Jean Louis Rodolphe Agassiz (1807– 73) founded the study of glaciology (and was known as the "father of glaciology"). After immigrating to the United States, Agassiz became director of the Museum of Comparative Zoology and professor at Harvard's Lawrence Scientific School. He had already traveled to the Amazon region in Brazil earlier in 1819 on a scientific expedition with German explorers Johann Baptist von Spix and Carl F. P. von Martius, who had been traveling through the Amazon between 1817 and 1820. Agassiz visited Brazil decades later in 1862, together with his (second) wife Elisabeth Cabot Cary Agassiz (1822–1907), a Bostonian blue blood; the two traveled several months through the Amazon region (1865–66) and coauthored a book, *Journey in Brazil*, in 1868—this trip was known as the Thayer Expedition, sponsored by American millionaire Nathaniel Thayer.[96]

One of Agassiz's students from Harvard, the young William James (the future, eminent philosopher), had joined them on this journey, along with Brazilian intellectual and politician Aureliano Cândido Tavares Bastos, a fierce supporter of immigration to Brazil and major proponent of opening the Amazon to foreign trade. After Agassiz completed the trip in 1866, Brazil finally opened the Amazon to foreign commercial navigation in 1867.

This Amazon trip had been inspired by Agassiz's furious attempt to disprove Darwin's theories, which ultimately failed. Agassiz died refusing to accept the theory of Darwinian evolution; according to Agassiz, as well as other scientists of the time who held Biblical narratives literally sacrosanct, the world could not be older than eight thousand years old (in modern vernacular, he was a creationist). In his study on Agassiz's daguerreotypes, Brian Wallis describes how in Agassiz's view "the Bible referred only to the Caucasian inhabitants of one portion of the Globe: Negroes, Indians, Hindus and the other 'species' he identified inhabited different and discrete geographical regions, having originated and evolved in unique ways."[97] Like his contemporary Swiss compatriot Arnold Guyot, Agassiz was an advocate of polygenesis, the theory that claims that "human races" were created separately, blacks and whites belonged to different species, and "monkeys and 'inferior' races were connected in a specially intimate way with particular regional environments."[98]

When he first encountered a black person in Philadelphia in 1846, Agassiz "experienced a pronounced visceral revulsion. This jarring experience coupled with his fears about miscegenation, apparently established his conviction that blacks are a separate species."[99] At the Houghton Library at Harvard University, Stephen Jay Gould found a letter that Agassiz had written to his mother, translated it verbatim into English, and published it in full for the first time in *Mismeasure of Man* in 1981:

> I experienced pity at the sight of this degraded and degenerate race, and their lot inspired compassion in me in thinking that they are really men. Nonetheless, it is impossible for me to repress the feeling that they are not of the same blood as us. In seeing their black faces with their thick lips and grimacing teeth, the wool on their head, their bent knees, their elongated hands, I could not take my eyes off their face in order to tell them to stay far away. And when they advanced that hideous hand towards my plate in order to serve me, I wished I were able to depart in order to eat a piece of bread elsewhere, rather than to dine with such service. What unhappiness for the white race—to have tied their existence so closely with that of negroes in certain countries! God preserve us from such contact![100]

Although many other scientists at that time shared some of his views, Agassiz's racism was extreme even for his day. Agassiz believed that black populations were inherently inferior and insisted that the United States should be a country for "whites only."[101] To further his case, Agassiz had collected several daguerreotypes in Brazil of naked black and Indigenous populations to prove white racial superiority.[102] He had asserted that the brain of an adult black person was comparable with that of a white fetus seven months old.[103] Ironically, Agassiz was working together with Rev. Fletcher and Tavares Bastos toward transitioning Brazil from slave labor to free labor.

Dom Pedro II was in direct contact with Agassiz for over a decade; the emperor was influenced by the latter's ideologies, particularly the type of environmental determinism Agassiz disseminated. Multiple letters written by Dom Pedro II extensively quote and mention Agassiz. One letter contained detailed lessons Agassiz had sent to the emperor. Dom Pedro II even boasted about having acquired Agassiz's autograph—the emperor was clearly enamored with Agassiz.[104]

In 1871 Dom Pedro II was interviewed by a special correspondent of the *New York Herald* (the interview was facilitated and arranged by none other than the U.S. chargé d'affaires at the time, Robert Clinton Wright of Maxwell, Wright & Co.). Dom Pedro II had asked the correspondent whether he had yet traveled to the southern provinces of Brazil (e.g., Santa Catarina, Rio Grande do Sul) and, when the interviewer told him he had not yet been there, the Emperor replied, "It is the finest part of Brazil, and is progressing very fast. It is best adapted to colonization and is being filled with colonists . . . the climate is more temperate and suits the emigrants better than the climate of the north, which is too tropical."[105]

Dom Pedro II then asked the interviewer, "Can you tell me if you heard anything lately of Professor Agassiz? What is he doing now?" The interviewer replied he had not heard of anything. The emperor then reported that he had received a letter from Agassiz, but it had been quite some time since he had heard back, and Dom Pedro II continued, "I expect the world will reap a great result from the Professor's investigation of the Amazon."[106]

Agassiz and his ideas of colonizing the Amazon were in line with Maury's thinking; Agassiz states, "two things are strongly impressed on the mind of the traveler in the Upper Amazons. The necessity, in the first place, of a larger population, and secondly, of a better class of whites, before any fair beginning can be made in developing the resources of the country." Agassiz explains, "not only is the white population too small for the task before it, but it is no less poor in quality than meagre in numbers." He concluded by affirming that the white population of the world "presents the singular spectacle of a higher race receiving the impress of a lower one, of an educated class adopting the habits and sinking to the level of the savage."[107]

It turned out that Agassiz was also wrong about his theories on glaciation during the Pleistocene age in Brazil (there is no active volcano in Brazil, a country that has been the least disturbed by earthquakes compared to any place else in the world with equal territory).[108]

Agassiz promoted and encouraged U.S. Southern emigration to Brazil by maintaining that "no country in the world is richer, more attractive, more fertile, *more salubrious*, more fit to be the focus of a numerous population that this magnificent valley of the Amazonas." However, in an interview published in the *Baltimore Sun* in 1866, he also expressed particular concern with the "transfer of land titles, delays and formalities and other forms of petty tyranny."[109]

Agassiz had influenced Brazilian intellectual and political elites as well as his students and disciples at Harvard University, such as his student Nathaniel Southgate Shaler, who became one of the forefathers of modern American geography. Like Agassiz, Shaler claimed that there were innate moral implications to the influx of the so-called "inferior races" entering the United States. Shaler became the vice-president of the Immigration Restriction League in Boston later in 1900, and he strongly advocated the separation of blacks and whites in public spaces.[110] Another student and disciple of Agassiz's at Harvard (as well as Shaler's student), Robert DeCourcy Ward (the first professor of climatology in the United States), was a key witness to the U.S. Congress favoring the Immigration Act of 1924 (a direct outcome of the U.S. eugenics movement). Ward, like Shaler, became head of the Boston Immigration Restriction League. Curiously, he and W. H. D. C. Wright (of Maxwell, Wright & Co.) shared a common ancestor. Robert DeCourcy Ward's father was Henry Veazey Ward, a governor of Maryland in the early nineteenth century. Henry's mother was Sarah DeCourcy Veazey of Cecil and Baltimore.

Ward claimed that serious moral and genetic implications justified his opposition to the immigration of "inferior" and "undesirable" racial groups. Ward became president of the Association of American Geographers in 1917 and the first president of the American Meteorological Society in 1920. He was an ardent advocate of eugenics ("race betterment") and directly helped to reduce the Jewish student enrollment at Harvard University.[111]

One common thread shared by the abovementioned scholars—the darlings of the Bostonian intelligentsia—was how their theological and teleological lines of geographical inquiry were inherently tied to racial ideology.

In an ironic twist, although the U.S. South is commonly associated with racialized politics and racial segregation (still to this day), deep in the heart of Cambridge, Massachusetts, a string of eminent professors at Harvard (Agassiz, Shaler, and Ward) vehemently and openly opposed racial equality and miscegenation. Adding to this irony, these same faculty members in Massachusetts peddled the idea that America should be a country for Christians and whites only (i.e., "desirable" immigrant populations), resulting in U.S. policies that restricted immigration. Their staunch racialized rhetoric was articulated and justified as "science." Nonetheless, this legacy stems directly from the epicenter of Brahmin blue bloods.

The deterministic frameworks pushed by Agassiz gained political weight and strongly influenced Brazilian intellectuals and politicians—for example, among others, Tavares Bastos as well as diplomat and politician Rui Barbosa, who, despite being a major abolitionist in Brazil, was a known admirer of Agassiz and his 1865 publication.[112] Agassiz (along with Gobineau) helped to lay the groundwork, pushing his ideological claims that the future of Brazil should hinge on the influx of "desirable" white immigrants.

Agassiz died in Cambridge, Massachusetts, in 1873. Today, several places and locations around the world are named after him. One of them is the Louis Agassiz Museum of Comparative Zoology at Harvard University. A plaza in the north zone of Rio de Janeiro is named Praça Agassiz, located, ironically, in the neighborhood of Abolição (Abolition).

Tavares Bastos

Louis Agassiz also influenced young Brazilian politician, public intellectual, and Freemason Aureliano Cândido Tavares Bastos. As a young man, Bastos had been profoundly influenced by the work of Matthew Fontaine Maury, which had been translated into Portuguese and which

Bastos had read as a young man. The policies advocated by Bastos and his direct personal relationship with Agassiz reflect the influence scientists had upon the former and later, more broadly, on Brazilian immigration policies. According to Alexandre Carlos Gugliotta's study in 2007, Tavares Bastos exerted a significant influence on immigration policy as well as Brazilian racial ideology from the 1860s until his death in 1875. Gugliotta describes Bastos's political ascension as rapid: while still in his twenties Bastos was already a *deputado* (state representative) for Rio from 1861 to 1870. He had also written several articles anonymously, publishing his *Cartas do solitário* (Letters from a recluse) in the *Correio mercantil* between 1861 and 1862.[113]

Bastos identified several challenges within Brazil's political structures at that time. He expressed his opposition to the Brazilian monarchy and its administrative centralization and pressed for the opening of the Amazon River to foreign navigation (clearly in line with Maury's treatise published nearly a decade earlier).

Bastos was a strong advocate of immigration to Brazil; however, he favored only white immigrants from Europe and the United States. He believed members of the "Germanic races," who flourished on Protestant individualism, were superior to those of the Iberian races, whose retrograde societies were forged by a "fanatical" style of Iberian Catholicism and absolutism. According to Bastos, all the "ills" of Brazil stemmed from a Portuguese Catholic colonial absolutism that created a generalized "degeneracy" (note Gobineau's strong influence here), and this was a direct result of the centuries-long legacy of Portuguese colonialism, which he found inferior to British colonialism.[114]

The collection of letters written by Bastos was eventually published in a book in 1863, in which he stresses the need to decentralize the Brazilian government and emancipate slaves. He portrays blacks and the descendants of Africans in Brazil in a highly negative tone, citing them as a reason to bring in more white immigrants to that nation.[115] Here the influence of Agassiz clearly comes through again.

Bastos was at the helm of creating the International Immigration Society (Sociedade Internacional de Imigração) in 1866, and the immigration of white U.S. Southerners and Europeans to Brazil became a "dream-come-true" for him—those migrants were, in his mind, the outcome of the "vigorous races" of Europe. The board of directors of the Sociedade Internacional de Imigração comprised the following individuals: Caetano Furquim de Almeida (president), Aureliano Cândido Tavares Bastos (minute taker), Herman Haupt (Prussian consul in Brazil), William Scully, Eduardo Pecher, José Corrêa de Aguiar, Rodrigo Ferreira Felício, and Fernando Castiço.[116] In 1866 Bastos published *O valle do Amazonas* (The valley of Amazonas), in which he promotes the opening of the Amazon region to foreign trade.[117]

Bastos thought that slavery was one of Brazil's biggest mistakes, because it had brought African populations into the country. At the same time, he thought that delaying the abolition of slavery had become an obstacle to promoting immigration to Brazil and that U.S. Southerners belonged to a "civilization of value."[118] Bastos was also in direct contact with Rev. Fletcher, who would discuss in public discourse the commercial implementation of steamship routes connecting Rio to New York.[119]

Whereas Agassiz was another scientist convinced that Brazilian miscegenation was a total disgrace, Bastos returned to Rio after the Amazonian Thayer Expedition of 1865–66 convinced that miscegenation was a favorable element in Brazilian society despite the "ills of slavery." Bastos was convinced that miscegenation was proof of Brazilian adaptability, albeit with the lingering idea that whites would still predominate over time. Bastos's posturing on racial politics reflects the broader dimension in which race in Brazil was already treated as a complicated, contested, and paradoxical narrative as early as 1861. Bastos staunchly believed that the only possible strides toward "progress" and "modernity" in Brazil were made through immigration.[120] Immigration to Brazil, according to Brazilians and especially for Bastos, would become a means to renew and replace the Brazilian labor system and to emancipate black slaves.

Aureliano Cândido Tavares Bastos, the politician from Alagoas and *deputado* in Rio, died of pneumonia in France in 1875. He would not live to see the eventual abolition of slavery in 1888, or immigration eventually reaching its peak in Brazil in 1891—both events that he ardently strived to achieve during his lifetime. Today, a *favela* (slum or shanty town) in the Catete neighborhood of Rio is named after him, as well as several streets throughout Brazil.

Ideological Impacts on Late Nineteenth-Century Brazil

Biological determinism began to dominate discussions of race in Brazil and influence Brazilian intellectuals and politicians such as Nina Rodrigues, Oliveira Vianna, Euclides da Cunha, and the Barão do Rio Branco.[121] By the 1870s the Brazilian government had taken an explicitly racialized turn.[122] For example, in Sven Schuster's research of Brazil's participation in World Fairs between 1862 and 1889, he describes how Brazil was clearly concerned with its world image as projected by its population makeup. According to Schuster, Brazil had deliberately silenced the existence of its black populations in those world fairs. However, the Brazilian government quickly decided to exhibit carefully selected photographs of Brazilian black populations in settings that promoted the country as a "racial paradise," striving to project the idea that Brazil was progressing into a gradual state of modernity. Brazil attempted to reassure the rest of the world that slavery in Brazil was different to the types of slavery that existed in the Caribbean or North America and that Brazil was engaged in a "civilizing project," a paternalistic enterprise to gradually turn slaves and blacks into citizens.[123] No doubt, the institution of slavery was as cruel and abhorrent in Brazil as it was in the United States or in any other place in the world.

Miscegenation had been long practiced (and encouraged) in Brazil. It was to become a lasting legacy of Portuguese colonial strategies and a contributing factor in the overall diverse population makeup of Brazil.[124] Due to the chronic shortage of European women in colonial Brazil, miscegenation was encouraged by Portuguese colonialists as a geostrategic approach for occupation and territorial annexation—hence, sexual intercourse between Portuguese men and Indigenous and African women was not taboo; much to the contrary, it was promoted.[125]

However—and this is the crux—miscegenation in Brazil was a paradox. It was only good for the nation so long as black populations eventually "dissipate[d]" so that white populations could predominate. Immigration then became a metaphor for "advancement" in Brazil and the only way to envision the country's transition into an imagined modernity. Henceforth, immigration to Brazil offered a solution to two problems: it strengthened the ideal of "whitening" Brazil and simultaneously quelled the old fear of Brazil's chronic lack of labor.[126]

Within three or four years after the first U.S. Southern settlers had arrived in Brazil, a wave of liberal ideology grew to strongly shape Brazilian economic and political landscapes. This was the decade when Auguste Comte's positivism entered Brazilian political and intellectual thought (to this day, Comte's motto *Ordem e progresso* (Order and progress) is stamped across a stripe on the Brazilian national flag). This new political slant also helped to end the old Brazilian colonial legal order and initiate the country's transition from a monarchy to a federal republic in 1889.[127]

Moreover, the theological embeddedness of all scientific enterprises up to the late 1850s was omnipresent; as geographer David N. Livingstone explains, "Scientific research was transacted within a framework derived from natural theology."[128] Livingstone notes that evangelicals "eagerly participated in early nineteenth century science." Among evangelicals, "all were convinced that the creation bore the unmistakable stamp of its Creator, whether expressed in the general laws of nature or in the detailed adaptations of creatures to their environment."[129] This interrelationship between early to mid-nineteenth-century evangelicalism and science tended to merge into political ideologies that surfaced racist tendencies and sentiments.[130] That is, scientists of that time conveyed ideologies considered patently racist in today's world, though they belonged to that era's scientific vernacular.

However, the intellectual and scientific world underwent a major paradigm shift in the last quarter of the nineteenth century after the publication of Charles Darwin's *On the Origin of Species* in 1859. Until 1855 nearly every U.S. scientist held a position of "God's divine plan mechanism"; however, after 1860 most of the scientific work that was produced was influenced by Darwinism or inspired by biology (in other words, they used metaphors drawn from biology—for example, the idea that the nation-state is akin to a living and growing "organism" that needs to survive).[131] Now climate, nation, and race were tied together (e.g., morally and intellectually "superior" white populations originated from temperate climates in Europe). This rhetoric added a new biological/racial layer to the existing evangelical supposition of hierarchical differences among human populations. Nonetheless, Europeans (specifically, the so-called "Nordic/Teutonic" populations) were deemed superior to the rest of the world. These ideologies spread to Brazil and strongly influenced Brazilian politicians and intellectuals.

Last, and to contextualize this chapter within the framework of the culture of the times, consider the words of Stephen Jay Gould: "Facts are not pure and unsullied bits of information: culture also influences what we see and how we see it. Theories, moreover, are not inexorable inductions from facts. The most creative theories are often imaginative visions imposed upon facts: the source of imagination is also strongly cultural."[132] Hence, the source of twentieth-century racism would soon emerge out of these scientific ideologies from the culture of the times.

It is also important to consider broader world economic transformations in the last quarter of the nineteenth century. This was the period spurred by the emergence of industrial capitalism, the dominance of the British, and the end of slavery, signaling the end of the Brazilian monarchy and the old colonial and slavery-based models. With growing urban centers and agriculture systems not based in slavery, wage labor became the new economic model, and "the transition to wage labor was unquestionably the crucial social issue in nineteenth century Brazil."[133]

The next chapter examines the Confederados and their descendants, particularly how Confederate symbols and meanings have transformed over time in syncretic, contested, and inconsistent ways in Brazil.

5

Protestantism, Education, and the Campo Cemetery Grounds

This chapter focuses on Campo, the settlement in Santa Bárbara, and the development of American schools and Protestant churches. Together, these reflect the cultural imprints left by Confederados in Brazil. As Confederado descendant Carolyn Smith Ward describes, "the newly arrived Southerners found themselves in an area where many Americans were already settled and which, at its peak, is reputed to have reached a population of 500 families, though the numbers fluctuated, and many did not remain there permanently. At times the area must have seemed almost like Dixie under the tropical sky."[1]

Santa Bárbara grew into a vital community, emerging as the most successful U.S. Southern settlement and the one that survived the longest out of all the Brazilian (and Latin American) Confederate settlement projects. This next section begins with a brief discussion about commonly held perceptions of Brazil as a "wilderness."

For example, publications written in the mid- to late nineteenth century by European travelers in Brazil were written "with the expectation of affording light and pleasure to thousands of readers."[2] Eminent figures such as William Henry Edwards, Henry Walter Bates, and Alfred Russel Wallace were among the many mid-nineteenth-century naturalists who traveled and wrote about the Amazon, and they helped to spur a new interest in that region.[3] In the late nineteenth century, publications on Brazil provided further geographical and commercial knowledge on that country. These include publications written by women; for example, the accounts of travelers to Brazil such as Adèle Toussaint-Samson in 1891 and, decades later, Lillian Elliott (Joyce), who wrote under the pen name "L. E. Elliott" in 1914. Although most travel writers carried their own set of gender, class, and racial biases, their insights are prolific and offer rich glimpses of Brazil from that period.

The discussion moves on here to examine the roles of Reverends Kidder, Fletcher, and Dunn. All three had convinced U.S. Southerners "that Brazil was a paradise wilderness where fruits were legion . . . and [that it was] a land, in short, that only required North American enterprise to pour out colossal riches and opportunities."[4] While I have already introduced Reverends Kidder, Fletcher, and Dunn in the introduction and in chapter 2, I reexamine their impact and influence here. U.S. Southern immigrants brought with them to Brazil still another ideology: Protestantism.

Mythic Brazil and the Tropics

Brazil has long been understood through a mythical lens dating back to the gaze of the first Europeans, who saw South America and Brazil as the epitome of the "exotic." For Europeans throughout the 1500s, for example, Brazil was a land of "ferocious cannibals." Surekha Davies points out that between 1500 and 1625, sixty out of the seventy maps and atlases produced in Spain, Portugal, France, and Germany include depictions of cannibalism in Brazil.[5] Moreover, many now taken-for-granted appellations stem from powerful imageries dating back to the first voyages of Columbus, which conveyed the geographies of the "Edenic New World," from the perspectives of "a plethora of mythic personae belonging to the Classical World."[6] As John Moffit and Santiago Sebastian explain, "The minds of Columbus and his men were unquestionably filled with predigested literary formulas. As applied to the tropical wonders of the Indies these set textual patterns were, of course, largely derived from Marco Polo and, especially, the fraudulent, pseudonymous traveler, Sir John Mandeville. That was the new or postclassical and medieval, literary formula of topography: Exoticism. . . . Thus was a raw America immediately invented in the conventional European poetic mold."[7]

These imageries informed and diffused a new geography of the Tropics, particularly the way in which Brazil was viewed by the rest of the world. For example, when the term "America" was first used in a European world map (Martin Waldseemüller's map of 1507), even the naming of the New World was loaded with intricate stories and controversies. Moreover, Waldseemüller's map of 1516 "depicted cannibalism as a defining feature of Brazil."[8] The first voyages of Columbus to the Americas produced geographical monikers that are used to this day.[9] Furthermore, Amerigo Vespucci was the European inventor of the iconographic myth of American Indian culture: that is, of "the melodramatic, libidinal and anarchic, and home of contemporary cannibal feasts and sexual orgies."[10] Today the continent "America" is named after him. In the early twentieth century, adventures fueled by a mythical El Dorado focused on the Amazon as a place of exotic mystique and "wilderness" (e.g., popular stories of a so-called, fabled "City of Gold").[11]

Such representations, fraught with provocative insights of the erotic and the exotic from the Tropics, were thus disseminated back to Europe and later to the United States, setting the tone and precedents under which Brazil has long been imagined and understood.[12] More important, such representations have influenced past studies of the Confederados in Brazil, who have also been viewed through the lens of the "exotic." For example, on the back cover of Dawsey and Dawsey's book *The Confederados: Old South Immigrants in Brazil*, published in 1995, two of the three review blurbs include the word "exotic" in their commentaries about the Confederados.

To the rest of the world, Brazil was a place of unknown "wilderness." For example, in their preface to *Brazil and the Brazilians* in 1857, Reverends Kidder and Fletcher state, "A very majority of general readers are better acquainted with China and India than with Brazil."[13] Generally speaking, this statement still holds true to this day.[14]

The Impact of Reverends Dunn, Fletcher, and Kidder

Reverends Dunn, Fletcher, and Kidder were directly invested in the proselytization enterprise in Brazil, and their work engaged in an imagined Protestant "civilizing" project. That is, they sought to bring a U.S. Protestant ideology to the "wilderness" of Brazil—a project that would also inherently dovetail later with the migration of U.S. Southerners to Brazil.

Rev. Kidder was outspoken about exposing what he considered the "evil practices" of the Catholic Church in Brazil.[15] Furthermore, the Brazilian Mission Monthly Bulletin of Missionary Intelligence articulated in 1819 their proselytizing objectives within this "civilizing" project:

> God knows how much poor Brazil needs the entire time and all the energies of the priesthood. When it is remembered, that those who have had the spiritual and educational interests of the people in their hands for near four hundred years, can only show a nation of illiterates, since statistics show that over 80 per cent, of the people can neither read nor write. Now these are the men who are furious, because they can no longer prostitute their sacred functions, by dedicating themselves to all the trickery and corruption of politics. Better far if the whole troop were swept into the sea, than play the role of blind guides to a people naturally docile and susceptible to the truths of the Gospel of our Lord Jesus.[16]

Therefore, despite the benevolence and well-intentioned Protestant mission projects in Brazil, one can also detect an inherent hubris projected in this sanctimonious perception that U.S. missionaries and ministers would become self-anointed "civilizing" agents in that country.

Rev. Kidder's book *Sketches of Residence and Travels in Brazil* (1845) and his coauthored publication with Rev. Fletcher *Brazil and the Brazilians* (1857) were both reprinted in later editions. The latter publication was specifically designed to influence and encourage U.S. Southern migration to Brazil, becoming so popular that it went through eight editions in less than ten years.[17] Both of their publications received special attention by Gilberto Freyre throughout his colossal publication *Ordem e progresso* (1949).

Rev. Kidder, missionary of the Methodist Episcopal Church, Louisiana, lived in Brazil from 1836 to 1840, when he returned to the United

States with his two children after his wife had died. The Mission Board in Brazil decided to close in 1842 due to financial pressure.[18]

Rev. Fletcher from Indiana, a friend of Dom Pedro II, lived in Brazil intermittently between 1851 and 1865 and was inducted into the prestigious Historical and Geographical Institute of Brazil (Instituto Histórico e Geográfico Brasileiro). He studied at Brown University and at Princeton Theological Seminary, and was sent to Brazil as the chaplain for the American Seamen's Friend Society at the age of twenty-seven. In 1855, he organized an exhibition of goods from the United States at the National Museum in Rio, which sparked both great interest in domestic items as well as Fletcher's interest in the potential for business and proselytization in Brazil. By 1856, Rev. Fletcher was already giving well-attended guest lectures about Brazil at the Maryland Institute in Baltimore and at the New-York Historical Society in 1860, establishing himself as an expert on Brazil.[19]

As we have seen earlier, Rev. Fletcher was a close friend of Louis Agassiz (Fletcher became one of his assistants, along with young Harvard student William James, in the Thayer Amazonian Expedition in 1865–66). Another close friend of Fletcher's was Brazilian politician Aureliano Cândido Tavares Bastos (not to be confused with José Tavares Bastos, his father, president of the province of São Paulo from 1866 to 1867). Bastos and Fletcher collaborated on a regular steamship–transportation line project between Brazil and New York, which culminated in the inauguration of the United States and Brazilian Steamship Company in 1865.[20] Last, Rev. Dunn, an Episcopal chaplain from Louisiana, published the widely read and influential *Brazil, the Home for Southerners* in 1866, which helped to galvanize U.S. Southern migration interest in settling in Brazil.

These publications by Kidder, Fletcher, and Dunn, along with their close associations with Brazilian political elites and their established relationships with eminent politicians and scientists of the day, created important networks, political capital, and influence in Brazil; at the same time, they marshaled U.S. Southerners to move to Brazil. They were keenly invested in the proselytization throughout Brazil of a U.S. capitalist style of Protestantism. All of them together—Kidder, Fletcher,

Dunn, and Bastos—were invested in bringing U.S. Southerners to Brazil.[21] Ultimately, they laid the groundwork for the Protestant missions, churches, and new American schools that emerged later in Brazil, especially in the western interior of São Paulo (Oeste Paulista)—the region of the Santa Bárbara Confederado settlement.

The Settlement in Santa Bárbara

Confederate army veteran, lawyer, and Freemason Col. William Hutchinson Norris was born in 1800 in Oglethorpe, Georgia, and was a former Alabama senator and member of the Alabama House of Representatives in the 1830s and 1840s.[22] Together with his son Robert Cicero Norris (1837–1913), William Hutchinson Norris left for Rio in late 1865 to search for suitable lands to settle. The pair was self-funded and left for Brazil independently—in contrast to most other U.S. Southerners, who were recruited and funded (or partially funded) by immigration agents or agencies.

Once they arrived in São Paulo, the pair found suitable lands in the interior near Campinas and Santa Bárbara.[23] Thereafter, "the Norris pair loaded their few chattels into an oxcart and walked eight miles to the northwest where they purchased lands for a settlement."[24] They eventually settled what was to become the colony of Santa Bárbara (where, ostensibly, the flat rolling hills and fertile soil were similar to that found in Alabama, Georgia, North Carolina, and South Carolina). Within a year, more than fifty families would join them, and soon about five hundred families lived within and around the settlement.[25] Beforehand in 1810 Santa Bárbara had been known as Ribeirão dos Toledos (Stream of Toledos), with a road that connected Vila Nova da Constituição (today the city of Piracicaba) to Vila de São Carlos de Campinas (today the city of Campinas). Dona Margarida da Graça Martins, wife of sergeant Francisco de Paula Martins, had acquired two square leagues—or sixty-seven square miles—and established a settlement and farm, Machadinho (named after its previous owner Domingos da Costa Machado). The lands were known for their fertile soil, and in 1818 the title transferred to her offspring and relatives.[26]

According to Helena Quintana Menchi's 2008 study, Confederado families living in the Santa Bárbara region comprised several clusters in 1875, as subsequently described—in the direction toward Limeira, in Funil: the Hardeman, Ellis, Keese, Bankston, and Dumas families. In Villa de Santa Bárbara (today, Santa Bárbara d'Oeste): the Domm and Tarver families. In Campo: the Miller, Whitaker, MacFadden, Smith, and Ferguson families. Toward the southwest, heading to Capivari, in Retiro: the McAlpine, Crisp, Wright, Pyles, Newman, Tanner, and Steagall families; and to the east, where Estação Santa Bárbara was located (today the city of Americana): the Thomas, Terrel, Ratcliff, Hawthorne, Baird, Mills, Scurlock, Rowe, Moore, Carlton, Cole, Whitaker, Pyles, Norris, and Fenley families.[27] These families cultivated beans, corn, cotton, and sugarcane, and they became successful cattle breeders; many of their descendants became the first dentists in the region.[28]

In a letter from June 5, 1869, John H. Crisp, a Confederado living in Santa Bárbara (in the Retiro subregion) wrote a report published in *O diário do Rio de Janeiro* providing valuable insights about the settlement and the agricultural capabilities in Santa Bárbara. Curiously, the report is addressed to "Mr. Chas.[Charles] Nathan," who had commissioned this report. Clearly Nathan was invested in the success of this settlement:

> The crops of cotton are nearly completely gathered and the corn crops full matured . . . my nearest neighbor, Mr. Lang, from 10 acres makes 8 bales; Mr. Taherne from 15 acres makes 14 bales; Mr. Hall from 27 acres makes about 30 bales; Mr. Perkins from 15 acres, 15 bales; Coln. Tanner from 28 acres, 30 bales; Coln. Oliver from 28 acres, 25 bales.
>
> My own crop, 32 acres, planted in the middle of November . . . is about 20 bales. The country generally is making good crops of Corn. I am the only one in the neighborhood cultivating Corn with the plow: it shows very plainly in the gathering that I shall make very nearly double the quantity produced to the acre by my neighbors, and the size of the ears resembles our old States corn. Mr. Provost planted Tobacco alone, which did remarkably well: the seed was from Cuba.

The Rice crop was good: the little Coffee and Sugar in this region looks well: people are gathering the one and grinding the other.

Coln. Norris will give you the results of this year in his vicinity . . . I think the Brazilian Government has a right to congratulate itself on the success of its immigration, forming so great a contrast to the Colonist settlements, which, at an undefined cost, have nearly all proved disgraceful failures: it is even reported here that many of the New York emigrants have left the Itajahy Colony and return[ed] to the U.S. in one of the vessels of war. This province only requires 100,000 Southerners more to place another 1% or 2% of this land in cultivation to make it the most important in the Empire.[29]

By 1874 William H. Norris had founded the first Freemason lodge in Santa Bárbara (Loja Maçônica), named the "Washington Lodge" No. 309, affiliated with the Grand Orient of Brazil, (Grande Oriente do Brasil); in 1891 Norris obtained permission to continue functions at the lodge in the English language. His son, Robert Cicero Norris—born in Perry County, Alabama, in 1837—was a member of the fifteenth and sixtieth Alabama Regiments during the U.S. Civil War. He participated in forty-four battles fought for Virginia (1862–64), principally under Stonewall Jackson, eventually becoming sergeant major in the Confederate States Army. He was already a Freemason in 1858 at the Fulton Lodge, Dallas County, before he left for Brazil.[30]

Robert Norris took an active role in organizing the Freemason lodge A. Y. M. in Santa Bárbara, became Senior Warden for two years, and then was elected to the position of Grand Master in Brazil, which he held until his death in 1913.[31] Robert Norris had returned to the United States in his forties, studied medicine at Medical College (now the University of Alabama), then returned to Brazil, becoming a well-known physician in Santa Bárbara.

The Freemasonry linkages mentioned throughout this treatise suggest that strong Freemason networks were already available to newly arrived U.S. Southern Freemasons in Brazil, which likely aided and facilitated Confederados such as the Norrises.

Today, Freemason symbols are conspicuously seen around Santa Bárbara, particularly on the grounds of Campo. They are visible on most headstones throughout the cemetery. Though the most commonly recognized Freemason symbol is a "compass and square," there are other Freemason symbols, such as the Maltese cross. At William H. Norris's tombstone at Campo, the plaque beneath the headstone reads: "William Hutchinson Norris. 'I wish I was in Dixie, Away, Away I'll take my stand to live and die in Dixie,'" with the traditional compass and square conspicuously etched on top of the headstone (see fig. 1).

Freemasonry became popular throughout nineteenth-century Brazil, particularly with the increasing dissatisfaction with the Catholic Church. Decades earlier Freemasonry had supported the movement for Brazilian independence in 1822. The Grand Orient of Brazil was founded in 1822 by Gonçalves Ledo, José Bonifácio (the first Grand Master), and, among others, the Visconde de Inhaúma, the Conde de Irajá, and numerous priests—including Padre Antonio Feijó—with the main objective of eliminating absolutism.[32] Positivists were among those who were attracted to Freemasonry, and their ideals dovetailed with those of the Protestant faith; for example, they believed in "individual liberty, the constant development of human personality, and the importance attached to morality and the development of a feeling of responsibility and justice."[33]

Some U.S. Southerners who migrated to Santa Bárbara were already Freemasons before they left, and most became Freemasons once they settled there. The scope and scale of the Freemasonry networks that existed among U.S. Southerners most likely provided automatic entrée with and ties to Brazilian elites. Consider that during the 1870s there were as many as 135 Masonic lodges throughout Brazil, in comparison to only 56 throughout the rest of Latin America.[34] The networks that Brazilian Freemasons provided and made available to the Norrises, for example, are a recurring theme that needs to be closely addressed in future scholarship. For now, although the evidence is inconclusive, this connection was undeniably an important network that opened doors for Confederado communities with Freemason ties. The next section looks at the development and expansion of American schools, Protestant churches in Brazil, and, more broadly, the diffusion of Protestantism in Brazil.

American Protestant Schools and Churches

Cyrus B. Dawsey and James M. Dawsey aptly point out that some scholarship has gone too far in crediting the American missionary schools to the Confederados, as American settlers were only brought into the Colégio Internacional as of 1872. In addition, they also point out that the Presbyterian religion in Brazil did not begin with the Confederados and that the Protestant churches did not radiate out of the Santa Bárbara settlement nucleus.[35]

British Anglicans had already established the first Protestant church in Rio de Janeiro as early as 1819.[36] Ultimately, it was the confluence of other European Protestant immigrants in the greater Santa Bárbara area, along with the Confederado settlements, that "opened the door also to the *confederados*' religion ... Moreover, since kinfolk had moved there, laypeople in the South of the United States took a special interest in Brazil and were more apt to support missions there than in any other place."[37]

Nonetheless, U.S. Protestant missions were attracted to the presence of Confederados in the interior of São Paulo, which consequently helped to expand U.S. Protestant pedagogies not only in São Paulo but also to other provinces throughout Brazil, where Protestants founded American Protestant schools. As Weaver remarks, the greatest concern of U.S. Southerners in Brazil, other than food and shelter, was "the establishment of adequate church and school facilities for their children."[38] Concern for these facilities evidently went hand-in-hand with the traditions of U.S. Presbyterians, which account for the proliferation of American schools in the interior of São Paulo.

According to a study by Maria L. S. H. Barbanti in 1977, the first American schools founded by U.S. Presbyterians were created in the province of São Paulo: the Escola Americana in 1870, Escola de Missão in 1871, Escola Presbeteriana in 1873, and the Colégio Internacional in 1869. Later, the American Baptists founded the Colégio Batista Brasileiro in

1902, and the American Methodists founded the Colégio Piracicabano (Piracicaba School) in 1881, which was an extension of Annie and Mary Newman's school, itself opened in 1879.[39]

Women were instrumental in administering and teaching in these newly created American schools. Take, for example, Annie Ayres Newman from Alabama (daughter of Rev. Junius Newman, discussed ahead)— arriving in Brazil at the age of eleven and becoming fully bilingual in Portuguese and English, she became a well-known pioneer educator in Brazil. She was one of the first students at the Colégio Internacional and, after graduating, she accepted a position at the Colégio Rangel Pestana, an elite women's school in São Paulo named after Rangel Pestana, one of Brazil's eminent education pioneers.

Newman would also teach Portuguese to John James Ransom (1853–1934), from Tennessee, at the Colégio Internacional. Ransom helped to diffuse Methodism in Brazil after his arrival in 1876 (and received the first Brazilians to a Methodist church in Brazil), and he married Newman in 1879. Annie Newman soon opened her own school, with the help of her sister Mary Newman, in Piracicaba. However, Annie died in 1880 of yellow fever. Ransom returned to the United States in 1884 and later married Ella Crowe of Pulaski, Tennessee, where he continued to make speeches about the work of Annie Newman and her efforts in the school she had opened in Brazil. As a result, successful partnerships and initiatives developed with the funding of the Woman's Missionary Society to restart Annie's school in Piracicaba. One of the educators they sent on that mission to restart the school was Martha Hile Watts, from Kentucky. This school became the well-known Colégio Piracicabano, where the nephew, niece, and children of Prudente de Morais (future president of Brazil and governor of São Paulo) would later attend as students.[40] Ransom returned to Brazil in 1885 with his new wife. Their son Richard Bruce was born in Rio. Ransom returned to Tennessee later, where he died in 1934. His other son, John Crowe Ransom, became a professor of English at Vanderbilt University in the 1950s and 1960s.[41]

Until 1930, with few exceptions Methodist missionary activities in Brazil had been conducted exclusively by U.S. Southerners.[42] As the success of Protestant American schools gained momentum, the U.S. Protestant ideal appealed largely to Brazilian Republicans. American schools opened throughout Brazil.[43] In São Paulo, the growth of Protestantism expanded simultaneously with the arrival of other European immigrants (e.g., German Lutheran immigrants).[44]

The U.S. Presbyterian Church established the first American Protestant church permanently rooted in Brazil in Rio in 1862, where Ashbel G. Simonton, A. L. Blackford, and George W. Chamberlain were sent as ministers. Even though many Protestant ministers were from the U.S. North, Confederados collaborated with them and jointly forged Protestant liaisons within Brazil. Many of the daughters of Confederados married missionaries or ministers (from both the U.S. South and U.S. "North"). Hervey Hall was one of the first Confederado settlers in the Santa Bárbara settlement (discussed ahead), and five of his daughters married Presbyterian missionaries.[45] Rev. Blackford (originally from Ohio) eventually married the daughter of Confederado Dr. James M. Gaston of South Carolina, and Blackford moved with her to establish a mission in Bahia.

The development of Protestantism and American schools emerged and flourished in Oeste Paulista. The first church at Campo was interdenominational, as there were no Protestant churches nearby in the region. By the early 1870s several more preachers had arrived at the Santa Bárbara community—for example, Robert P. Thomas, Elijah H. Quillen, Samuel M. Pyles, James R. Baird, and William C. Emerson.[46] By 1869 the U.S. Southern Presbyterian Church commenced a mission of its own, sending Rev. G. N. Morton and Rev. E. Lane to Campinas. The Southern Baptist Church entered Brazil much later, in 1881, and "the action was in response to an appeal for help from a small church of American Baptists who had gone to Brazil after the war and settled in or about Santa Bárbara, in the province of São Paulo." Its board soon appointed Rev. E. H. Quillen as its missionary to Santa Bárbara, and "among the refugees from the South, to Brazil soon after the war, was Gen. (now Rev.) A. T. Hawthorne."[47]

The Igreja do Campo (Church of Campo) was founded in 1871 by Confederado and Freemason Junius C. Newman (father of Annie and

Mary Newman), born in Virginia and raised in Mississippi. This church became the first Methodist church in Brazil.

Newman had gone to Brazil in 1867 to do ministerial work with the U.S. Southerners in Santa Bárbara. However, it was not until 1875 that Newman was officially recognized as the first Methodist missionary in Brazil. The first U.S. Methodist mission in Brazil, however, had begun decades earlier in 1836. The Missionary Society decided to send Rev. Fountain E. Pitts, of the Tennessee Conference, for a trip to Brazil and South America. In 1836 Rev. James Spaulding of the New England Conference went to Rio and began service with a congregation of thirty or forty people; a year later Rev. Daniel Parish Kidder of the Genesee Conference was sent to join him—Rev. Kidder was the first Protestant missionary to reach São Paulo.[48]

Rev. Ashbel Green Simonton of Pennsylvania was the pioneer missionary to Brazil of the U.S. Presbyterian Church, arriving in Rio in 1839 (at that time, the only other Protestant missionary in Brazil was Rev. Robert R. Kalley from Scotland). By 1862 Simonton had organized the Presbyterian Church of Rio, and in that same year Rev. A. L. Blackford and his wife joined the mission.[49]

In 1869 an overture was sent to the General Assembly by Bethel Presbytery in South Carolina to make Brazil "the second mission field of the Southern Presbyterian Church," as it had been informed of the significant number of U.S. Southern populations residing there. George Morton and Edward Lane were the first ministers to volunteer to migrate to Santa Bárbara.[50] The U.S. Southern Presbyterian Church then sent its first ministers to Brazil in the late 1860s. Edward Lane and George Nash Morton were sent in 1869 to initiate activities and religious services.[51] Together, they opened the Colégio Internacional in Campinas.

By 1871 American teachers such as Mary Videau Kirk and Nannie Henderson had arrived in the interior of São Paulo specifically to teach in Confederado communities. At first, only American students were enrolled, and classes were taught in English. Later classes were taught in Portuguese, and Brazilian-born pupils could enroll—including female pupils, which was rare in Brazil at that time.[52]

By 1875 the Colégio Internacional in Campinas had expanded into a two-story building, financed by the Presbyterian church.[53] In 1877 Miss Annie Lou Vincent from Alabama was sent to teach at a new school in Santa Bárbara (Retiro), which eventually burned in a fire. After the fire, she left to lecture at the Colégio Piracicabano and the Escola de Agronomia de Piracicaba (Agricultural School of Piracicaba).[54] The year of 1875 was a unique year for Confederados and their families, as this was the year that Dom Pedro II visited Campinas to inaugurate the first stretch of the railway between Campinas and Santa Bárbara; Dom Pedro II also visited the Colégio Internacional of Campinas.[55] The region surrounding the railway station in Santa Bárbara eventually became known as Villa dos Americanos (Village of the Americans) and later as the city of Americana.

In 1873 only 5,066 primary schools (private and public) existed in all of the Empire of Brazil, with 114,014 male pupils and 46,246 female pupils.[56] Today the impact of Confederados and the legacy of the U.S. Protestant ministers, missionaries, and teachers who went to Brazil is broadly reflected throughout the country, with English-speaking (and bilingual) American schools in virtually every Brazilian state.[57]

By 1891 there were three boarding schools for girls in Rio, Taubaté, and Piracicaba under the Woman's Missionary Society of the Methodist Church—the last had a total of 146 pupils, nine missionaries and five assistants, and the property was valued at $45,000. Among the U.S Presbyterian missionaries in Campinas were Rev. Edward Lane and his future wife Miss Charlotte Kemper, Miss K. E. Bias, and Rev. S. R. Gammon—and, in Botucatu, Miss Nannie Henderson.[58]

Although Catholics are still the majority in Brazil today, the country is currently home to the world's second largest Protestant population, with the world's largest Pentecostal population—*evangélicos* (evangelicals), known in popular vernacular as *crentes* (believers)—with a large membership in the Assembléia de Deus (Assembly of God). Many, if not most, Pentecostals are associated with U.S. Southern churches.[59] While at first Confederados spoke English in their homes and churches and created English-speaking schools, after the 1940s their descendants spoke Portuguese as their first language—today, "there are no longer monolingual English speakers in the region."⁶⁰

Early Twentieth-Century Confederados

Almost half a century after the Confederados had arrived in Brazil, Grover G. Pyles of Santa Bárbara wrote in 1911 to the *Confederate Veteran Magazine* in Nashville about the living Confederates in the Santa Bárbara colony. These include Dr. Robert C. Norris, Clay Norris, Lieut. Joseph Whitaker, N. B. McAlpine, George Worthrop, John Wessinger, Joseph Minchin, J. Partridge, William McCann, William Pyles, and Ezekiel B. Pyles. He concluded his letter by stating, "The Confederate veteran has been a power in peace, even as he helped to make the Confederate army one of the most invincible that ever faced the foe."⁶¹

However, in 1917 a letter from Cicero Jones stated that many Confederados were ready to enlist to fight in World War I for the United States. This letter suggests that Confederados felt a strong loyalty to the United States, even though some were aging Confederate veterans from the U.S. Civil War or Brazil-born Confederado descendants. Hence, this act of loyalty can be construed as another inconsistency in this story—that is, the antithesis of the archetypal "recalcitrant Confederate" with a "hatred" for the U.S. government. Brazil had also declared war against Germany in 1917, and this proposal to volunteer to fight for the United States would emerge as a lingering and contradictory tension between U.S. Southern identity and loyalty to the United States. Adding to this convoluted narrative, the offspring of immigrants, and even a few original migrants, were able to claim U.S. citizenship based on their parents' having been born in the United States. For example, Confederado descendants Hiram Fenley, John McFadden, Edward Minchin, Franklin Pyles, and James Ulrich Terrell were all born in Brazil but claimed U.S. citizenship (listed at the U.S. consulate in Santos).

This letter continued to state that after a meeting, the thirty men from the settlement in Santa Bárbara wrote a resolution. They sent this resolution to the Brazilian U.S. Consul in São Paulo: "We the undersigned sons and grandsons of Confederate veterans, most respectfully offer through our consul in São Paulo our services to the American government to be used as it may see fit during the war between the United States and Germany, promising the same loyalty to the Stars and Stripes that our fathers gave to the Stars and Bars."[62]

The letter was signed by Lieut. Joseph E. Whitaker, then eighty-one years old and a Confederate veteran from the U.S. Civil War. His two sons and grandson also signed, and among other signatories were Oscar Pyles; George Darvil; Frank Hawthorn; Edgar, Julian and Leroy McFadden; Rev. Maxwell; Edward Carlton; Ernest and Lee Rowe Lock; and Cicero Jones and his sons Robert, Yancey, Carroll, and George. They concluded, "We are now awaiting the order of the United States."[63] It is unknown who exactly enlisted in the U.S. forces during World War I.

By 1921 most of the first-generation settlers had already died. Among the surviving Confederates was Joseph Long Minchin, of the Fourth Florida Infantry & Orderly Sergeant, and prison guard at Andersonville, Georgia, who had left Santa Bárbara for the neighboring municipality of Nova Odessa, São Paulo. Born in 1841 near Thomasville, Georgia, and the son of a Baptist preacher, he first moved to Florida. In 1866 he married Julia Antoinette Pyles (born in Macon, Georgia, in 1849), and they moved to Brazil in 1867, where they had eight children. Employed by *fazendas* (coffee plantations) as an overseer or *administrador* (foreman), he eventually became the owner of a farm of nine hundred acres. He said: "We make a good living raising hogs, corn, rice, watermelons, potatoes, mandioca [manioc], etc. . . . I should like to visit my native land, but am too old and feeble and do not think I could stand the climate there now."[64] He died a few years later in 1927 and was buried at Campo.

Confederados had re-created a *place* within a different space and context, gradually creating a unique, "multiplicitous" postbellum U.S. Southern–Brazilian community—one that was inconsistent with the ideologies and symbolisms that had been produced in the Reconstruction-era postbellum U.S. South. By maintaining strong ties and loyalties to the antebellum U.S. South as well as to the United States, they held on to convoluted symbolic cultural and national connections while at the same time remaining "Brazilian."

Absence and Presence

Geographers have long discussed the humanistic aspects of place and have been at the forefront of articulating how sense of place is experienced.[65] For example, in 1947 John Kirtland Wright coined the term "geopiety" to describe the sense of piety aroused by human consciousness and geographical space.[66] In addition, in his milestone publication *Topophilia*, published in 1974 and closely related to Wright's ideas, Yi-Fu Tuan further explores the awareness of human emotional attachments and sentiments experienced in certain places and spaces of care (either natural spaces or constructed) and how place-based experiences have been known to invoke powerful emotions in different beholders. Therefore, the deliberations of Tuan and Wright, for example, give us a basic conceptual insight in order to explore the complex symbolism of Santa Bárbara's Campo as a sacred site and as a site of piety and pilgrimage.

The understanding of place also presumes the power of the geographical imagination, which according to geographer Denis Cosgrove is "part of the common experience of [humans]."[67] Humans have long conjured up powerful images of places in the form of the geographical imagination, and this type of imagination has been observed in the decision-making progression made by immigrants in migration processes.[68] Take, for example, the process by which immigrants imagine what their lives will be like in another place and, at the same time, how they imagine what their lives would be like if the migration project did not take place. Yet after arriving at their places of destination, immigrants and their descendants often turn to imagining what their old homeland had been like, often with sentimental nostalgia, as seen in the case of the Confederados. Therefore, the geographical imagination provides valuable insights into the bearing of human agency, often multifaceted with complex symbolic interpretations and understandings of place(s).[69]

For another example, in *Imagined Communities* (1983) Benedict Anderson elaborates on the development of world nations as "imagined communities." By definition, nations are political communities and, according to Anderson, "imagined communities" because the individuals of one nation will never meet every single person from the same nation or even hear from them—therefore, these other individuals are "imagined." Anderson examines how the territorialization of nationalism has prompted people to live and die for nations.[70] This idea of imagining nationhood then becomes a powerful thought process. In this sense, Confederado settlements were also "imagined communities," in which community members imparted their perceptions of a shared common ancestral homeland in the U.S. South, with cultural similarities forged by the shared sense of belonging to a nation—the Confederate States of America.

The Millers, the Halls, and Campo

Most of those who stayed in Santa Bárbara died in Brazil without being able to return to the United States. For example, after living in Brazil for twenty years in Santa Bárbara, Sarah Miller died at the age of sixty-five in 1889. She longed for her homeland in South Carolina, and this homesickness is reflected on her tombstone at the cemetery at Campo:

> Asleep in Jesus! Far from thee
> Thy kindred and their graves may be:
> But here is still blessed sleep
> From which none ever wakes to weep.

The Millers and Halls were among the first settlers in the Confederado community of Santa Bárbara, along with Col. William H. Norris. James Williamson Miller boarded the *South America* along with his daughters Lizzie, Anna, and Gena for the month-long voyage to Brazil. William McFadden and his wife Sarah (James Miller's sister), also from South Carolina, joined them on that voyage. However, Sarah Miller's family opposed her leaving for Brazil and cut her off completely. The party headed on the long trip to Santa Bárbara: from Rio by ship to the port of Santos, onward to the capital of São Paulo Province by train, and then finally by ox carts, mules, and horses to Santa Bárbara.[71]

Lizzie Miller eventually married Charles Moses Hall in 1873, and Anna Miller married LeRoy King Bookwalter, a former Confederate from Ohio who later would own a publishing house in São Paulo. Bookwalter would purchase a farm in Santa Bárbara (previously owned by the Olivers and then the Millers). He died in 1900 from a brain tumor, and Anna was left with a large farm to manage and seven children to raise; she effectively took over the duties of the farm and family as well as the cemetery and the church at Campo. The Millers soon bought Col. Oliver's plantation in Santa Bárbara, where they lived, built a home (which they attempted to make resemble their old South Carolina residence), and raised their family of seven children. A century later in 1978, the property was still owned by one of their descendants, owned and farmed by Ross Pyles (Sarah and Hervey Miller's great-grandson).[72]

Sarah and James Miller had lost two small children before leaving for Brazil, and their three grown sons, John, Robert, and William, died not long after their arrival in Brazil. John eventually moved to Rio, where he became vice consul of the U.S. Embassy; he contracted smallpox soon after and died in 1887, twenty-three years old and unmarried. Robert lived in Santos with his wife Theresa Coulter, and he died from a farm accident at the age of thirty-four in 1885 with no children. Theresa eventually returned to Alabama. A third son, William Baskin, committed suicide in 1913. James Miller died in 1897 and was buried at the cemetery at Campo beside his wife, Sarah.[73]

The story of Col. Anthony Thompson Oliver of Georgia is inherently tied to the development of the grounds at Campo today. Oliver owned the land where he buried his wife, Beatrice—who died after arriving in Brazil in 1867—as well as his two daughters, Inglianna and Mildred, who died of tuberculosis. Not too long afterward Oliver too died and was buried at Campo.[74] James Williamson Miller of South Carolina then bought the Oliver Plantation with the stipulation that the grounds will always be reserved as a cemetery for American Protestant immigrants. In 1873, James Miller's daughter Anna Miller (who married LeRoy King Bookwalter, mentioned above) purchased the land from James Miller.[75] The property where the Olivers are buried became known as Cemitério do Campo, or the Protestant cemetery. In 1954 the Bookwalter family donated the land to the Fraternidade de Descendência Americana (Fraternity of

American Descendants), a private organization that overlooks the cemetery grounds and organizes reunions of Confederado descendants.[76] Today more than 430 of their descendants have been buried there.[77]

Sense of Belonging

Examples of imagining and longing for the homeland are commonly found among other immigrant communities in Brazil and are not unique to Confederados. For example, German, French, British, and Japanese descendants of immigrants in Brazil hold strong ties to their "homelands" while still considering themselves fully Brazilian. German immigrant communities in Brazil have for a long time published several of their own German-language newspapers in Brazil, beginning as early as the 1850s (e.g., *Der kolonist, Der Deutsche einwanderer, Kolonie zeitung, Der Deutsche beobachter, Allgemeine Deutsche zeitung für Brasilien,* and *Der Deutsche kolonist*). This sense of belonging to two places translates into a social mechanism that facilitates, strengthens, and solidifies family bonds and social networks within immigrant communities in Brazil over long periods of time.

Like Confederados, other immigrant groups in Brazil also hold family reunions, fairs, or parades, and they dress in costumes (e.g., the German immigrant community's Oktoberfest celebrations in the south of Brazil)—in the same way the Irish Americans in Boston, New York City, and all over the United States act during a St. Patrick's Day Parade, exhibiting with great esteem, for example, the shamrock as a symbolic enforcement of Irishness. Yet many, if not most, third-, fourth-, and fifth-generation Irish Americans have never even set foot in Ireland, nor do they speak Gaelic. John C. Dawsey explains, "Just like being Italian during Columbus Day parade in the United States is a way of being American, so also being American or Confederate at the Campo cemetery in Brazil is a way of being Brazilian."[78] However, in the case of the Confederado descendants, perhaps there has been more cultural capital in the act of highlighting and exaggerating one's American ancestry rather than one's Portuguese, African, or Italian ancestries, or other ancestries perceived in Brazil as having less cultural capital than American ancestry (the "cherry-picking" of one's ancestry).

In another example, British immigrant communities in Brazil, including second- and third-generation immigrants in São Paulo and Rio, have also re-created places and spaces. They have long established and maintained their own cricket clubs and social clubs (São Paulo Athletic Club, Rio Cricket Club in Niterói), private schools (St. Paul's School in São Paulo, the British School in Rio); churches (the Anglican Church of Rio), cemeteries (Gamboa in Rio), and several British societies (St. Andrews Society, British Society, etc.).[79] These communities gather annually, most with Union Jack flags in hand, to celebrate the Queen's birthday, sing "God Save the Queen," and revel in Guy Fawkes Day, Burns Supper, Scottish kilts, and Scottish dancing. Much of the British expat community has then become exaggeratedly British; they have become almost more "British" than the British themselves, in order to maintain and strengthen immigrant ties to an imagined homeland despite being rooted in Brazil.[80]

In summary, Campo gradually became an important site for Confederados and their descendants. The cemetery, grounds, and Protestant Church at Campo emerged with the deeply embedded concepts of absence and presence, as well as a sense of belonging.

Campo

The idea of the lingering presence of Confederados and their descendants buried at Campo is palpably expressed by their absence.[81] The cemetery has received frequent negative publicity in foreign newspapers recently and in the past, even though Confederado descendants regard Campo as a sacred place or "hallowed ground"—the place where their families are buried. For them, it is a place imbued with sentimentalism and emotional attachment. Foreign coverage in newspapers, television, and magazines, however, have typically portrayed Confederado descendants as "alienated," "retrograde," or "calcified in time" within the remoteness of a resilient antebellum Confederacy. Some scholars have pointed out that this portrayal is misleading. For example, anthropologist John C. Dawsey claims that "it seems that the Confederate flag has come to mean something quite different among descendants in Brazil than whatever meanings it might have in the United States."[82] That is, in the United States, the Confederate flag has become synonymous with public and political controversy, and its symbolism there today is inherently associated with the institution of slavery, racism, racial segregation, and Lost Cause ideologies.

This controversy also stems from the conspicuous presence of Confederate flags displayed throughout Campo, the pavilion, and the obelisk monument at the site. The display of the flag has become a poignant topic of contention, given that the Confederate flag has also been appropriated by militant U.S. white supremacists and contemporary neo-Nazi groups (who often display the Confederate flag beside Nazi swastikas) and has come to symbolize hatred and racism (as seen in the violent demonstrations in Charlottesville, Virginia, in 2017). Nonetheless, researchers such as Dawsey have pointed to how these symbols are represented and interpreted differently *within* Brazil; they neither were nor are tied to the same symbolic racist meanings in the minds of Confederado descendants. Instead, Confederado descendants associate these symbols (including the flag) with ties of kinship and immigrant heritage in what is perhaps a convoluted and murky understanding that developed *within* Brazil. Despite their conspicuous displays of Confederate flags, Confederado descendants do not espouse racial hatred or political extremism, as researchers such as Dawsey have found. During family reunions at Campo, for example, individuals of all ethnic backgrounds attend, and Confederado descendants have long accepted interracial marriage, as is common in Brazil.

However, in a new article published recently in 2019, "Contesting the Confederacy: Mobile Memory and the Making of Black Geographies in Brazil," geographer Jordan Paul Brasher has pointed out that Brazilian black resistant groups—for example, as mentioned earlier, the União de Negros pela Igualdade (UNEGRO; Union of Blacks in Favor of Equality)—led a protest in 2019 against the use of Confederate symbols at Campo. They used the slogan, "Take Down the Confederate Flag," taken directly from the Black Lives Matter movement in the United States. This leads me to believe that researchers in the future will likely see a change in either two ways. One scenario: the organization that oversees Campo and its reunions will ultimately decide to remove any public display of Confederate symbolism (including the Confederate flag) on the grounds at Campo, especially in light of recent protests and the strong negative association of the Confederate symbolism with U.S. racism and slavery in recent public discourses. Conversely, the other scenario is that failing to take down any Confederate symbolism at Campo will likely exacerbate polarized tensions between different camps (i.e.; the old adage of "heritage" versus "racist symbolism" arguments), and in fact, Campo reunions might even attract a growing attendance of militant white supremacist groups who are familiar with U.S.-based racist political and cultural rhetoric from outside the Confederado descendant community, precisely because of this magnified negative association.

Nonetheless, the annual reunions of Confederado descendants at Campo offer insights into the ideas of presence and absence. These reunions generate a sense of place among the Confederados and their descendants and, at the same time, galvanize descendants to visit Campo as a site of pilgrimage and piety, by way of the absence of about 430 Confederates and their descendants buried there. The largest family reunion is held in April each year, sponsored and supported by the Fraternidade Descendência Americana.

Researchers interviewed Confederado descendants after a visit to Alabama in the 1990s. Two of the descendants articulated sentiments of attachment to "the home of their immigrant ancestors—after a hundred years' absence."[83] Cyrus B. Dawsey maintains, "*Campo* is a shrine with special meaning only to the descendants."[84] Hence, the emotional attachment to this place and the symbolism of the Confederado cemetery hold a vital role for descendants today, who experience a sense of belonging and of place.

In 1972 Jimmy Carter, the then governor of Georgia and future U.S. president—visited Campo in what would be described as an emotional visit. Eugene C. Harter, a Confederado descendant as well as U.S. diplomat and former U.S. Consul in Rio, was present during Carter's visit. According to Harter, Carter shed a tear after he spoke to the Confederado community, whose members came out to greet him at Campo. One of the tombstones at Campo belonged to the great-uncle of Carter's wife Rosalynn, W. S. Wise (d. 1888). Carter's visit received Brazilian media attention, yet much to the chagrin of Santa Bárbara locals, virtually all coverage in newspapers mistook Santa Bárbara for Americana. Harter had introduced Jimmy Carter to his cousins and other Confederado descendants who were present for his visit. He described Carter's address to the community from the obelisk on the grounds at Campo: "His face showed happiness, not sadness. Yet he paused, and tears ran down his cheeks. Starting again, he told them he would never forget this scene and would tell Americans about it when he returned to his country."[85]

For Confederado descendants, Campo's grounds have been transformed into a place where there is a palpable sense of belonging to Brazil, the United States, and the U.S. South at the same time—with a special sense of sentimental nostalgia for the U.S. South homeland. This sense of nostalgia between the U.S. South, United States, and Brazil is multifaceted and complex. Yet this relationship is also viewed and interpreted through the lens of identity tensions between Brazilian cultural interpretations of Confederate symbolism and its contemporary significance in the United States.

The act of "remembering" is filled with political synergies, viewed through the lens of Brazilian syncretic components, and muddled through Brazilian cultural complexes over generations. These synergies are often contradictory and have been transformed and reshaped over time. In this way, Confederados and their descendants have engaged in a process of re-creating a sense of place in Brazil.

The Miller family in Santa Bárbara reminisced on the cultural artifacts and activities that reminded them of the U.S. South; as Confederado descendant Carolyn Ward describes, "The life was just a bit of Confederate life in the States. They had their quilting parties, spelling bees, candy pulls, etc."[86] As Ward puts it, "the longing for the familiar places and yearning for family and friends so far away who would never be seen again."[87] Campo has become more than just a place of final repose for the dead. It has been transformed into a symbolic place of pilgrimage and piety, a place to (re)imagine the U.S. South homeland, and, at the same time, a vital community center, bringing Confederado descendants together in Brazil (see figs. 1–8 in the gallery).

Fig. 1. Col. William Hutchinson Norris's grave at Cemitério do Campo. "In Memory of Wm. H. Norris. Born in Oglethrop Co., GA, U.S.A, 17th September 1800, died July 13th, 1893, age 93 years old." The plaque beneath the headstone reads, "William Hutchinson Norris. 'I wish I was in Dixie, Away, Away I'll take my stand to live and die in Dixie.'" Note the Freemasonry symbol on the headstone. Santa Bárbara d'Oeste, Brazil. Photo by Debbie Marcus, 2017.

Fig. 2. Igreja do Campo, the first Methodist church in Brazil (now renovated), adjacent to the Cemitério do Campo. The church was founded in 1871 by Confederado Junius C. Newman, born in Virginia and raised in Mississippi. Santa Bárbara d'Oeste, Brazil. Photo by Debbie Marcus, 2017.

Fig. 3. Grounds of the cemetery pavilion where descendants of Confederados hold annual gatherings and family reunions. A large Confederate flag is painted on the grounds. Santa Bárbara d'Oeste, Brazil. Photo courtesy of the author, 2017.

Fig. 4. Obelisk monument at Cemitério do Campo, Santa Bárbara d'Oeste. Photo courtesy of the author, 2017.

Fig. 5. Monument honoring Col. William Norris (note his name is misspelled with an *n*). Also note the conspicuous Freemasonry symbol above the name. Photo by Debbie Marcus, 2017.

Fig. 6. Confederados who were from Louisiana preferred to be buried on the cemetery's elevated section at Campo because they were accustomed to floods from the Mississippi River; they believed this position would be safe from flooding during the rainy season. Photo by Debbie Marcus, 2017.

Fig. 7. View of the Campo grounds. In the backdrop are the hills of Santa Bárbara d'Oeste. Author in the middle. Photo by Debbie Marcus, 2017.

Fig. 8. The Backwoods at Cemitério do Campo, Santa Bárbara d'Oeste. Photo courtesy of the author, 2017.

Conclusion

This synthesis of former Confederates and their postbellum migration to Brazil to start new lives in a foreign land adds to growing scholarship on the international dimensions of the U.S. Civil War, Brazil, and migration studies as well as to the literature just coming into publication on broader Antebellum ties between the United States and South America. This event also informs us about later U.S.-backed ventures into Brazil, most notably Henry Ford's failed Amazonian project, Fordlândia (located about twenty-five miles from Lansford W. Hastings's Confederado settlement in Santarém, established decades earlier), described in a recent book written by Greg Grandin.[1]

Given that recent contested discussions on immigration policies and immigrants in the United States have appeared at the forefront of national debates, this treatise shows a different perspective. It offers a reflection on the lives of thousands of *American immigrants in Brazil* after the U.S. Civil War (often referred to in reports as "exiles" or "refugees"). Like many immigrants in the United States today, they too faced many challenges as immigrants in Brazil, including living in another land with a different language, soil, vegetation, and culture. Those who remained in the country would eventually become fully "Brazilian."

While the questions posed at the beginning of this book were answered, more questions emerge. Confederados were certainly trying to avoid and escape a dystopia they would have faced had they decided to remain in the U.S. South. What we do know is that they eventually integrated into Brazilian society as their descendants became Brazilian, and they found relative peace and fulfillment in the Santa Bárbara settlement particularly (here we must make a distinction between Santa Bárbara and rest of the settlements).

One question remains unanswered: Whatever happened to those ideologies that influenced racial and immigration policies in Brazil? A few anthropologists and geographers later in the 1920s voiced their opposition to the environmental-deterministic frameworks espoused by scholars such as Agassiz, Guyot, Shaler, and several others. For example, geographer Carl O. Sauer and anthropologist Franz Boas proposed a theoretical approach of "Possibilism": the "possibilities" of human agency and human culture. Sauer headed the famed Berkeley School of Cultural Geography at the University of California, Berkeley, for almost three decades—this program would become the epicenter of cultural geography.[2] Their major counterargument to the environmental-deterministic stance, in its simplest terms, was to highlight the important role of human culture and its interrelationship with the environment as well as the fact that the environment (e.g., place of birth or ancestry) alone does not determine the perceived moral and intellectual success of human populations. In addition, Gilberto Freyre, although a controversial figure in his own right—and one was directly influenced by Franz Boas as a student of Boas's at Columbia University—famously defended Brazilian hybridity as a symbol of nationhood, contrary to determinists such as Gobineau. Freyre asserted that miscegenation was, in fact, beneficial to Brazil and Brazilians—and that it was to be interpreted with a sense of pride and not shame.

Yet as we notice, the ideologies disseminated at different points in time by Maury, Guyot and Agassiz (and his student disciples at Harvard) propagated "scientific" claims about racial differences between human populations—and herein lies the peril. These thinkers made deliberations on human differences, vehemently opposing racial equality and miscegenation, with long-lasting public, intellectual, and political consequences; they influenced Brazilian elites and Brazilian immigration policies. They understood a world in which human populations can be grouped into neatly pigeonholed biological and taxonomical categories and hierarchies, which helped to shape and produce a myopic and racist world cartography—and, in today's vernacular, one without human agency or broader cultural and social structures. Such ideologies evidently transferred into political realities. They laid the groundwork for U.S. immigration restriction policies and the rise of the eugenics movement in the United States. Remarkably, such dangerous ideologies persist today, whether explicitly in recent xenophobic and neo-Nazi movements around the world or veiled in U.S. policies or in academia. More important, these ideologies helped to shape Brazilian policies that favored white immigration as a "solution" to Brazil's chronic lack of human capital and its agricultural lag.

As John Kirtland Wright warns, "a powerful imagination is a dangerous tool in geography unless it be used with care. Indeed, the imagination might better be compared to a temperamental horse than to an instrument that operates precisely and with objectivity."[3] This "dangerous tool" continues to play a salient role in world geographies to this day indeed. Hence, amid contemporary discussions about race and racism, this narrative of the Confederados in Brazil may provide a starting point, instead of an end, to furthering and deepening difficult conversations.

Racialized turmoil has surfaced to a boiling point in the United States recently. Stemming from public reactions to Lost Cause ideologies, associated with racism and oppression, cities throughout the United States have taken critical measures to remove the names of parks and monuments associated with the Confederacy. By 2018, 113 Confederate memorials had been taken down, with 1,700 remaining. In Baltimore alone, for example, three memorials—including the statues of Robert E. Lee and Stonewall Jackson—were taken down quietly overnight on the orders of former mayor Catherine E. Pugh in 2017.[4] Pugh explained to the *Baltimore Sun* that this action "probably kept [the city] from a whole lot of protesters."[5] However, Pugh has not revealed where the statues are currently kept. At the locations where the statues had been—in Wyman Park, Bolton Hill, Mount Vernon, and Tuscany-Canterbury—only the pedestals remain now.

As for Brazil, it is now home to one of the most genetically diverse populations in the world.[6] Brazil's hybrid national construct of miscegenation continues to be celebrated as a symbol of nationhood. However, Brazil has also long struggled with its contradictory racial attitudes and the "myth of racial democracy." The historical process of "whitening" Brazil clearly points to the country's stance on "blackness," which fanned anxiety about its own racialized world image. That is, Brazil wanted to become "whiter" (and still does). Moreover, with the election of President Jair Bolsonaro, who has been publicly vocal with his incomparable and explicitly racist, misogynist, antiblack, antigay stances, Brazil has ostensibly turned the clock back to the boorish, dark days of the Brazilian military dictatorship period (1964–85).

Even though widespread racism is a political reality in Brazil—and thousands of *favelas* as well as dire poverty and indigence exist throughout most of the country (disproportionally comprising nonwhite populations)—Brazil has paradoxically not yet experienced institutionalized segregation or groups such as the Ku Klux Klan, since racist organizations are not allowed to exist in Brazil by law. However, although rare in the past, in recent years there has been an increase in white supremacist and neo-Nazi activities in Brazil, particularly in southern and southeastern Brazilian states.[7] Conversely, in the United States, the Ku Klux Klan has certainly not been confined to the U.S. South; much to the contrary, its membership today is found scattered throughout the rest of the country, extending from Oregon, Idaho, Colorado, and California to New Hampshire, Maine, and Pennsylvania.[8] Furthermore, even more than half a century after the U.S. Civil Rights Act had taken effect, the United States remains the nation with the largest incarcerated population in the world, a population that is disproportionally black; indeed, an estimated one-third of the total black male U.S. population will likely be incarcerated in their lifetimes. If these populations serve time in prison, in most cases when they are released, they cannot vote and are not easily employable, thus finding themselves effectively disenfranchised (a process known as "felon disenfranchisement").[9] While Brazilian and U.S. racialized politics emerged from fundamentally different historical, cultural, and political standpoints and constructs, the bottom line is that realistically speaking, black populations have clearly been indirectly or directly ostracized politically, socially, and economically, in *both* Brazil and the United States—race and racism still matter today and are important political realities in both countries.[10]

What overall conclusions, then, can we draw from this Confederado story? First, the end of the U.S. Civil War was unquestionably the catalyst that prompted the mass migration to Brazil. Second, agriculture and trade played important roles in the migration enterprise, becoming two of the most important pull factors in this story. With favorable inducements offered by the Brazilian government, U.S. Southerners and Brazil participated in a mutually beneficial enterprise. At the same time, U.S. Southerners saw their homeland in a state of disarray, rubble, and destruction after the U.S. Civil War, which counts among a few of the migration push factors they faced. Third, without the help of various networks, communities, institutions, societies, and individuals from both Brazil and the United States, the migration of U.S. Southerners would not have been possible—at least not on a large scale.

Fourth, two Confederado contributions to Brazil stand out: the dissemination of Protestantism (e.g., the Methodist, Baptist, and Presbyterian faiths) in Brazil and the resulting American schools created by Protestant missions in Brazil, with Confederados helping in their proliferation and administration. The schools and their introduced pedagogies expanded into other Brazilian states and, as a result, there are American schools throughout Brazil today, in virtually every Brazilian state. Confederado contributions to agriculture were also significant—for instance, the usage and spread of agricultural implements and, especially, the creation of new agricultural schools in São Paulo (*escolas de agronomia*) and in the western interior of São Paulo (e.g., Piracicaba).

Fifth, the most successful Confederado community was in the Santa Bárbara region, where the cemetery and Campo grounds are located and where Confederado descendants still gather for their family reunions. The settlements in the Oeste Paulista became the epicenter from which Confederado contributions to Brazil developed;

they are where the notions of absence, presence, and sense of place can be palpably observed.

Sixth, the Confederados who stayed in Brazil were not major slaveholders. Like their European immigrant counterparts, who arrived at the same time in Brazil by the thousands—these Confederados were not seeking a "white utopia." Confederados moved to Brazil under multiple circumstances and reasons rather than because of any single factor. Confederado descendants eventually intermarried with local and other immigrant groups—a reflection of today's racially diverse Brazilian society. In this regard, it is important to highlight that the immigration of U.S. Southerners to Brazil should not be viewed in isolation, nor should it be divorced from the various interrelated push/pull factors that induced them to move to Brazil.

Finally, a common thread that emerges throughout this treatise is the theme of "inconsistency." This inconsistency involves the topic of race in Brazil and the interpretation of Confederate symbols and ideologies, including the conspicuous presence of the Confederate flag at Campo. Take, for example, the fact that at Campo, the U.S. national flag can be seen flying alongside the Confederate flag and the Brazilian flag. These contradictions and inconsistencies strongly suggest how the syncretic, elastic, and hybrid elements that evolved out of the Confederado community in Brazil came to embody cultural interpretations that are far more Brazilian than they are American or Southern.

In summary, Maury's idea to take over the Amazon and transplant U.S. Southern socioeconomic systems to Brazil never happened. Maury never went to Brazil, abandoning the idea of a Brazilian destination for U.S. Southerners altogether and favoring Mexico instead—though he later abandoned that idea as well.

Religious leaders, missionaries, and ministers from the United States had focused their interests with the mindset of proselytizing Protestant religions throughout Brazil, as they viewed proselytization as a moral duty given the widely held perceptions of Brazil as a vast "wilderness" and of how the predominant style of Luso-Brazilian folk-Catholicism was "backward." They provided encouragement for U.S. Southerners to migrate, especially through their widely read publications on Brazil, which were intended to promote the migration of U.S. Southerners to Brazil.

Moreover, the ideologies of Maury, Gobineau, and Agassiz disseminated the idea that miscegenation was abhorrent and that Brazilians in general were "degenerate" and "imbecile." They influenced Brazilian intellectuals and politicians such as Tavares Bastos, Rui Barbosa, Barão do Rio Branco, and Dom Pedro II. Brazil therefore underwent policy transformations and shifted its stance on race matters. These ideologies propelled Brazilian politicians and agriculturalists to induce the coming of "industrious" immigrants of "European stock," since their goal was to transition into an imagined and desired "modernity" and "prosperity."

Baltimoreans in Brazil had long established contacts with key figures among the Brazilian elite and politicians, gaining capital and political clout in Brazil (e.g., the Wright family members associated with Maxwell, Wright & Co.). At the same time, they shared an interest in welcoming U.S. Southern immigrants to Brazil, as they aided and facilitated these immigrants' searches for and obtaining of suitable lands to settle. The backdrop of trade, agriculture, and sociocultural mores altogether transformed physical landscapes in both Brazil and the United States (e.g., coffee drinkers in the United States and the high demand and consumption of wheat flour in Brazil)—and this transformation solidified commercial, political, and kinship networks in Brazil as well as trade ties between Baltimore and Rio. Baltimorean connections in Brazil, based on family and commercial ties, helped to consolidate a strong network within that country, which ultimately facilitated the mobility of U.S. Southerners.

Immigration promoters such as Charles Nathan, Quintino Bocaiúva, William Scully, Tavares Bastos, Maj. Wood, Dr. Gaston, Maj. Meriwether, and Dr. Shaw—and the immigration societies created in both the U.S. South and Brazil (e.g., Edgefield Immigration Society, International Immigration Society)—were eagerly invested in agroeconomics and global capitalism. That is, they believed that U.S. Southerners would bring profitable dividends to Brazilian coffers and, at the same time, that immigration was a mutually beneficial enterprise from which they would likely stand to gain financially, as individuals and collectively.

These insights highlight the roles of each stakeholder and the access each maintained with trade, commercial, social, kinship, and institutional networks. Each of these networks is identified here to understand their importance and respective roles in this migration enterprise. The stakeholders framed their views in favor of immigration from various angles—through ideological, religious, commercial, capitalist, or agrarian standpoints—anticipating the financial and agrarian benefits of the immigration of thousands of U.S. Southerners to Brazil. Hence, each of the stakeholders helped to systematically shape, promote, encourage, facilitate, aid, and finance U.S. Southern mobility to and within Brazil—ultimately fueling the migration of the largest organized group (of white populations) who ever voluntarily emigrated out of the United States.

NOTES

PREFACE

1. Campo is just outside of the city of Santa Bárbara d'Oeste.
2. For more details, see Dawsey and Oliveira, "Campo."
3. Ho, *Graves of Tarim*, 26.
4. Ho, *Graves of Tarim*, 10.
5. My maternal grandfather migrated from England to Brazil to work for the Leopoldirona Railway Co. in 1921.
6. Coincidently, John Wilkes Booth is also buried at the Green Mount Cemetery, in the Booth family plot.
7. Dr. Wilkie studied under the supervision of Dr. Richard Morrill at the University of Washington in the late 1960s, at a time when that university was a well-known epicenter of geography's so-called "quantitative revolution." Later Dr. Wilkie's research work would focus on humanistic geography, spirit of place, and sense of place.
8. See, for example, Marcus, "Brazilian Immigration" and "(Re)Creating Places and Spaces."
9. Dr. Strait has been directing this fieldtrip for almost two decades and is an innovator in the geography of the blues. For more details, see Strait et al., "Students Experience the Blues."
10. See Strait, "Geographical Study."
11. Campbell, *Providence*, 9.
12. As a result of the Great Migration, U.S. Southern sociocultural mores (e.g., food, the blues, etc.) diffused via the relocation of millions of black Southerners who moved into northern cities like Chicago, Detroit, Milwaukee, Baltimore, New York, and Detroit, just to name a few.
13. Gaddis, *Landscape of History*, 3.

INTRODUCTION

1. Kidder and Fletcher, *Brazil and the Brazilians*, 105.
2. "Brazilian Emigration," *Gazette & Comet*, February 18, 1868, 1.
3. "Terrible Sufferings of the Planters Who Went to Brazil. A Picture of Despair, Depravity and Destitution," *New York Times*, May 21, 1871, 5.
4. Except for the U.S. repatriation project that sent about fifteen thousand American free blacks to Liberia in the early and mid-nineteenth century, discussed in chapter 4.
5. While I use the term "race" here, it is interpreted and understood as a sociopolitical construction without any scientific validity. However, "race" remains a powerful *political reality* in both Brazil and the United States.
6. For exceptions where race is discussed briefly, see, for example, Dawsey, "Constructing Identity"; Harter, *Lost Colony*.
7. Surprisingly, the International Society of Woman Geographers (ISWG) in Washington DC has no information on Elliott, and ISWG members have not heard of her either.
8. Jefferson, "American Colony in Brazil," 231.
9. As Eric Hobsbawm puts it, "In the 1860s, a new word entered the economic and political vocabulary of the world: 'capitalism.'" Hobsbawm, *Age of Capital*, 1.
10. *Pau-Brasil*: a tree known for its red dye and from whence the word "Brazil" allegedly gets its name.
11. The major Brazilian economic booms were Brazilwood, sugar, tobacco, gold, cacao, coffee, and rubber. For more details, see Alden, "Late Colonial Brazil."
12. For more details, see Boxer, *Golden Age of Brazil*.
13. Russell-Wood, "Gold Cycle," 201. See also McCreery, *Frontier Goiás*.
14. Mauro, "Political and Economic Structures," 59–61.
15. Stein, *Vassouras*, 29.
16. Pommeranz and Topik, *World That Trade Created*, 87.
17. Bethell, "Decline and Fall," 74. See also Dean, *Rio Claro*. For a discussion on the coffee boom in the twentieth century in Paraná, see Margolis, *Moving Frontier*.
18. Pommeranz and Topik, *World That Trade Created*, 89.
19. For more details about the illegal transatlantic slave trade, see Conrad, "Contraband Slave Trade."
20. For a discussion of this transition in racial policies in Brazil, see Skidmore, "Brazilian Intellectuals."
21. Hill, "Confederate Exodus to Latin America I," 103.
22. Jack Tarver, "Way Down South toward Rio Dixie's Still Unreconstructed," *Baltimore Sun*, September 17, 1949, 9.
23. See Hill, "Confederate Exodus to Latin America I"; Dawsey and Dawsey, *Confederados*; Griggs, *Elusive Eden*; Harter, *Lost Colony*; Wahlstrom, *Southern Exodus*.

24. See Wahlstrom, *Southern Exodus*.
25. Smith, *Brazil*, 137.
26. Bureau of the American Republics, *Brazil*, 50.
27. Harter, *Lost Colony*, 11.
28. Graham, "Slavery and Economic Development," 647.
29. Levy, "O papel da migração," 52.
30. For example, see C. Silva, "Confederates and Yankees," 370.
31. See Conselho de Imigração e Colonização, Ministério das Relações Exteriores, "Imigração norte-americana."
32. Jarnagin, "Fitting In," 224; see Jarnagin, *Confluence of Transatlantic Networks*.
33. Jarnagin, "Fitting In," 224.
34. Jarnagin, "Fitting In," 224. See also Thornton, *Politics and Power*.
35. Freyre, *Ordem e progresso*, 693. Translations from Portuguese by this author.
36. Jarnagin, "Fitting In," 222.
37. Jarnagin, *Confluence of Transatlantic Networks*, 35.
38. Quoted in Brannon, "Southern Emigration to Brazil," 83.
39. Brannon, "Southern Emigration to Brazil," 83.
40. Gaston, *Hunting a Home*, 373.
41. Dawsey, "Constructing Identity," 165.
42. Saba, "American Mirror," 186.
43. Dawsey, "Constructing Identity," 165–66.
44. See Murray, "William Scully."
45. Weaver, "Confederate Emigration to Brazil," 36.
46. Hill, "Confederate Exodus to Latin America I," 102.
47. Tarver, "Way Down South."
48. See Ferguson, "Journey."
49. See Horne, *Deepest South*.
50. Unfortunately (perhaps inadvertently), Gerald Horne mistook Americana for Santa Bárbara and ignored the correct Brazilian-Portuguese orthographic accents and spelling for place names in Brazil (e.g., names of Brazilian states, towns, and cities).
51. A comprehensive list of publications is far too long to include here. However, for "classic" scholarly publications on slavery, race, and race relations in Brazil, see Degler, *Neither Black nor White*; Freyre, *Masters and the Slaves*; Nobles, *Shades of Citizenship*; Sansone, *Blackness without Ethnicity*; Skidmore, *Black into White*; Schwartz, *Slaves, Peasants, and Rebels*; Schwarcz, *O espetáculo das raças*; and Tannenbaum, *Slave and Citizen*.
52. See Kidder and Fletcher, *Brazil and the Brazilians*, 132–33.
53. Nascimento, *O genocídio do negro Brasileiro*.
54. Scheper-Hughes, *Death without Weeping*, 90.

55. For a contemporary discussion on the geography of Brazilian racial categories, see Marcus, "Sex, Color, and Geography."
56. See Marcus, "Sex, Color, and Geography."
57. These quasi-ethnic categories are arbitrarily used in various Brazilian rural regions. For a detailed discussion on the formation of the Brazilian peasantry, see Forman, *Brazilian Peasantry*.
58. By 1800 the Amerindian population had been reduced by three quarters to about six hundred thousand. By the time the Confederados arrived in Brazil, most of the Amerindians had either died, fled, or been forced into the hinterlands, mainly to the central-west and north Amazonian regions. For more details, see Hemming, *Red Gold*, 492–501.
59. Metcalf, *Go-Betweens*, 129.
60. See Marcus, "Sex, Color, and Geography."
61. See Wagley and Harris, "Typology of Latin American."
62. For example, see Kendi, *Stamped from the Beginning*. However, it is also important to point out that historically the U.S. treatment of Indigenous populations was no less abhorrent, albeit under different circumstances. Suffice to mention, consider the unabated broken treaty agreements and the infamous Sioux massacre committed by the U.S. government at Wounded Knee in 1876. It was only with the Indian Citizenship Act of 1924 that full U.S. citizenship was granted to Indigenous peoples. However, public and academic discourses on racism tend to focus on a U.S. biracial framework (black/white), much to the neglect of Indigenous populations—dispossessed and displaced within their own homeland, Indigenous populations tend to be completely absent from most current U.S. political discussions that involve the terms "racism" and "race." Yet, even more than a decade after the U.S. Emancipation Act had been signed, thousands of Indigenous populations who survived cultural genocide were still confined and disenfranchised, without even being granted U.S. citizenship, forced to move from place to place, then restricted by the U.S. government to live within imposed U.S. Indian reservations, where they remain to this day.
63. See Ravenstein, "Laws of Migration."
64. For a detailed explanation, see Castles and Miller, *Age of Migration*.
65. Castles and Miller, *Age of Migration*, 28.
66. Jones, *Folhas esparsas*, 404.
67. For a discussion on the "culture of times" and contemporary immigration, see Cwerner, "Times of Migration."
68. Cresswell, *In Place/Out of Place*, 13.
69. Fleming, *Gone with the Wind*.
70. It is likely that Confederados had not been exposed to the screening of *Birth of a Nation* or to the ideology it disseminated. They had long been living in Brazil

at the time of the release of the film. To my knowledge, the film did not screen in Brazil at the time of its release.
71. Wright, "Terra Incognitae," 3–4.
72. Dawsey and Dawsey, "Heritage," 86–87.
73. "Advertisement," *Jornal do commercio Rio de Janeiro*, November 29, 1854, 3.
74. *Correio mercantil*, September 26, 1856, 1.
75. Conniff, "Foreword," xii–xiii.
76. Hill, "Confederate Exodus to Latin America II," 173.
77. Gussi, *Os norte-americanos*.
78. Jones, *Folhas esparsas*, 91.
79. "Notice from the Correio Paulistano," *O diário do Rio de Janeiro*, September 7, 1869, 1.
80. *O diário de S. Paulo*, May 3, 1872, 2.
81. *O diário de S. Paulo*, May 3, 1872, 2.
82. Jones, *Folhas Esparsas*, 90.
83. See Rizzolli, *A imigração norte-americana*.
84. Medeiros, "American Brazilian English," 152.
85. Dawsey, "O espelho Americano," 223.
86. Weaver, "Confederate Immigrants," 462.
87. Weaver, "Confederate Immigrants," 465.
88. See Harter, *Lost Colony*, 73–74.
89. See Marcus, *Towards Rethinking Brazil*.
90. See Dawsey and Dawsey, "Leaving," 21.

1. THE BALTIMORE CONNECTION

1. Alison Knezevich, "Museums Celebrate Immigrant Role in City. Event Marks 150 Years since Ship's Journey from Germany to Locust Point," *Baltimore Sun*, March 24, 2018, 2.
2. For more information on the Birckheads, see Jarnagin, *Confluence of Transatlantic Networks*, 123–29.
3. "From Rio de Janeiro; Interesting Celebration of the Fourth of July the United States Minister Not Present Arrival of Prince Alfred Wreck of an American Vessel Political, Naval, and General Intelligence," *New York Times*, August 20, 1860, 5.
4. "From Rio de Janeiro."
5. Merchants Manufacturers Association of Baltimore, Maryland, *A reciprocidade commercial: Baltimore e Brazil*, 9.
6. Majewski and Wahlstrom, "Geography as Power," 344.
7. Maxwell, Wright & Co., "Commercial Formalities," 5.
8. Henry A. Houghton Papers, 1838, MS 467. H. Furlong Baldwin Library, Maryland Historical Society, Baltimore.

9. Rood, "Bogs of Death," 21.
10. Stein, *Vassouras*, 296.
11. Schley, "Natural History," 448.
12. Rutter, *South American Trade*, 10.
13. Beirne, *Amiable Baltimoreans*, 38.
14. Park, "Development of the Clipper Ship," 54.
15. Rutter, *South American Trade*, 9.
16. Rutter, *South American Trade*, 9–10.
17. Rutter, *South American Trade*, 20.
18. Rutter, *South American Trade*, 21.
19. Rutter, *South American Trade*, 31.
20. See Baker, *View of the Commerce*.
21. Alden, "Late Colonial Brazil," 325.
22. See *Hunt's Merchants' Magazine and Commercial Review*.
23. Smith, "Navy before Darwinism," 48.
24. Mitchell, "Matthew Fontaine Maury," 633.
25. Hobsbawm, *Age of Capital*, 62.
26. For more details see, for example, Horne, *Deepest South*.
27. Rutter, *South American Trade*, 9.
28. Kidder and Fletcher, *Brazil and the Brazilians*, 65.
29. In addition to the Maxwell, Wright & Co. pamphlets titled *Commercial Formalities of Rio de Janeiro*—published since 1828, throughout the 1830s, and up to 1842—several other books were published: *A View of the Commerce between the United States and Rio de Janeiro, Brazil* was published in 1838, *The Empire of Brazil at the Universal Exhibition of 1876 in Philadelphia* in 1876, *South American Trade* in 1887, and *A reciprocidade commercial: Baltimore e Brazil* (Brazilian reciprocity: Baltimore and Brazil) in 1892.
30. See *Almanak administrativo, mercantil e industrial do Rio de Janeiro*.
31. Exports of flour from Baltimore to Brazil from 1861 to 1864 amounted to 129,895 barrels (representing 47 percent of total exports from Baltimore to Brazil); from 1865 to 1869: 115,248 barrels (50 percent); from 1870 to 1874: 229,171 barrels (58 percent); from 1875 to 1879: 283,702 barrels (62 percent); from 1880 to 1884: 243,813 barrels (54 percent); and from 1885 to 1887: 312,843 barrels (17 percent). Rutter, *South American Trade*, 27–51.
32. Phipps & Co., *Cypher Code Compiled*, 3.
33. Quoted in Jarnagin, *Confluence of Transatlantic Networks*, 111.
34. See Perkins, "Financing Antebellum Importers."
35. Perkins, "Financing Antebellum Importers," 437.
36. Alexander Brown, born in Ireland in 1764, founded the house of Alexander Brown & Sons. He left for Baltimore with his eldest son, William, in 1800, where he imported

Irish linens. His son William and another brother, James, founded William & James Brown & Co., and, later, Brown, Shipley & Co. in London. William died in Liverpool in 1864. In 1811 Alexander Brown & Sons was formed in Baltimore, where his son George S. Brown and his son-in-law William H. Graham established a branch in Philadelphia under the name "John A. Brown & Co." in 1825; James Brown settled in New York City and established Brown Brothers & Co, while George Brown continued in Baltimore with his father. John A. Brown retired in 1839. Alexander Brown died in 1834. For more details, see Scharf, *Chronicles of Baltimore*.

37. Perkins, "Financing Antebellum Importers," 444.
38. Howard, *Monumental City*, 267.
39. For more details, see Brown, *Hundred Years*.
40. Jarnagin, *Confluence of Transatlantic Networks*, 123–24.
41. William Henry DeCourcy Wright, MS 2416, letterbook, box 1.
42. Sharrer, "Flour Milling," 326.
43. Rood, "Bogs of Death," 39.
44. Rood, "Bogs of Death," 25.
45. Rood, Reinvention of Atlantic Slavery, 123.
46. "Commercial Record. Correspondence of the Journal of Commerce," *American and Commercial Daily Advertiser*, April 26, 1831, 1.
47. Maxwell, Wright & Co., "Commercial Formalities," 26. Due to the Civil War, total imports to Baltimore decreased in 1862 to $3,696,620, whereas total exports remained relatively the same, just decreasing very slightly to $8,375,303. Wheat flour was the largest Brazilian import from the United States in 1885, amounting to $3,369,074. Total imports of coffee from Brazil to the United States also increased from $30,861,906 in 1873 to $45,664,127 in 1890. Bureau of the American Republics, *Brazil*, 130–39.
48. Sharrer, "Merchant-Millers," 138.
49. Rood, "Bogs of Death," 21.
50. Sharrer, "Flour Milling," 332.
51. Howard, *Monumental City*, 133.
52. Howard, *Monumental City*, 137.
53. For more details, see Rutter, *South American Trade*.
54. Sharrer, "Merchant-Millers," 138.
55. Sharrer, "Merchant-Millers," 148.
56. Olson, *Baltimore*, 85.
57. Sharrer, "Merchant-Millers," 148.
58. Olson, *Baltimore*, 103.
59. Sharer, "Merchant-Millers," 150.
60. Rood, "Bogs of Death," 21.
61. Schley, "Natural History," 445.

62. Schley, "Natural History," 446.
63. Jarnagin, *Confluence of Transatlantic Networks*, 224.
64. Sharrer, "Flour Milling," 332.
65. Graham, "Slavery and Economic Development," 622. Rood, *Reinvention of Atlantic Slavery*, 129.
66. Leff, "Economic Retardation," 495.
67. Jarnagin, *Confluence of Transatlantic Networks*, 122.
68. Rood, *Reinvention of Atlantic Slavery*, 33.
69. See dedication in Emory, *Colonial Families and Their Descendants*.
70. William Henry DeCourcy Wright, MS 2416, letterbook, box 1.
71. Several of the Wright family members shared the same first names, particularly "Robert" and "William" (also popular first names at the time), which can be confusing. One of the few ways to distinguish one from the other is by the spelling of their middle names.
72. Maryland State Archives, *Daniel Giraud Wright*.
73. "Our Coffee Trade: How It Was Built Up and Maintained—Judge Wright's Recollections," *Baltimore Sun*, November 18, 1889, 1.
74. William Decourcy Thom, MS 2416, box 15.
75. Warfield, *Founders of Anne Arundel*, 253–54; Emory, *Colonial Families*, 140–48.
76. Emory, *Colonial Families*, 140–48.
77. William Henry DeCourcy Wright, MS 2416, letterbook, box 1.
78. William Henry DeCourcy Wright, MS 2416, letterbook, box 1.
79. William Henry DeCourcy Wright, consular documents, MS 2416, box 4.
80. Henry A. Wise to William H. D. Wright, 1845–46, William Henry DeCourcy Wright Papers, MS 1467, H. Furlong Baldwin Library, Maryland Historical Society, Baltimore.
81. William Henry DeCourcy Wright, MS 2416, letterbook, box 1.
82. William Henry DeCourcy Wright, MS 2416, letterbook, box 1.
83. See A. Ribeiro, "Leading Commission-House."
84. Jarnagin, *Confluence of Transatlantic Networks*, 111–14.
85. Kidder and Fletcher, *Brazil and the Brazilians*, 36.
86. Kidder and Fletcher, *Brazil and the Brazilians*, 36.
87. More recently in 2014 Alan dos Santos Ribeiro also researched the firm in his doctoral dissertation. See A. Ribeiro, "Leading Commission-House."
88. "Mr. Joseph Maxwell," *Richmond Enquirer*, October 17, 1854, 2. Laura Jarnagin Pang now recognizes that the date she had to work with in *A Confluence of Transatlantic Networks* was erroneous and that she found it far more credible that a newly arrived foreign merchant would have been in his mid-thirties in order to have gone on to realize the success that Joseph Maxwell did. Laura Jarnagin Pang, email message to author, March 2, 2020.
89. Kidder and Fletcher, *Brazil and the Brazilians*, 114–16.

90. Kidder and Fletcher, *Brazil and the Brazilians*, 144.
91. William Henry DeCourcy Wright, MS 2416, box 3.
92. "Died," *Baltimore Sun*, March 26, 1864, 2.
93. Kidder and Fletcher, *Brazil and the Brazilians*, 240.
94. Warfield, *Founders of Anne Arundel*, 116–17.
95. "Dom Pedro II. Interview of a Herald Special Correspondent with His Majesty the Emperor of Brazil," *New York Herald*, June 20, 1871, 5.
96. Kidder and Fletcher, *Brazil and the Brazilians*, 140.
97. Gaston, *Hunting a Home*, 51.
98. See Jacob and John A. Humbird Papers, *Jacob Humbird*.
99. Dunn, *Brazil*, 148.
100. John James Aubertin, "The Province of S. Paulo and American Immigration," *Anglo-Brazilian Times*, March 24, 1866, 4.
101. Howard, *Monumental City*, 914.
102. Howard, *Monumental City*, 915.
103. See Jacob and John A. Humbird Papers, *Jacob Humbird*.
104. "The word 'lodge' means both a group of Masons meeting in some place and the room or building in which they meet. Masonic buildings are also sometimes called temples' because much of the symbolism Masonry uses to teach its lessons comes from the building of King Solomon's Temple in the Holy Land." Maryland Freemason Lodge, "Amicable St. John's Lodge."
105. See Maryland Freemason Lodge, "Amicable St. John's Lodge."
106. "A. F. & A. M." stand for "Ancient Free" and "Accepted Masons," respectively. Permission was granted by Edward Heimiller, Curator at the Stephen J. Ponzillo, Jr. Memorial Library & Museum of the Grand Lodge of A. F. & A. M. of Maryland, Maryland Masonic Museum.
107. Jarnagin, *Confluence of Transatlantic Networks*, 126.
108. See Cândido, "O rito de York no Brasil."
109. Maryland Freemason Lodge, "Amicable St. John's Lodge."
110. By permission of Edward Heimiller, Curator at the Stephen J. Ponzillo, Jr. Memorial Library & Museum of the Grand Lodge of A. F. & A. M. of Maryland, Maryland Masonic Museum.
111. Jarnagin, *Confluence of Transatlantic Networks*, 251.
112. Michael Dresser, "150 Years Ago the Bloodshed Started Here," *Baltimore Sun*, April 11, 2011, https://www.baltimoresun.com/maryland/bs-md-pratt-street-riot-20110418-story.html.
113. "Southern Emigration to Brazil," *New York Herald*, March 5, 1866, 4.

2. MOVING TO BRAZIL

1. Elliott, *Brazil Today and Tomorrow*, 63.

2. See Hill, "Confederate Exodus to Latin America III."
3. Harmon, "Confederate Migration to Mexico," 487.
4. For more details, see Schwarcz, *As barbas do imperador*.
5. Griggs, *Elusive Eden*, viii.
6. *Papers relating to Foreign Affairs*.
7. See Sampaio, "Emancipação, expulsão e exclusão," 9; and Hopperstad, "Confederate Exiles in Brazil," 11.
8. Elliott, *Brazil Today and Tomorrow*, 52.
9. Dom Pedro II was the son of Emperor Dom Pedro I and Empress Dona Maria Leopoldina. Dom Pedro I declared independence from Portugal in 1822. See Schwarcz, *As barbas do imperador*.
10. Dawsey and Dawsey, "Leaving," 11.
11. Harter, *Lost Colony*, 8.
12. Flynt, "Baptists," 106.
13. Sutherland, "Looking for a Home," 153.
14. Hill, "Confederate Exodus to Latin America I," 103.
15. Lowe, "Reconstruction Revisited," 6.
16. Dunn, *Brazil*, 71. Capt. Shippey, however, abandoned the Brazilian migration project and returned to Kansas, where he became Treasurer of the Kansas City and Northwestern Railway and where he died at the age of fifty-nine, in 1900. See "Capt. William Francis Shippey," 268.
17. *Jornal do commercio*, September 27, 1867, 1.
18. *Jornal do commercio*, September 27, 1867, 1.
19. "Immigration," *Anglo-Brazilian Times*, July 24, 1865, 1.
20. "A Trip to Dixie. The Confederates in Brazil," *Chicago Tribune*, August 31, 1866, 2.
21. Although Maj. Meriwether and Dr. Shaw went to Brazil, there is no record of who went to Brazil from this society. The governing body of the Southern Colonization Society was as follows: President, Maj. Joseph Abney; vice-president, Col. D. L. Shaw; secretary, Col. A. P. Butler; corresponding secretary, Maj. John E. Bacon; treasurer, Thomas B. Reese. Its members included Dr. Hugh A. Shaw; Maj. Isaac Boles; Mr. B. C. Bryan; Mr. William M. Williams; Mr. T. B. Durisoe; Benjamin F. Mays; Henry G. Arthur; D. F. McEwin; Thomas J. Davis; S. J. M. Clark; Capt. Tilman Watson Jr.; W. J. Gardner, Charles Glover; John Sentell, Esq.; Capt. W. H. Brunson; Dr. W. D. Jennings; Mr. G. W. Morgan; John R. Carwile; and Maj. Robert Meriwether. See Brannon, "Southern Emigration to Brazil," 76.
22. Hill, "Confederate Exodus to Latin America I," 116.
23. Gaston, *Hunting a Home*, 30.
24. See Weaver, "Confederate Emigration to Brazil," and Hill, "Confederate Exiles to Brazil."

25. William and Carlota had four sons—Henrique (Henry), Carlos (Charles), João (John) and Guilherme (William)—and one daughter, Carlota.
26. Gaston, *Hunting a Home*, 52. Spelling corrections in italics by this author.
27. Gaston, *Hunting a Home*, 52.
28. Gaston, *Hunting a Home*, 50.
29. Gaston, *Hunting a Home*, 374.
30. "Shall Southerners Emigrate to Brazil?," *Debow's Review*, January 1866, 36–37.
31. "Shall Southerners Emigrate to Brazil?," *Debow's Review*, January 1866, 36–37.
32. Conselho de Imigração e Colonização, Ministério das Relações Exteriores, "Imigração norte-americana," 301–2.
33. Rios, "Assimilation of Emigrants," 146.
34. Griggs, *Elusive Eden*, xii.
35. "Brazil and Southern Emigration," *Baltimore Sun*, August 6, 1866, 2.
36. Weaver, "Confederate Emigration to Brazil," 37.
37. "Emigration of Southerners to Brazil," *New York Herald*, November 18, 1865, 5.
38. Weaver, "Confederate Emigration to Brazil," 38.
39. Conselho de Imigração e Colonização, Ministério das Relações Exteriores, "Imigração norte-americana," 277–86.
40. "Immigration," *Anglo-Brazilian Times*, July 24, 1865, 1.
41. "Immigration."
42. Weaver, "Confederate Emigration to Brazil," 47.
43. "Advertisement," *Anglo-Brazilian Times*, June 19, 1865, 4.
44. Weaver, "Confederate Emigration to Brazil," 44.
45. Weaver, "Confederate Emigration to Brazil," 44.
46. "The 'Castel Garden' of Rio," *Anglo-Brazilian Times*, April 23, 1867, 3.
47. "Praça do Commercio. Associação Internacional de Emigração," *O diário do Rio de Janeiro*, February 1, 1866, 3.
48. "Extracts from the Relatório of Conselheiro Manoel Pinto de Souza Dantas, Minister of Agriculture, Public Works. North American Immigration," *Anglo-Brazilian Times*, July 9, 1867, 2.
49. "Extracts from the Relatório."
50. See Murray, "William Scully."
51. See Murray, "William Scully."
52. Gaston, *Hunting a Home*, 42.
53. "Emigration of Southerners to Brazil."
54. Kelsey, *Seven Keys to Brazil*, 110.
55. Dunn, *Brazil*, 26.
56. Conselho de Imigração e Colonização, Ministério das Relações Exteriores, "Imigração norte-americana," 328.
57. Hill, "Confederate Exodus to Latin America I," 127.

58. Quoted in Hill, "Confederate Exodus to Latin America II," 176.
59. Neeley, *Works of Matthew Blue*, 153. See also Brannon, "Southern Emigration to Brazil," 77.
60. Jarnagin, *Confluence of Transatlantic Networks*, 226.
61. H. L., "Sea Island Cotton," *Anglo-Brazilian Times*, October 22, 1870, 1.
62. "American Immigration," *Anglo-Brazilian Times*, February 24, 1866, 1.
63. "American Immigration."
64. Hill, "Confederate Exodus to Latin America I," 130.
65. "Southern Emigration to Brazil," *New York Herald*, March 5, 1866, 4.
66. "Southern Emigration to Brazil."
67. "Southern Emigration to Brazil."
68. See *Correio Mercantil*, June 29, 1867, 3.
69. "President on Immigration," *Anglo-Brazilian Times*, December 7, 1869, 1.
70. Again, not to be confused with Horace Manley Lane of Maine, who was the first president of Mackenzie College and director of the Escola Americana in São Paulo.
71. "Dr. J. H. Blue and his brother, H. L. Blue[,] arrived in Rio on May 10, 1865," *Jornal do commercio*, May 10, 1865, 3.
72. Dawsey and Dawsey, "Leaving," 20–21.
73. Aguiar, "Imigrantes norte-americanos," 30.
74. "Terrible Sufferings of the Planters Who Went to Brazil. A Picture of Despair, Depravity and Destitution," *New York Times*, May 21, 1871, 5.
75. "Emigration to Brazil," *Pulaski Citizen*, February 1, 1867, 1.
76. "Emigration to Brazil," *Pulaski Citizen*, February 1, 1867, 1.
77. Among the doctors, for example, was Dr. Gaston, whom after settling in the interior of São Paulo with his family practiced medicine in the city of Campinas. Gaston eventually returned with his family to Atlanta, Georgia, and taught at the Southern Medical College.
78. "New Steamboat Lines," *Anglo-Brazilian Times*, September 7, 1867, 3.
79. Hill, "Confederate Exiles to Brazil," 196.
80. "The 'Castel Garden' of Rio."
81. "New Steamboat Lines."
82. "Editorial," *Brazilian World*, April 24, 1869, 1.
83. "Terrible Sufferings."
84. "Terrible Sufferings." Translation corrections in brackets by this author.
85. "Brazil and Emigration," *Daily Dispatch*, February 15, 1865, 1.
86. Tate, "Robert E. Lee Letter," 255.
87. Sutherland, "Looking for a Home," 355.
88. Kidder and Fletcher acknowledge Ferdinand Coxe for his helpful contributions in their preface to *Brazil and the Brazilians*, 5.

89. "Emigration and Brazil," *Anglo-Brazilian Times*, October 10, 1865, 1.
90. Nash, *Conquest of Brazil*, 91.
91. IBGE, "Espírito Santo, Iguape. Histórico." January 2018, https://cidades.ibge.gov.br/brasil/sp/iguape/historico.
92. Prefeitura de Linhares, *Linhares*.
93. Southey, *History of Brazil*, 851.
94. Reclus, *Earth and Its Inhabitants*, 226.
95. Reclus, *Earth and Its Inhabitants*, 226.
96. Jarnagin, "Fitting In," 80.
97. Gaston, *Hunting a Home*, 368.
98. Jarnagin, *Confluence of Transatlantic Networks*, 206.
99. "The Right Place: The Right Sort," *Correio Mercantil*, June 29, 1867, 3.
100. "The Right Place."
101. Conselho de Imigração e Colonização, Ministério das Relações Exteriores, "Imigração norte-americana," 318.
102. Conselho de Imigração e Colonização, Ministério das Relações Exteriores, "Imigração norte-americana," 318.
103. Conselho de Imigração e Colonização, Ministério das Relações Exteriores, "Imigração norte-americana," 327.
104. Conselho de Imigração e Colonização, Ministério das Relações Exteriores, "Imigração norte-americana," 327.
105. Four original letters written by William Bowen, dated between October and November 1867, were archived randomly and incorrectly without protection, folder, or label at the Arquivo Público do Estado de São Paulo (Regional Archives of the State of São Paulo). By sheer chance, I found them on January 6, 2018, in a miscellaneous "immigration box" dated 1909. I never got an explanation by any of the staff for why they were misplaced and found without an adequate protective folder, when I inquired. They did not inform me where they would later archive the letters, either. This letter was the first of the four letters found, numbered here, "Letters 1–4." See Arquivo Público do Estado de São Paulo, "Acervo 1909 Imigrantes," letter 1.
106. Arquivo Público do Estado de São Paulo, letter 1.
107. Arquivo Público do Estado de São Paulo, letter 3. Translations in italics by this author.
108. Arquivo Público do Estado de São Paulo, letter 4. Translations in italics by this author.
109. Andrews, "Ambitions of Lansford," 473.
110. Andrews, "Ambitions of Lansford," 474.
111. See Gravois and Weisbrod, "Annotated Bibliography," 248.
112. See Hill, "Confederate Exodus to Latin America II," 189.

113. Hopperstad, "Confederate Exiles in Brazil," 86.
114. Hopperstad, "Confederate Exiles in Brazil," 90.
115. "The Swatara's Mission," *New York Herald*, October 30, 1875, 11.
116. See Dawsey and Dawsey, *Confederados*.
117. "Twenty-One Years in Brazil: Report from the American Colony by One of the Southern Refugees," *Baltimore Sun*, June 25, 1888, 4.
118. There has been some uncertainty about whether Charles Nathan was born in England or Brazil, as different sources have cited either. His parents were born in England and migrated to Rio in 1820; it therefore would seem unlikely that he was born in England. Charles Nathan eventually left Brazil and took up full residency with his family in New Orleans (he was not born in New Orleans, as some sources have incorrectly cited). However, under the Nathan household listed, the U.S. Census of 1880 states, "Born in England" and, referring to all Charles Nathan's children, "Born in the United States." Other documents show that three of his children were born in Rio. Under the list of foreigners living in Rio at the Arquivo Nacional in Rio de Janeiro, Nathan's brothers are listed, and all of them were born in London; however, Charles Nathan's name is not listed, and the archives have no records of his date of birth either (though this might have been obtainable by researching a list of baptisms in Rio at that time, Charles Nathan was Jewish, and this would have made it implausible). It is more than likely that he was born in Rio.
119. Gaston, *Hunting a Home*, 369.
120. See Nathan, *Exposição que faz*.
121. "Advertisements," *Anglo-Brazilian Times*, June 4, 1865, 4.
122. Dunn, *Brazil*, 16.
123. Dunn, *Brazil*, 20–22.
124. "Southern Emigration to Brazil," *Baton Rouge Tri-Weekly Gazette & Comet*, November 5, 1867, 2.
125. *Correio mercantil*, June 29, 1867, 3.
126. Burton, *Explorations of the Highlands*, 5.
127. Hopperstad, "Confederate Exiles in Brazil," 57.
128. Quoted in Brannon, "Southern Emigration to Brazil," 83.
129. "Brazilian Emigration," *Gazette & Comet*, February 18, 1868, 1.
130. Jarnagin, *Confluence of Transatlantic Networks*, 239.
131. Antonio Silva, *Entre a cruz*, 74.
132. Quoted in Antonio Silva, *Entre a cruz*, 74. Translations from Portuguese by this author.
133. Antonio Silva, *Entre a cruz*, 87. Translations from Portuguese by this author.
134. *Jornal do commercio*, May 3, 1828, 4.
135. Gaston, *Hunting a Home*, 368.

136. Gaston, *Hunting a Home*, 221.
137. In 1875 Charles Nathan wrote an article for the *New Orleans Republican*, in which he stated, "Flour is at present moment only sometimes purchased by owners of sailing vessels to endeavor to earn a higher freight out. This must cease with steamers as carriers, as then it becomes necessary and profitable for millers to ship the flour. And this has been the case in most instances by sailing vessels . . . with very many of the Baltimore mills." He continued, "The St. Louis millers can only expect to compete with others in this important trade by accommodating themselves to the change of system brought by the introduction of steam and the telegraph into commercial pursuits. The millers are right to combine in the selection of an agent to look after their interests in Rio." He concluded, "Let him be the man who understands the process of milling wheat into flour, so that he may point out to the millers any defect that may be easily corrected and improve the value of their brands." Charles Nathan, "St. Louis Flour—Brazil Coffee," *New Orleans Republican*, September 7, 1875, 1.
138. "Pioneer Teacher Passes Away," *Times Democrat*, November 25, 1910, 3.
139. "Pioneer Teacher Passes Away."
140. "Pioneer Teacher Passes Away."

3. CONDITIONS IN BRAZIL

1. Johnson, "Portuguese Settlement," 2.
2. For more details, see Burns, *History of Brazil*, 9–10.
3. For more details, see Boxer, *Golden Age of Brazil*, 227–28; Bethell, *Brazil*, 9–10.
4. See Boxer, *Golden Age of Brazil*.
5. For further discussion, see Dean, "Latifundia and Land Policy"; Ridings, "Class Sector Unity"; Leff, "Economic Retardation."
6. See Burns, *History of Brazil*; Boxer, *Golden Age of Brazil*. For a map of the Brazilian *capitanias*, see Johnson, "Portuguese Settlement," 15.
7. For an in-depth discussion, see Boxer, *Golden Age of Brazil*, 227–28; Bethell, *Brazil*, 9–10.
8. Dean, "Latifundia and Land Policy," 608.
9. Freyre, "Social Life in Brazil," 600. Translation by this author.
10. Pang, "State and Agricultural Clubs," 145.
11. Schwartz, "Plantations and Peripheries," 69.
12. Schwartz, "Plantations and Peripheries," 77.
13. Dawsey and Dawsey, "Leaving," 17.
14. See Alden, "Late Colonial Brazil," 318–22.
15. See "Romantic Circles: A Refereed Scholarly Website Devoted to the Study of Romantic-Period Literature and Culture," Romantic Circles, last updated 2018, University of Maryland, College Park, http://www.rc.umd.edu.

16. "Arrived at Liverpool," *Lancaster Gazette*, March 13, 1802, 3; "Liverpool Imports. Brazil," *Manchester Mercury*, December 2, 1817, 2.
17. Brannstrom, "Forests for Cotton," 169.
18. See Andrews, "Slavery and Race Relations," 3.
19. See Mauro, "Political and Economic Structures."
20. Mauro, "Political and Economic Structures," 55.
21. Tannenbaum, *Slave and Citizen*, 5.
22. Mattosso, *To Be a Slave*, 12.
23. Stein, *Vassouras*, 25.
24. Stein, *Vassouras*, 65.
25. Stein, *Vassouras*, 66.
26. Alencastro and Renaux, *Caras e modos*, 327.
27. Bethell, "Decline and Fall," 78.
28. Bethell, "Decline and Fall," 88.
29. Elliott, *Brazil Today and Tomorrow*, 73.
30. Dom João was Prince Regent in 1808 when the Portuguese court relocated to Brazil to escape Napoleon's invasion of Portugal; he then became king of Portugal, Brazil, and the Algarves in 1816. He was Dom Pedro II's grandfather. For more details, see Burns, *History of Brazil*.
31. Elliott, *Brazil Today and Tomorrow*, 57.
32. Elliott, *Brazil Today and Tomorrow*, 61.
33. Elliott, *Brazil Today and Tomorrow*, 57.
34. Bureau of the American Republics, *Brazil*, 49.
35. Bethell, "Decline and Fall," 79.
36. Smith, *Brazil. People and Institutions*, 137.
37. *Bureau of American Republics*, 50.
38. For more details, see Stein, *Vassouras*.
39. See Graham, "Slavery and Economic Development."
40. The article was originally published in the *Brasilian Reflector* and reprinted in *O diário do Rio de Janeiro*.
41. "Transcrição. Imigração dos Estados-Unidos," *O diário do Rio de Janeiro*, November 26, 1868, 2.
42. Ridings, "Class Sector Unity," 433.
43. For details on Brazilian nineteenth-century business associations, see Ridings, "Class Sector Unity."
44. In archaic Portuguese orthography, it would have been spelled *Queiroz*.
45. For more details, see Dean, *Rio Claro*.
46. Laura Jarnagin provides an excellent and extensive genealogical examination of the Dabney / Avelar Brotero families. See Jarnagin, *Confluence of Transatlantic Networks*, 220–23.

47. Mendes, "Ibicaba revisitada outra vez," 336–38.
48. Kidder and Fletcher, *Brazil and the Brazilians*, 404–7.
49. Mendes, "Ibicaba revisitada outra vez," 336–38.
50. Dean, *Rio Claro*, 30.
51. Dean, *Rio Claro*, 31.
52. Dean, *Rio Claro*, 31.
53. Saba, "American Mirror," 190.
54. See Dawsey and Dawsey, "Heritage," 85–86.
55. Barbanti, "Escolas Americanas de confissão," 106. See also Weaver, "Confederate Immigrants."
56. Levy, "O papel da migração," 51.
57. Smith, *Brazil*, 130.
58. Saba, "American Mirror," ix.
59. Saba, "American Mirror," x.
60. "Advertisements," *Anglo-Brazilian Times*, June 4, 1865, 4.
61. Saba, "American Mirror," 213.
62. For example, see C. Silva, "Confederates and Yankees," 370–84.
63. Graham, "Slavery and Economic Development," 628–30.
64. Graham, "Slavery and Economic Development," 629.
65. For example, see Fragoso, "A roça e as propostas"; Pang, "State and Agricultural Clubs"; Ridings, "Class Sector Unity"; Ridings, "Interest Groups and Development"; and "Agricultura," *A aurora Paulista*, October 10, 1851, 1–4.
66. For more details, see Pang, "State and Agricultural Clubs."
67. Ridings, "Interest Groups and Development," 246.
68. Sodré, *História da imprensa do Brasil*, 227.
69. For example, see "Agricultura," *A aurora Paulista*, October 10, 1851, 1–4.
70. Pang, "State and Agricultural Clubs," 24.
71. Pang, "State and Agricultural Clubs," 48.
72. For more details see Ridings, "Interest Groups and Development"; Fragoso, "A roça e as propostas"; Pang, "State and Agricultural Clubs."
73. In speeches to the Sociedade Círculo Agrícola de São João de Cacaria, its founder Pedroso and the society's spokesmen identified that the greatest causes of the deterioration in Brazil's agricultural conditions were largely bad roads and lack of labor, in addition to lack of farming technology and techniques. However, knowledge of those farming techniques did exist in Brazil, as one of the society's members, Miguel Antonio da Silva, pointed out. This knowledge, for example, included farming techniques published in Burlamque's manuals *Manual dos agentes fertlisantes* (Manual of fertilizing agents, 1858) and *Manual de machinas: Instrumentos e motores agricolas* (Manual of machines: Instruments and agricultural motors, 1859). However, these were only available in the journal

O auxiliador da indústria nacional, and the information was not made available in the other major and more accessible newspapers for wider dissemination. Moreover, ostensibly the use of the plow in Brazilian soil contributed to the acceleration of soil erosion, due to its detrimental effects on soil composition and soil productivity, leaving the fertile components of the soil exposed to the excessive heat of the tropical sun. See Fragoso, "A roça e as propostas," 139–40.

74. See "Agricultura," *O commercio*, March 15, 1851, 2; "Agricultura," *A aurora Paulista*, October 10, 1851, 1–4.
75. For example, see "Provincia do Rio de Janeiro," *O diário do Rio de Janeiro*, July 20, 1850, 2; "Aos Fazendeiros," *O diário do Rio de Janeiro*, May 25, 1852, 4.
76. Pang, "State and Agricultural Clubs," 58.
77. As early as 1798 Rodrigo de Sousa Coutinho, Brazilian Secretary of State for the Navy and for the Overseas Territories (1796–1801), from the prominent Sousa Coutinho family, had promoted several projects in Brazil, including the use of the ox-drawn plow, the use of cleaning and shelling machinery for cotton and coffee, and a push to "popularize 'scientific' agriculture among Brazilian landowners by distributing free pamphlets on agronomy printed in Lisbon and specially written in, or translated into, Portuguese." Andrée Silva, "Imperial Re-Organization," 274.
78. Dunn, *Brazil*, 108.
79. Dunn, *Brazil*, 138.
80. Dunn, *Brazil*, 187–88.
81. See Dunn, *Brazil*.
82. Gaston, *Hunting a Home*, 87. Translations in italics by this author.
83. Take another example: the series of articles published in the *A aurora Paulista* (1851–52) newspaper, written by an anonymous author and simply signed, "S. (Do *Commercio de Nictheroy*.)." According to the anonymous author, the knowledge acquired in farming technologies and methods developed and published by European and American authors—who had based their research in foreign soil in northern temperate climates—was different to that based in Brazilian tropical soils, which are extremely diverse and different soils from the soils used in research based in northern hemispheric countries. The same author claimed, therefore, that the use of the plow in hot climates in the southern hemispheres was detrimental to the environment and the soil, especially tropical Brazilian soils. He claimed that foreigners were mistaken to criticize Brazil's "backwardness" in agriculture, with their insistence that the mere use of the plow (*arado*) would bring agricultural advancement and improvement (the same type of commentary that Confederados made when they first visited Brazil). He contended that even the thousands of active European immigrant agriculturalists in Brazil had not adopted the plow in climates such as Rio de

Janeiro's, after all, because it was not adequate to the region's native soil, and they had to adapt to indigenous agricultural practices. The plow, he concluded, did not suit Brazilian soil because it exposed the soil—as new fertile surfaces are damaged by the heat of the tropical sun, this would destroy their rich and fertile vegetation. See "Agricultura," *A aurora Paulista*, October 10, 1851, 1–4.

84. Hecht and Cockburn, *Fate of the Forest*, 2.
85. Kidder and Fletcher, *Brazil and the Brazilians*, 66.
86. Skidmore, *Brazil*, 36. Also see Sodré, *História da imprensa do Brasil*.
87. Stein, *Vassouras*, 296.
88. Ridings, "Interest Groups and Development," 232.
89. Ridings, "Class Sector Unity," 445.
90. Alden, "Late Colonial Brazil," 309.
91. Hahner, *Emancipating the Female Sex*, 21–22.
92. Kent, "Revolt in Bahia," 341.
93. Jeha, "Anphiteatrical Rio!," 116.
94. Kent, "Revolt in Bahia," 341.
95. Hobsbawm, *Age of Capital*, 43.
96. Hobsbawm, *Age of Capital*, 192.
97. Skidmore, *Brazil*, 85.
98. Jarnagin, *Confluence of Transatlantic Networks*, 221–22. See also Dean, *Rio Claro*.
99. Quoted in Ward, *American-Brazilian Odyssey*, 26.
100. Ward, *American-Brazilian Odyssey*, 26.
101. Ward, *American-Brazilian Odyssey*, 32.
102. "Southerners in Brazil," *Public Ledger*, April 7, 1877.
103. Ward, *American-Brazilian Odyssey*, 55.
104. Tarver, "Way Down South."
105. Graham, "Slavery and Economic Development," 630.
106. Weaver, "Confederate Emigration to Brazil," 34.
107. Bethell, "Decline and Fall," 74.
108. A figure who was considered the "J. P. Morgan of Brazil"; however, in his case, he ended up bankrupt.
109. Filho, *O Rio de Janeiro Imperial*, 148.
110. Leff, "Economic Retardation," 501.
111. Railroad lines in Brazil differed starkly from those in the U.S. South. For example, Richard Graham points out that in 1850 there were no railroads in existence in Brazil. In contrast, a total extent of 2,079 miles of railroads was already available that same year in the U.S. South. Ten years later there was only a total of 109 miles of railroad in Brazil, in comparison to 9,165 miles in the U.S. South. By 1890 there was still only 5,994 miles of railroad networks in all of Brazil (mostly in Brazil's southeast region) in comparison to 29,256 miles in all of the U.S.

South—almost five times as extensive. Graham, "Slavery and Economic Development," 626.
112. Graham, "Slavery and Economic Development," 654.
113. *Debow's Review*, "Shall Southerners Emigrate to Brazil?" 32.
114. Elliott, *Brazil Today and Tomorrow*, 130.
115. See Rothschild Archives, "June 2017."
116. "The Brazils: The Don Pedro II. Railway Portion Built by American Contractors an Imperial Visit," *New York Times*, July 16, 1860, 1.
117. Dunn, *Brazil*, 210.
118. William Milnor Roberts Papers.
119. William Milnor Roberts Papers.
120. William Milnor Roberts Papers.
121. Pang, "State and Agricultural Clubs," 132.
122. Pang, "State and Agricultural Clubs," 49–50.
123. Ridings, "Class Sector Unity," 440.
124. "The Great Migration Question IV," *Anglo-Brazilian Times*, August 7, 1865, 1.
125. "The Great Migration Question IV."
126. See U.S. Department of State Archive, "Visits to the U.S."
127. Comissão Brasileira na Exposição Universal de Philadelphia, Centennial Exhibition, *Empire of Brazil*, 382.
128. Kidder and Fletcher, *Brazil and the Brazilians*, 6.
129. On a far broader scale at the macro level, between the 1880s and 1930s an estimated thirty to forty million immigrants arrived in ports throughout the Americas—for example, Ellis Island, Locust Point, Buenos Aires, Rio de Janeiro, Santos, just to name a few. See Oliveira, *O Brasil dos imigrantes*, 11.
130. Hill, "Confederate Exodus to Latin America I," 114.
131. Hill, "Confederate Exodus to Latin America I," 123.
132. Williams, *Dom Pedro the Magnanimous*, 236–37.
133. IBGE, *Populational Statistics*, 225.
134. Oliveira, *O Brasil dos imigrantes*, 18.
135. Oliveira, *O Brasil dos imigrantes*, 18.
136. Dunn, *Brazil*, 5.
137. Jarnagin, "Fitting In," 83.
138. Gaston, *Hunting a Home*, 53.
139. Hobsbawm, *Age of Capital*, 174.

4. IDEOLOGIES

1. Skidmore, *Brazil*, 56.
2. Skidmore, *Brazil*, 56.

3. See Sutherland, *Confederate Carpetbaggers*.
4. Jarnagin, "Fitting In," 69.
5. Horne, *Deepest South*, 201.
6. Simmons, "Racist Americans," 34.
7. Wolnisty, "Austral Empires," 4–5.
8. Weaver, "Confederate Emigration to Brazil," 33.
9. Bethell, "Decline and Fall," 75.
10. Kidder and Fletcher, *Brazil and the Brazilians*, 187.
11. Gussi, *Os norte-americanos*, 102.
12. Hopperstad, "Confederate Exiles in Brazil," 77.
13. Quoted in Hill, "Confederate Exodus to Latin America II," 170.
14. Jarnagin, "Fitting In," 69.
15. Wolnisty, "Austral Empires," 4.
16. See Wahlstrom, *Southern Exodus*.
17. Hill, "Confederate Exodus to Latin America II," 174.
18. See Wahlstrom, *Southern Exodus*.
19. Gaston, *Hunting a Home*, 227.
20. Conselho de Imigração e Colonização, Ministério das Relações Exteriores, "Imigração norte-americana," 325.
21. Conselho de Imigração e Colonização, Ministério das Relações Exteriores, "Imigração norte-americana," 374.
22. *Debow's Review*, "The Empire of Brazil," January, 1858, 1–27.
23. John James Aubertin, "The Province of S. Paulo and American Immigration," *Anglo-Brazilian Times*, March 24, 1866, 4.
24. Although the laws stated one thing on paper, the reality was that widespread antipathy among the Brazilian public existed toward black populations, especially toward slaves, throughout Brazil.
25. If there had been one individual who clearly voiced his virulent racism and anti-Semitism, it was a member of the clergy: Rev. Ballard S. Dunn (see Dunn, *Brazil*). Yet Dunn did not stay in Brazil; he returned to the United States within two years, abandoning the settlement of Iguape, and was accused of absconding with many of the settlers' funds.
26. Gilberto Freyre and Frank Tannenbaum have been criticized in the past by other scholars for their shortsightedness and Eurocentric perspectives and of downplaying the insidious nature of slavery in Brazil by not portraying the reality of Brazilian slavery as a cruel and horrendous institution. Moreover, for more on how Freyre and Tannenbaum perpetuated Brazil's "myth of racial democracy," see Nascimento, *O genocídio do negro Brasileiro*, 38.
27. See Hill, "Confederate Exiles to Brazil."

28. Shalhope, "Race, Class, Slavery," 568.
29. The postbellum concern with racial politics in the U.S. South happened after the Confederate migration to Brazil had taken place.
30. Hale, *Making Whiteness*, xi.
31. See Whitney Benns, "American Slavery, Reinvented," *Atlantic*, September 21, 2015, https://www.theatlantic.com/business/archive/2015/09/prison-labor-in-america/406177/.
32. See Benns, "American Slavery, Reinvented."
33. Hale, *Making Whiteness*, 9. See also Foster, *Ghosts of the Confederacy*; Wilson, *Baptized in Blood*.
34. Degler, *Neither Black nor White*, 9.
35. Skidmore, "Brazilian Intellectuals," 2; Skidmore, *Brazil*, 70.
36. Kidder and Fletcher, *Brazil and the Brazilians*, 133.
37. Dawsey and Dawsey, "Conclusions," 194.
38. Padoveze, *Boletim*.
39. For an example of the new literature on recent protests at Campo, see Brasher, "Contesting the Confederacy." For another perspective, see Dawsey, "Constructing Identity."
40. For a comparative discussion of racial politics in Brazil and in the United States, see Nobles, *Shades of Citizenship*.
41. See Degler, *Neither Black nor White*; Nobles, *Shades of Citizenship*; Marcus, "Sex, Color, and Geography"; Sansone, *Blackness without Ethnicity*.
42. For an examination of racialized politics in Brazil, see Nobles, *Shades of Citizenship*; Skidmore, *Black into White*.
43. "Brazil and Emigration," *Daily Dispatch*, February 15, 1865, 1.
44. Kidder and Fletcher, *Brazil and the Brazilians*, 132.
45. For more details, see Schwartz, "Plantations and Peripheries," 137; Dean, *Rio Claro*.
46. For more details, see Andrews, *Afro-Latin America*; Blauner, *Still the Big New*.
47. See Skidmore, *Black into White*.
48. Skidmore, *Black into White*, xii.
49. Samantha Pearson, "Demand for American Sperm Is Skyrocketing in Brazil: Explosive Growth Spurred by More Wealthy Single Women and Lesbian Couples Turning to U.S. Donors," *Wall Street Journal*, March 22, 2018, https://www.wsj.com/articles/in-mixed-race-brazil-sperm-imports-from-u-s-whites-are-booming-1521711000.
50. Take, for example, "Brazil and the Negro," an article published later in 1910, written by former U.S. president Theodore Roosevelt in *The Outlook*. Roosevelt quotes a Brazilian public official in the article without naming him; the Brazilian diplomat clearly reflects the racialized mindset that was common among Brazilian elites:

> Of course the presence of the Negro is the real problem, and a very serious problem, both in your country, the United States, and in mine, Brazil. Slavery was an intolerable method of solving the problem and had to be abolished. But the problem remained, in the presence of the Negro. It was not the slave-owner who inherited his slaves who was responsible for the problem. The slave-trader who brought the slaves into the country was the man who inflicted the ghastly wrong, not only upon the blacks but upon the whites. We, like you, have merely inherited the problem . . . the pure Negro is constantly growing less and less in numbers, and after two or more crosses of the white blood the Negro blood tends to disappear, so far as the physical, mental and moral traits of the race are concerned.

Roosevelt had been concerned about U.S. race relations; he turned to Brazil (after his Amazonian exploration of the so-called River of Doubt in 1914) to look for ideas and solutions and ultimately took a positively favorable view to this Brazilian statesman's claim, which exemplified the Brazilian elite's perception of the racialized rhetoric that had emerged by that time. Roosevelt, "Brazil and the Negro," 409.

51. Lesser, *Negotiating National Identity*, 9.
52. Ralston, "Return of Brazilian Freedmen," 578.
53. Vorenberg, "Lincoln," 25.
54. Hutton, "Economic Considerations," 378.
55. Hutton, "Economic Considerations," 378.
56. Ralston, "Return of Brazilian Freedman," 583.
57. Ralston, "Return of Brazilian Freedmen," 592.
58. "The Colonization of People of African Descent (Interview with President Lincoln)," *New York Tribune*, August 15, 1862, 1. Also see Horne, *Deepest South*.
59. "Colonization of People," 1.
60. Vorenberg, "Lincoln," 23.
61. Quoted in Sampaio, "Emancipação, expulsão e exclusão," 18–19.
62. Magness and Page, *Colonization after Emancipation*, 1.
63. Livingstone, *Darwin's Forgotten Defenders*, 25.
64. Horne, *Deepest South*, 197.
65. Kidder and Fletcher, *Brazil and the Brazilians*, 580.
66. Maury, *Amazon*, 5.
67. Bell, "Relation of Herndon," 498.
68. See Sternberg, "'Manifest Destiny' and the Brazilian Amazon."
69. Hecht and Cockburn, *Fate of the Forest*, 231.
70. Maury, *Amazon*, 6.
71. Hecht and Cockburn, *Fate of the Forest*, 231–32.

72. Matthew Fontaine Maury Papers, "Letter his children, mail to Will or Corbin, Havana Arrived 9, Veracruz, Mexico, 1 March 1866, 24450," VMI Archives manuscript no. 00103, Lexington: Virginia Military Institute Archives, 1866, http://digitalcollections.vmi.edu/cdm/singleitem/collection/p15821coll6/id/5.
73. Hill, "Confederate Exodus to Latin America I," 120.
74. Matthew Fontaine Maury Papers, "Letter son-in-law S. Wellford Corbin, 24450," VMI Archives manuscript no. 00103; "Letter son-in-law S. Wellford Corbin, August 11, 1866," Lexington: Virginia Military Institute Archives, 1866, http://digitalcollections.vmi.edu/cdm/singleitem/collection/p15821coll6/id/5.
75. Majewski and Wahlstrom "Geography as Power," 344.
76. Bell, "Relation of Herndon," 503.
77. For example, Maury's *The Amazon, and the Atlantic Slopes of South America* was published four years later in 1858; followed by a scientific exploration that turned into a popular publication, *Journey in Brazil*, coauthored in 1868 by Louis Agassiz and his wife Elisabeth Cabot Agassiz.
78. Dozer, "Matthew Fontaine Maury's Letter," 212.
79. Sternberg, "'Manifest Destiny' and the Brazilian," 25.
80. Dozer, "Matthew Fontaine Maury's Letter," 226.
81. Dozer, "Matthew Fontaine Maury's Letter," 217.
82. Dozer, "Matthew Fontaine Maury's Letter," 219.
83. Along with Karl Marx, Élisée Reclus, and Frederich Ratzel, Guyot was a student of German geographer Karl Ritter (who is considered, along with Alexander von Humboldt, one of the forefathers of modern geography). For more details, see Livingstone, *Geographical Tradition*.
84. Today first-year students at the U.S. Naval Academy in Annapolis, Maryland, climb up the Herndon Monument to place a cap on top of the monument during the "plebes-no-more" ceremony, which takes place every year.
85. Sternberg, "'Manifest Destiny' and the Brazilian," 33.
86. Williams, *Dom Pedro the Magnanimous*, 261.
87. Williams, *Dom Pedro the Magnanimous*, 261.
88. Raeders, *D. Pedro II*, 28.
89. See Sousa, "A extinção dos Brasileiros," 21.
90. Skidmore, "Brazilian Intellectuals," 410.
91. See Gobineau, *Essai sur l'inégalité*.
92. Raeders, *D. Pedro II*, 13.
93. Skidmore, "Brazilian Intellectuals," 410.
94. See Raeders, *D. Pedro II*.
95. Sousa, "A extinção dos Brasileiros," 29.
96. Agassiz and Elisabeth met at the time when Agassiz had still been married to Cecile Braun, his first wife, whom he left behind in Switzerland and with whom

he had already had three children. Braun died within two years of his departure from Switzerland, and Agassiz was able to marry Elisabeth in Boston. For more details, see Irmsher, *Louis Agassiz*.

97. Wallis, "Black Bodies, White Science," 44.
98. Quoted in Livingstone, *Geographical Tradition*, 166.
99. Gould, *Mismeasure of Man*, 44.
100. Quoted in Gould, *Mismeasure of Man*, 45.
101. Irmsher, *Louis Agassiz*, 3–4.
102. For more details, see Wallis, "Black Bodies, White Science."
103. Gould, *Mismeasure of Man*, 115.
104. See Museu Imperial, Arquivo Histórico, *Documentos textuais*.
105. "Dom Pedro II. Interview of a Herald Special Correspondent with His Majesty the Emperor of Brazil," *New York Herald*, June 20, 1871, 5.
106. "Dom Pedro II."
107. Agassiz, *Journey in Brazil*, 246.
108. Nash, *Conquest of Brazil*, 51.
109. "Brazil and Southern Emigration," *Baltimore Sun*, August 6, 1866, 2. Italics are in the original.
110. See Livingstone, *Geographical Tradition*, 238.
111. See Buchholz, 125–29; Livingstone, *Geographical Tradition*, 238.
112. Freyre, *Ordem e progresso*, 363.
113. Gugliotta, "Entre trabalhadores imigrantes," 26.
114. Gugliotta, "Entre trabalhadores imigrantes," 27–29.
115. Gugliotta, "Entre trabalhadores imigrantes," 127.
116. Gugliotta, "Entre trabalhadores imigrantes," 74.
117. Gugliotta, "Entre trabalhadores imigrantes," 82.
118. Gugliotta, "Entre trabalhadores imigrantes," 128.
119. Gugliotta, "Entre trabalhadores imigrantes," 150.
120. Gugliotta, "Entre trabalhadores imigrantes," 107.
121. For more details, see Schwarcz, *O espetáculo das raças*.
122. For more details on the "whitening" of Brazil, see Skidmore, *Black into White*.
123. Schuster, "Envisioning a 'Whitened' Brazil," 20–22.
124. For more details, see Marcus, "Sex, Color, and Geography."
125. See Marcus, "Sex, Color, and Geography."
126. Gugliotta, "Entre trabalhadores imigrantes," 108.
127. Hobsbawm, *Age of Capital*, 120.
128. Livingstone, *Darwin's Forgotten Defenders*, 3.
129. Livingstone, *Darwin's Forgotten Defenders*, 27.
130. Livingstone, *Darwin's Forgotten Defenders*, 60.
131. See Livingstone, *Darwin's Forgotten Defenders*, 27. Also see Gould, *Mismeasure of Man*.

132. Gould, *Mismeasure of Man*, 22.
133. Dean, *Rio Claro*, xi.

5. PROTESTANTISM, EDUCATION, AND THE CAMPO

1. Ward, *American-Brazilian Odyssey*, 28.
2. Hamilton, "English-Speaking Travelers," 533.
3. Although traditionally Alexander von Humboldt has been closely associated with South America through his publications, he never set foot in Brazil, as he was not allowed to enter Brazilian territory. The Portuguese Crown had put a price on his head if he ever entered the country; he faced suspicions of his possible intentions on Brazilian soil, because the Spanish Empire funded him. See Marcus, "Rethinking Brazil's Place within Latin Americanist Geography," 133.
4. Kelsey, *Seven Keys to Brazil*, 111.
5. Davies, "Depictions of Brazilians," 317.
6. Moffit and Sebastian, *O Brave New People*, 206.
7. Davies, "Depictions of Brazilians," 63–64.
8. Metcalf, *Go-Betweens*, 49.
9. Believing he had arrived in the "Orient," Columbus named the inhabitants he encountered *índio* (Indian; an inhabitant from the Indian subcontinent). Other geographical terms, now calcified in geographical vernacular, include "Caribbean" (from *canibas* [cannibals]; Columbus mistook a tribe named "Canibas" of the Greater Antilles for Asian Tartars or Mongols, subjects of the Gran Khan, since he believed he had arrived in Asia rather than the Americas; from the information he had, the Canibas tribe were known cannibals—this is where the term Caribbean derives from); "Patagonia" (from *patagón* [bigfoot], meaning "giant"), and "Amazon" (from the highly sexualized mythical female warriors said to have been seen along the Amazon river during the first European explorations—however, these observations were likely of naked male Amerindians with long hair, whom European explorers had perhaps confused with mythic breastless "Amazon" women). See Moffit and Sebastian, *O Brave New People*, 117–19.
10. Moffit and Sebastian, *O Brave New People*, 146.
11. See Hecht and Cockburn, *Fate of the Forest*.
12. Such geographical imageries of Brazil that stemmed from the European gaze were not, of course, unique to Brazil. Similar patterns are observed in Orientalism, for example—imaginative geographies of patronizing European representations of the Middle East and the East, aptly articulated by Edward Said in his classic *Orientalism*.
13. Kidder and Flecther, *Brazil and the Brazilians*, 3.

14. For example, in an early U.S. government exploration document of South America on the frigate *Congress*—published as *Voyage to South America* (1817–18)—the first U.S. mission of its kind to Brazil and headed by H. M. Brackenridge (secretary to the mission), the document's description of Brazil is conspicuously minute, as the mission's exploration of Brazil had been limited to the port in Rio without exploration of the rest of the country. Throughout the document's two volumes, pages are devoted to the Spanish Empire and its colonies in South America. The historical and sociocultural treatment of Brazil in this publication was so negligible to the point that the reader would naturally assume that Brazil was part of an imagined and monolithic Spanish-speaking continent, forged exclusively by the Spanish Empire—there was no contextualization of Luso-Brazilian historicity.
15. Weaver, "Confederate Immigrants," 450.
16. *Brazilian Missions*.
17. Weaver, "Confederate Emigration to Brazil," 38.
18. Weaver, "Confederate Immigrants," 450.
19. "Maryland Institute Lecture," *Baltimore Sun*, December 12, 1856, 1.
20. Weaver, "Confederate Immigrants," 451.
21. Rosi, "James Cooley Fletcher," 73–74.
22. See Jarnagin, *Confluence of Transatlantic Networks*.
23. Gussi, *Os norte-americanos*, 90.
24. Hill, "Confederate Exiles to Brazil," 205.
25. See Ward, *American-Brazilian Odyssey*, 28.
26. For more details, see Dawsey and Oliveira, "Campo."
27. See Menchi, "Os Confederados e o ciclo," figs. 9 and 10.
28. Jones, *Folhas esparsas*, 94.
29. John H. Crisp, "Crops of Southerners in S. Paulo," *O diário do Rio de Janeiro*, July 23, 1869, 1.
30. "Robert Cicero Norris," 401.
31. Hill, "Confederate Exiles to Brazil," 169.
32. Filho, *O Rio de Janeiro Imperial*, 196.
33. Weaver, "Confederate Immigrants," 449.
34. Jarnagin, *Confluence of Transatlantic Networks*, 219.
35. Dawsey and Dawsey, "Heritage," 99.
36. Weaver, "Confederate Immigrants," 448.
37. Dawsey and Dawsey, "Heritage," 100.
38. Weaver, "Confederate Immigrants," 454.
39. Barbanti, "Escolas Americanas," 106.
40. Dawsey, "Methodists," 126–29.
41. *Ransom Family Papers*.

42. Dawsey, "Methodists," 116.
43. For example, Colégio Escola de Jaú (1887), Escola Americana de Curitiba (1892), Colégio Americano de Natal (1892), Colégio Americano de Recife (1904), Escola de Ponte Nova (1906), Colégio Metodista de Ribeirão Preto (1889), Colégio Lineiro de Juiz de Fora (1891), Colégio Americano de Petrópolis (1895), Isabel Hendrix de Belo Horizonte (1904), O Bennett, of Rio (1921), Porto Alegre College (1919), and Colégio de Friburgo (1910). See Barbanti, "Escolas Americanas," 106.
44. The first American Protestant churches founded in São Paulo emerged in the following cities and towns: São Paulo (1862), Brotas (1865), Lorena (1868), Sorocaba (1869), Campinas (1870), and, Santa Bárbara (1870). Methodist churches were established in Santa Bárbara (1871) and Piracicaba (1881), and Baptist churches were inaugurated in Santa Bárbara (1871) and São Paulo (1899). Barbanti, "Escolas Americanas," 106.
45. Ward, *American-Brazilian Odyssey*, 459.
46. Ward, *American-Brazilian Odyssey*, 77.
47. *Brazilian Missions*.
48. *Brazilian Missions*.
49. *Brazilian Missions*.
50. Ward, *American-Brazilian Odyssey*, 88.
51. Jones, *Folhas esparsas*, 95.
52. Jones, *Folhas esparsas*, 95.
53. Jones, *Folhas esparsas*, 95.
54. Jones, *Folhas esparsas*, 96.
55. Jones, *Folhas esparsas*, 97.
56. Hahner, *Emancipating the Female Sex*, 21.
57. For example, from just a casual Internet search, the following American English–speaking schools exist today throughout several states in Brazil. In São Paulo, Chapel International School, Pan American Christian Academy, Escola Americana de Campinas, Associação Graduada de São Paulo (American Graded School of São Paulo). In Rio: American School of Rio de Janeiro, Our Lady of Mercy School, ICS (International Christian School of Rio). In Minas Gerais: Escola Americana de Belo Horizonte. In Brasília: American School of Brasília, Brasília International School. In Paraná: International School of Paraná. In Rio Grande do Sul: Pan-American School of Porto Alegre, and the North American School. In Bahia: Pan-American School of Bahia. In Pernambuco: the American School of Recife. And in Pará: Amazon Valley Academy. In Amazonas: International School of Amazonas.
58. *Brazilian Missions*.
59. Recent research conducted with Brazilian immigrants in Atlanta, Georgia, has pointed to the ongoing transnational connections between Brazilian

Protestantism (particularly Pentecostalism) and its close relationships with pastors and missionaries from the U.S. South (most Brazilians were recruited by U.S. Southern pastors influenced by the new theology of prosperity and Pentecostal churches). For more details, see Marcus, "Convenient Liaisons."
60. Montgomery and Melo, "Language," 176.
61. "Confederates Who Went to Brazil," 108.
62. "Patriotism of the American Colony in Brazil," 392.
63. "Patriotism of the American Colony in Brazil," 392.
64. "Confederate in South America," 86.
65. For example, see Entrikin, "Contemporary Humanism in Geography"; Lowenthal, "Geography, Experience, and Imagination"; Tuan, *Topophilia* and "Humanistic Geography"; Wright, *Human Nature in Geography*. See also Wilkie, "'Sense of Place.'"
66. See Wright, "Terra Incognitae."
67. Cosgrove, "John Ruskin and the Geographical Imagination," 43.
68. See, for example, Marcus, "Brazilian Immigration."
69. For a discussion on race and landscapes written by geographers, see Schein, *Landscape and Race*.
70. Anderson, *Imagined Communities*, 6.
71. Ward, *American-Brazilian Odyssey*, 28.
72. Ward, *American-Brazilian Odyssey*, 28.
73. Ward, *American-Brazilian Odyssey*, 33.
74. During my visit to Campo, I saw all four gravestones of the Oliver family, located side by side.
75. Ward, *American-Brazilian Odyssey*, 32.
76. Confederados were not the first immigrants to create a Protestant cemetery in Brazil; these had existed throughout Brazil long before their arrival. The British Cemetery, for example—known as the Cemitério dos Ingleses (the English Cemetery)—was the first Protestant cemetery built in Brazil in 1809, in Gamboa, Rio. Other provinces of the empire followed suit in cities such as São Luís (1817), Recife (1819), Santos (1846), Joinville (1851), Porto Alegre (1856), and São Paulo (1858). Fajardo, "Brasil Imperial Católico," 10.
77. Fajardo, "Brasil Imperial Católico," 27. Also see Dawsey and Oliveira, "Campo."
78. Dawsey, "Constructing Identity," 157.
79. In current vernacular, immigrant communities in Brazil who hail from Europe or the United States or the British Commonwealth commonly call themselves "expats" (expatriots) but, curiously, never "immigrants."
80. See Marcus, "Transnational Rio de Janeiro."
81. I visited Campo on January 5, 2017, which turned out to be a difficult task. The first hurdle to my visit to Campo was scheduling an appointment, which took

several telephone calls. When I arrived in Santa Bárbara, I was prompted to make additional calls to make necessary arrangements at the last minute with a Confederado descendant. This descendant oversaw visits to Campo and would open the gate for me, but this person was noticeably reluctant to arrange my visit. I assume the ongoing negative press reports from foreign journalists may have precipitated suspicion. Getting to Campo alone was no easy task, either. After about a two-hour drive by car from the city of São Paulo, and after arriving at Santa Bárbara (110 miles away), Campo was another 5.5 miles on a long, rough, dusty, unpaved dirt road on the outskirts of Santa Bárbara (heading in the direction of the city of Campinas). It was an eerie ride, with random horses walking in the middle of the road and no residential houses along the way. Though I was allowed into the cemetery grounds, I was immediately interrogated sternly by the same Confederado descendant about my intentions and what I planned to do with my findings. I explained yet again that I was researching material for an academic book. I was then allowed to walk through the rows of tombstones at Campo and to take several photographs. I observed the conspicuous Freemason symbols on most of the tombstones. Nonetheless, temperatures on that hot summer day had soared to a humid ninety-five degrees Fahrenheit. Much to my surprise, my wife and I were charged for a cup of water we each drank—something I had never experienced in Brazil before. In addition, before I left Campo, this same descendant staunchly told me that as soon as I returned to the United States, I was to immediately send my report with my findings in the mail. Clearly, I was treated with great suspicion as an outsider. Nonetheless, I was grateful that in the end, I was finally able to visit Campo.
82. Dawsey, "Constructing Identity," 174.
83. Montgomery and Melo, "Language," 178.
84. Dawsey, "Community Center," 153.
85. Harter, "Postscript," 209.
86. Ward, *American-Brazilian Odyssey*, 30.
87. Ward, *American-Brazilian Odyssey*, 31.

CONCLUSION

1. See Grandin, *Fordlandia*. For new scholarship just coming out, see Brasher, "Contesting the Confederacy" and "From South of the Mason-Dixon"; Wolnisty, *Different Manifest Destiny*.
2. See Denevan and Mathewson, *Carl Sauer*.
3. Wright, "Terra Incognitae," 5.
4. Jean Marbella, "Civil War Monuments Are Gone, Not Forgotten," *Baltimore Sun*, August 16, 2018, 1.
5. Marbella, "Civil War Monuments."

6. See Marcus, "Sex, Color, and Geography," 1284.
7. A Brazilian law enacted in 1989 named Lei Caó (Lei 7.716)—after Carlos Alberto de Oliveira, *deputado* and activist of the Movimento Negro (Black Movement)—includes *injúria racial* (racial slurs; article 140 of the Penal Code); that is, it is unlawful to offend the honor of anybody in reference to race, color, ethnicity, religion, or origin. In São Paulo, for example, a police station (Delegacia de Crimes Raciais e Delitos de Intolerância) deals specifically with racial crimes and intolerance, including homophobia. See Governo do Brasil, "Cidadania e Justiça."
8. See, for example, Southern Poverty Law Center, "Groups."
9. Whitney Benns, "American Slavery, Reinvented," *Atlantic*, September 21, 2015, https://www.theatlantic.com/business/archive/2015/09/prison-labor-in-america/406177/.
10. See Marcus, "Sex, Color, and Geography."

BIBLIOGRAPHY

ARCHIVAL MATERIALS

Arquivo Público do Estado de São Paulo. Letters 1–4. Box (*Caixa*) "Acervo 1909 Imigrantes." Regional Archives of the State of São Paulo, São Paulo, Brazil.

Auburn University Libraries. "Buford, John R. Correspondence, J. M. F. Gaston (1868, June 15)." Buford, John R., correspondence RG 958, box 1, fols. 1 & 2. Special Collections and Archives, accessed 2017. Confederados Papers, Auburn University, Auburn AL. Confederados: A Digital Collection of the Auburn University Digital Library. http://content.lib.auburn.edu/cdm/compoundobject/collection/confederado/id/2619/rec/2.

Henry A. Houghton Papers, 1838, MS 467, H. Furlong Baldwin Library, Maryland Historical Society, Baltimore.

Henry A. Wise Correspondence to William H. D. Wright, 1845–46, William Henry DeCourcy Wright Papers, MS 1467, H. Furlong Baldwin Library, Maryland Historical Society, Baltimore.

Jacob and John A. Humbird Papers, 1868–1893. *Jacob Humbird, 1811–1893*. Rare Books and Special Collections, University of British Columbia Library. http://rbscarchives.library.ubc.ca/uploads/r/university-of-british-columbia-library-rare-books-and-special-collections/6/7/67391/Humbird_Family.pdf.

Library and Museum of Freemasonry. *St. John's Lodge, Rio de Janeiro: Charles Nathan*. n.d. Description: Register of Admissions, Country and Foreign "G," no. 656–765, fols. 1–312. Freemasonry Membership Registers, London, UK.

Library of Congress. "Dom Pedro II and America Dom Pedro II e os Estados Unidos." Library of Congress (website), accessed 2017. http://international.loc.gov/intldl/brhtml/br-1/br-1-5-2.html.

Maryland Freemason Lodge. Amicable St. John's Lodge. "Amicable St. John's Lodge." Freemason Lodge, Baltimore ma. Accessed June 18, 2018, https://www.asj25.org/.

Maryland State Archives. *Daniel Giraud Wright (1840–1922) MSA SC 3520–14407, Judge, Baltimore City Supreme Bench 1888–1910*. n.d. Biographical Series, Maryland State Archives, Anapolis. Accessed October 2019. http://msa.maryland.gov/megafile/msa/speccol/sc3500/sc3520/014400/014407/html/14407bio.html.

Museu Imperial, Arquivo Histórico. *Documentos textuais (DBM) PEDRO II, Imperador do Brasil, 1825–1891*. 1867. Sociedade de Amigos do Museu Imperial, Rio de Janeiro. http://200.159.250.2:10358/handle/acervo/8599.

National Archives and Records Administration. "General Services Administration 1971." 1971. Washington DC. Accessed February 2018. https://www.archives.gov/files/research/microfilm/m121.pdf.

Papers Relating to Foreign Affairs. Accompanying the Annual Message of the President to the First Session of the Thirty-Eighth Congress. Part 2, 1171–81. Washington DC, U.S. Government Printing Office, 1864. Digital Collections, University of Madison–Wisconsin Libraries. http://digital.library.wisc.edu/1711.dl/FRUS.FRUS1864p2.

Ransom Family Papers, 1833–1957. Microfilm. State of Tennessee, Department of State, Tennessee State Library Archives, Nashville. https://sos-tn-gov-files.tnsosfiles.com/forms/RANSOM_FAMILY_PAPERS_1833-1957.pdf.

Rothschild Archives. "June 2017: Brazilian Bond and Scrip, 1824." Online Archival Collection, Rothschild Archives Collection. Accessed April 2017. www.rothschildarchive.org/collections/treasure_of_the_month/june_2017_brazilian_bond_and_scrip_1824.

Southern Historical Collection. James McFadden Gaston Papers, 1852–1946. Collection Number: 01470. Louis Round Wilson Special Collections Library, University of North Carolina, Chapel Hill.

U.S. Department of State Archive. "Visits to the U.S. by Foreign Heads of State and Government, 1874–1939." Accessed March 11, 2017. https://2001-2009.state.gov/r/pa/ho/34912.htm.

William Decourcy Thom. MS 2416, box 15. Genealogical notes, Barclay Family. Wright-May-Thom Family Papers, n.d., H. Furlong Baldwin Library, Maryland Historical Society, Baltimore.

William Henry DeCourcy Wright. Consular documents, MS 2416, box 4. Wright-May-Thom Family Papers, 1825–34. H. Furlong Baldwin Library, Maryland Historical Society, Baltimore.

———. MS 2416, box 3. Incoming Letters, Wright-May-Thom Family Papers, 1846–49. H. Furlong Baldwin Library, Maryland Historical Society, Baltimore.

———. MS 2416, letterbook, box 1. Wright-May-Thom Family Papers, 1829–33. H. Furlong Baldwin Library, Maryland Historical Society, Baltimore.

William Milnor Roberts Papers. Archives West series 1: Biographical Material, 1857–1923, box 1, folder 1, autobiography 1859. Special Collections and Archives, Montana State University. https://www.lib.montana.edu/archives/about/index.html.

PUBLISHED WORKS

Agassiz, Louis, and Elisabeth Cabot Agassiz. *Journey in Brazil*. Boston: Tickner and Fields, 1868.
Aguiar, Letícia. "Imigrantes norte-americanos em Santa Bárbara d'Oeste, 1866–1920." Curso de Ciências Econômicas. Monografia. UNESP, Faculdade de Ciências e Letras, Campus Araraquara, Universidade Estadual Paulista, São Paulo, 2004.
Alden, Dauril. "Late Colonial Brazil, 1750–1808." In Bethell, *Colonial Brazil*, 284–343.
Alencastro, Luiz Felipe, and Maria Luiza Renaux. *Caras e modos dos migrantes e imigrantes*. In *História da vida privada no Brasil. Império: A corte e a modernidade nacional*, edited by Fernando Novais, 2:291–336. São Paulo: Schwarcz, 1997.
Almanak Administrativo, Mercantil e Industrial do Rio de Janeiro. "Commercio." *Almanak administrativo, mercantil e industrial do Rio de Janeiro* 6, no. 1 (January 1849): 34.
Anderson, Benedict. *Imagined Communities. Reflections on the Origin and Spread of Nationalism*. 1983. Rev. ed. London and New York: Verso, 2006.
Andrews, George Reid. *Afro-Latin America, 1800–2000*. New York: Oxford University Press. 2004.
———. "Slavery and Race Relations in Brazil." The Brazilian Curriculum Guide Specialized Bibliography, Series 2. Albuquerque: Latin American Institute, University of New Mexico Press, 1997.
Andrews, Thomas F. "The Ambitions of Lansford W. Hastings: A Study in Western Myth-Making." *Pacific Historical Review* 39, no. 4 (1970): 473–91.
Baker, John M. *A View of the Commerce between the United States and Rio de Janeiro, Brazil*. Washington DC: U.S. Office of Democratic Review, 1838.
Barbanti, Maria Lúcia Spedo Heldsdorf. "Escolas Americanas de confissão Protestante na provincia de São Paulo: Um estudo de suas origens." Master's thesis, Universidade de São Paulo, 1977.
Beirne, Francis F. *The Amiable Baltimoreans*. Baltimore MA: Johns Hopkins University Press, 1951.
Bell, Whitfield J. "The Relation of Herndon and Gibbon's Exploration of the Amazon to North American Slavery, 1850–1855." *Hispanic American Historical Review* 19, no. 4 (November 1939): 494–503.
Bethell, Leslie. *Brazil: Empire and Republic, 1822–1930*. Cambridge MA: Cambridge University Press, 1989.
———, ed. *Colonial Brazil*. 1984. Reprint, Cambridge MA: Cambridge University Press, 1991.
———. "The Decline and Fall of Slavery in Nineteenth Century Brazil." *Transactions of the Royal Historical Society* 1 (1991): 71–88.

Blauner, Bob. *Still the Big News: Racial Oppression in America*. Philadelphia PA: Temple University Press, 2001.

Boxer, C. R. *The Golden Age of Brazil, 1695–1750*. 1962. Reprint, Berkeley: University of California, 1973.

Brannon, Peter A. "Southern Emigration to Brazil." Edited by Peter A. Brannon. *Alabama Historical Quarterly* 1 (Winter 1930): 79–94, 280–305, 467–88.

Brannstrom, Christian. "Forests for Cotton: Institutions and Organizations in Brazil's Mid-Twentieth-Century Cotton Boom." *Journal of Historical Geography* 36, no. 2 (2010): 169–82.

Brasher, Jordan Paul. "Contesting the Confederacy: Mobile Memory and the Making of Black Geographies in Brazil." Focus on Geography (website). 2019. http://www.focusongeography.org/publications/articles/brazil_confederacy/index.html.

———. "From South of the Mason-Dixon Line to South of the Equator: A Critical Exploration of the Transnational Contours of Confederate Memory." PhD diss., University of Tennessee-Knoxville Knoxville Tennessee, May 2020.

Brazilian Missions: *A Monthly Bulletin of Missionary Intelligence* 4, no. 2 (1891): 10–13.

Brown, Jack Crosby. *A Hundred Years of Merchant Banking*. New York: Printed by the author, 1909.

Buchholz, Heinrich Ewald. *Governors of Maryland: From the Revolution to the Year 1908*. Baltimore MA: Williams and Wilkins, 1908.

Bureau of the American Republics. *Brazil*. Bulletin 7. Washington DC: Bureau of the American Republics, June 1891.

Burns, E. Bradford. *A History of Brazil*. 3rd ed. New York: Columbia University Press, 1993.

Burton, Richard F. *Explorations of the Highlands of Brazil*. London: Tinsley Brothers. 1869.

Buttimer, Anne. "Grasping the Dynamism of Lifeworld." *Annals of the Association of American Geographers* 66, no. 2 (1976): 277–92.

Campbell, Will D. *Providence*. Waco TX: Baylor University Press, 2002.

Cândido, Guilherme. "O rito de York no Brasil, Blue Lodges." Pavimento Mosaico (website). January 25, 2016. https://pavimentomosaico.wordpress.com/2016/01/25/o-rito-de-york-no-brasil-blue-lodges.

Castles, Stephen, and Mark J. Miller. *The Age of Migration*. New York: Guildford Press, 2003.

"Capt. William Francis Shippey." *Confederate Veteran* 9, no. 6 (1901): 268.

Comissão Brasileira na Exposição Universal de Philadelphia, Centennial Exhibition. *The Empire of Brazil at the Universal Exhibition of 1876 in Philadelphia*. Rio de Janeiro: Typ. e Lithographia do Imperial Instituto Artístico, 1876.

"A Confederate in South America." *Confederate Veteran* 29, no. 3 (1921): 86.

"Confederates Who Went to Brazil." *Confederate Veteran* 19, no. 1 (1911): 108.

Conniff, Michael L. Foreword to Dawsey and Dawsey, *Confederados*, xi–xiii.

Conrad, Robert. "The Contraband Slave Trade to Brazil, 1831–1845." *Hispanic American Historical Review* 49, no. 4 (1969): 617–38.

Conselho de Imigração e Colonização, Ministério das Relações Exteriores. "Imigração Norte-Americana para o Brasil." *Revista de imigração e colonização*, edição 2, ano 4, 264–333. Rio de Janeiro, BR: Imprensa Nacional, 1943.Cosgrove, Denis E. "John Ruskin and the Geographical Imagination." *Geographical Review* 69, no. 1 (1979): 43–62.

Cresswell, Tim. *In Place/Out of Place. Geography, Ideology, and Transgression.* Minneapolis: University of Minnesota Press, 1996.

———. *Place: A Short Introduction.* Malden: Blackwell, 2004.

Cwerner, Saulo B. "The Times of Migration." *Journal of Migration Studies* 27, no. 1 (2001): 7–36.

Davies, Surehka. "Depictions of Brazilians on French Maps, 1542–1555." *Historical Journal* 55, no. 2 (2012): 317–48.

Dawsey, Cyrus B. "A Community Center." In Dawsey and Dawsey, *Confederados*, 138–54.

Dawsey, Cyrus B., and Betty Antunes de Oliveira. "Campo: A North American Cemitery in Brazil." *Tap Roots. The Genealogical Society of East Alabama, Inc.* 36, no. 3 (1999).

Dawsey, Cyrus B., and James M. Dawsey. "Conclusions." In Dawsey and Dawsey, *Confederados*, 191–205.

———. "Introduction." In Dawsey and Dawsey, *Confederados*, 1–10.

———. "Leaving." In Dawsey and Dawsey, *Confederados*, 11–23.

———, eds. *The Confederados: Old South Immigrants in Brazil.* Tuscaloosa: University of Alabama Press, 1995.

Dawsey, James M. "Constructing Identity." In Dawsey and Dawsey, *Confederados*, 155–75. Tuscaloosa: University of Alabama Press, 1995.

———. "The Methodists." In Dawsey and Dawsey, *Confederados*, 116–37.

Dawsey, James M., and Cyrus B. Dawsey. "The Heritage." In Dawsey and Dawsey, *Confederados*, 84–104.

Dawsey, John Cowart. "O espelho Americano: Americanos para Brasileiro ver e Brazilians for Americans to see." *Revista de antropología* 37 (1994): 203–56.

Dean, Warren. "The Empire of Brazil." *Debow's Review.* January 1858, 1–27.

———. "Latifundia and Land Policy in Nineteenth-Century Brazil." *Hispanic American Historical Review* 51, no. 4 (1971): 606–25.

———. *Rio Claro. A Brazilian Plantation System, 1820–1920.* Stanford CA: Stanford University Press. 1976.

———. "Shall Southerners Emigrate to Brazil?." *Debow's Review.* July 1866, 30–38.

Degler, Carl N. *Neither Black nor White: Slavery and Race Relations in Brazil and the United States.* New York: Macmillan, 1971.

Denevan, William H., and Kent Mathewson, eds. *Carl Sauer on Culture and Landscape: Readings and Commentaries.* Baton Rouge: Louisiana State University Press, 2009.

Dozer, Donald Marquand. "Matthew Fontaine Maury's Letter of Instruction to William Lewis Herndon." *Hispanic American Historical Review* 28, no. 2 (1948): 212–28.

Dunn, Reverend Ballard S. *Brazil, the Home for Southerners. Or a Practical Account of What the Author, and Others, Who Visited That Country, for the Same Objects, Saw and Did while in That Empire.* New Orleans: Bloomfield and Steel, 1866.

Elliott, L. E. *Brazil Today and Tomorrow.* 1917. Rev. ed. New York: MacMillan. 1922.

Emory, Mary Bourke. *Colonial Families and Their Descendants.* Baltimore MA: Press of the Sun Printing Office, 1900.

Entrikin, J. Nicholas. "Contemporary Humanism in Geography." *Annals of the Association of American Geographers* 66, no. 4 (1976): 615–32.

Fajardo, Alexander. "Brasil imperial Católico e o surgimento dos cemitérios Protestantes." *Integratio* 1, no. 1 (2015): 5–17.

Ferguson, Sarah Bellona Smith. "The Journey. The Sarah Bellona Smith Ferguson Narrative." In Dawsey and Dawsey, *Confederados*, 24–49.

Filho, Adolfo Morales de los Rios. *O Rio de Janeiro Imperial.* Rio de Janeiro: Topbook Editora, 2000.

Fleming, Victor. *Gone with the Wind.* Film. Directed by Victor Fleming. Los Angeles: Metro-Goldwyn Meyer, 1939.

Flynt, Wayne. "The Baptists." In Dawsey and Dawsey, *Confederados*, 105–15.

Forman, Shepard. *The Brazilian Peasantry.* New York: Columbia University Press, 1975.

Fragoso, João Luís Ribeiro. "A roça e as propostas de modernização na agricultura Fluminense do século xix: O caso do sistema agrário escravista-exportador em Paraíba do Sul." *Revista Brasileira de história, São Paulo* 6, no. 12 (1986): 140–41.

Freyre, Gilberto. *The Masters and The Slaves: A Study in the Development of Brazilian Civilization.* Translated by Samuel Putnam. 1933. 2nd English language rev. ed. Berkeley: University of California Press, 1986.

———. *Ordem e progresso.* São Paulo: Global Editora e Distribuidora, 2004.

———. "Social Life in Brazil in the Middle of the Nineteenth Century." *Hispanic American Historical Review* 5, no. 4 (1922): 597–630.

Gaddis, John Lewis. *The Landscape of History: How Historians Map the Past.* New York: Oxford University Press, 2002.

Gaston, James McFadden. *Hunting a Home in Brazil: The Agricultural Resources and Other Characteristics of the Country; Also, the Manners and Customs of the Inhabitants.* Philadelphia PA: King & Baird, 1867.

General Commission on Archives and History. *Timeline of United Methodist History, 1703–1996.* Madison NJ: General Commission on Archives and History, 1996.

Gobineau, Arthur de. *Essai sur l'inégalité des races humaines.* Paris: Libraire de Firmin Didot Fréres, 1853.

Gould, Stephen Jay. *The Mismeasure of Man.* New York: Norton, 1981.

Governo do Brasil. Secretaria da Justiça, Trabalho e Direitos Humanos. "Promoção da Igualdade Racial." Governo do Brasil (website). Accessed August 15, 2018. http://www.dedihc.pr.gov.br/modules/conteudo/conteudo.php?conteudo=96.

Graham, Richard. "Slavery and Economic Development: Brazil and the United States South in the Nineteenth Century." *Comparative Studies in Society and History* 23, no. 4 (1981): 620–55.

Grandin, Greg. *Fordlandia*. New York: Picador, 2009.

Gravois, James M., and Elizabeth J. Weisbrod. "Annotated Bibliography." In Dawsey and Dawsey, *Confederados*, 247–65.

Griggs, William C. *The Elusive Eden. Frank McMullan's Confederate Colony in Brazil*. Austin: University of Texas Press, 1987.

———. "Settling." In Dawsey and Dawsey, *Confederados*, 50–65.

Gugliotta, Alexandre Carlos. "Entre trabalhadores imigrantes e nacionais: Tavares Bastos e seus projetos para a nação." Têse de mestrado submetida ao programa de Pós-Graduação em Historia Social, Instituto de Ciencias Humanas e Filosofia, Universidade Federal Fluminense, Niterói, Rio de Janeiro, 2007.

Gussi, Alcides Fernando. *Os norte-americanos (Confederados) do Brasil. Identidades no contexto transnacional*. Campinas, BR: Universidade Estadual de Campinas, Unicamp, 1997.

Hahner, June Edith. *Emancipating the Female Sex: The Struggle for Women's Rights in Brazil, 1850–1940*. Durham NC: Duke University Press, 1990.

Hale, Grace Elizabeth. *Making Whiteness. The Culture of Segregation in the South, 1890–1940*. New York: Vintage Books, 1998.

Hamilton, Charles Granville. "English-Speaking Travelers in Brazil, 1851–1887." *Hispanic American Historical Review* 40, no. 4 (1960): 533–47.

Harmon, George D. "Confederate Migration to Mexico." *Hispanic American Historical Review* 17, no. 4 (1937): 458–87.

Harter, Eugene C. *The Lost Colony of the Confederacy*. 1985. Reprint, College Station: Texas A&M University, 2000.

———. "Postscript." In Dawsey and Dawsey, *Confederados*, 206–10.

Hecht, Susanna B., and Alexander Cockburn. *The Fate of the Forest: Developers, Destroyers, and Defenders of the Amazon*. London: Verso, 1989.

Hemming, John. *Red Gold: The Conquest of the Brazilian Indians*. Cambridge MA: Harvard University, 1987.

Herndon, William Lewis, and Lardner Gibbons. *Exploration of the Valley of the Amazon*. 2 vols. Washington DC: Robert Armstrong, 1854.

Hill, Lawrence F. "Confederate Exiles to Brazil." *Hispanic American Historical Review* 7, no. 2 (1927): 192–210.

———. "The Confederate Exodus to Latin America I." *Southwestern Historical Quarterly* 39, no. 2 (1935): 100–134.

———. "The Confederate Exodus to Latin America II." *Southwestern Historical Quarterly* 39, no. 3 (1936): 161–99.

———. "The Confederate Exodus to Latin America III." *Southwestern Historical Quarterly* 39, no. 4 (1936): 309–26.

Hobsbawm, Eric. *The Age of Capital, 1848–1875.* 1975. Reprint, New York: Vintage Books. 1996.

Ho, Enseng. *The Graves of Tarim: Genealogy and Mobility Across the Indian Ocean.* Berkeley: University of California Press, 2006.

Hopperstad, Shari Estill. *Confederate Exiles in Brazil.* Master's thesis, Montana State University, 1963.

Horne, Gerald. *The Deepest South: The United States, Brazil, and the African Slave Trade.* New York: New York University Press, 2007.

Howard, George W. *The Monumental City, Its Past History and Present Resources.* Baltimore MA: J. D. Ehlers, 1873.

Hunt's Merchants' Magazine and Commercial Review. Vol. 41. New York: Geo. W. & Jno. A. Wood, Freeman Hunt, 1859.

Hutton, Frankie. "Economic Considerations in the American Colonization Society's Early Effort to Emigrate Free Blacks to Liberia, 1816–36." *Journal of Negro History* 68 no. 4 (1983): 376–89.

IBGE (Instituto Brasileiro de Geografia e Estatística). "Iguape." https://cidades.ibge.gov.br/brasil/sp/iguape/panorama.

———. *Populational Statistics and Total Immigration—Annual Periods.* "Estatísticas de Povoamento." Rio de Janeiro: Instituto Brasileiro de Geografia e Estatística, 225. https://brasil500anos.ibge.gov.br/estatisticas-do-povoamento/imigracao-total-periodos-anuais.html.

Irmsher, Christoph. *Louis Agassiz: Creator of American Science.* Boston: Houghton Mifflin Harcourt, 2013.

Jarnagin, Laura. *A Confluence of Transatlantic Networks: Elites, Capitalism, and Confederate Migration to Brazil.* Tuscaloosa: University of Alabama Press, 2008.

———. "Fitting In." In Dawsey and Dawsey, *Confederados,* 66–83.

Jefferson, Mark. "An American Colony in Brazil." *Geographical Review* 18, no. 2 (1928): 26–231.

Jeha, Silvana Cassab. "Anphiteatrical Rio! Maritimos Americanos na baía do Rio de Janeiro; Seculo XIX." *Almanack* 6, no. 2 (2013): 110–32.

Johnson, H. B. "Portuguese Settlement, 1500–1580." In Bethell, *Colonial Brazil,* 1–38.

Jones, Judith MacKnight. *Folhas esparsas.* Sao Paulo: Editora Scortecci, 1996.

———. *Soldado, descansa! Uma epopéia Norte Americana sob os céus do Brasil.* São Paulo: Jarde, 1967.

Kelsey, Vera. *Seven Keys to Brazil.* New York: Funk and Wagnalls, 1941.

Kendi, Ibram X. *Stamped from the Beginning: The Definitive History of Racist Ideas in America*. New York: Nation Books, 2016.

Kent, R. K. "Revolt in Bahia: 24–25, January 1835." *Journal of Social History* 3, no. 4 (1970): 334–56.

Keyes, Julia L. "Our Life in Brazil." Edited by Peter A. Brannon. *Alabama Historical Quarterly*. 28, nos. 3/4 (1966): 127–37.

Kidder, Rev. Daniel P. *Sketches of Residence and Travels of Brazil. Embracing Historical and Geographical Notices of the Empire and Its Several Provinces*. Philadelphia PA: Sorin & Ball, 1845.

Kidder, Daniel P., and James C. Fletcher. *Brazil and the Brazilians: Portrayed in Historical and Descriptive Sketches*. Philadelphia PA: Childs & Peterson, 1857.

Koster, Henry. *Travels in Brazil*. London: Longman, Hurst, Rees, Orme, and Brown, 1816.

Leff, Nathaniel. "Economic Retardation in Nineteenth-Century Brazil," *Economic History Review* 25, no. 3 (1972): 489–507.

Lesser, Jeffrey. *Negotiating National Identity: Immigrants, Minorities, and the Struggle for Ethnicity in Brazil*. Durham NC: Duke University Press, 1999.

Levy, Maria Stella Ferreira. "O papel da migração internacional na evolução da população Brasileira (1872 a 1972)." *Revista de saúde pública, São Paulo* 8 (1974): 49–90.

Livingstone, David N. *Darwin's Forgotten Defenders*. Vancouver, CA: Regent College Publishing, 1984.

———. *The Geographical Tradition: Episodes in the History of a Contested Enterprise*. Malden: Blackwell, 1992.

Lowe, John. "Reconstruction Revisited: Plantation School Writers, Postcolonial Theory, and Confederates in Brazil." *Mississippi Quarterly* 51, no. 1 (2003): 5–26.

Lowenthal, David. "Geography, Experience, and Imagination: Towards a Geographical Epistemology." *Annals of the Association of American Geographers* 51, no. 3 (1961): 241–60.

Magness, Phillip W., and Sebastian N. Page. *Colonization after Emancipation: Lincoln and the Movement for Black Resentment*. Columbia: University of Missouri Press, 2011.

Majewski, John, and Todd W. Wahlstrom. "Geography as Power: The Political Economy of Matthew Fontaine Maury." *Virginia Magazine of History and Biography* 120, no. 4 (2012): 340–71.

Marcus, Alan P. "Brazilian Immigration to the United States and the Geographical Imagination." *Geographical Review* 99, no. 4 (2009): 481–98.

———. "Convenient Liaisons: Brazilian Immigration/Emigration and the Spatial-Relationships of Religious Networks." *Space, Populations, Societies* 2, no. 3 (2015): 2–13.

———. *Navigating Autobiographies: Transnational Geographers in the United States*. Lantham MD: Lexington Books, 2016.

———. "(Re)Creating Places and Spaces in Two Countries: Brazilian Transnational Migration Processes." *Journal of Cultural Geography* 26, no. 2 (2009): 173–98.
———. "Rethinking Brazil's place within Latin Americanist Geography." *Journal of Latin American Geography* 10, no. 1 (2011): 131–49.
———. "Sex, Color, and Geography: Racialized Relations in Brazil and its Predicaments." *Annals of the Association of American Geographers* 103, no. 5 (2013): 1282–99.
———. *Towards Rethinking Brazil: A Thematic and Regional Approach.* New Jersey: John Wiley & Sons, 2011.
———. "Transnational Rio de Janeiro: (Re)Visiting Geographical Experiences." In *Growing Up Transnational: Identity and Kinship in a Global Era,* edited by May Friedman and Silvia Schultermandl, 21–35. Toronto, CA: University of Toronto Press, 2011.
Margolis, Maxine L. *The Moving Frontier: Social and Economic Change in a Southern Brazilian Community.* Gainesville: University of Florida Press, 1973.
Martin, Percy Alvin. "The Influence of the United States on the Opening of the Amazon to the World's Commerce." *Hispanic American Historical Review* 1, no. 2 (1918): 146–62.
Mattosso, Katia M. de Queirós. *To Be a Slave in Brazil 1550–1888.* Translated by Arthur Goldhammer. New Jersey: Rutgers University Press, 1986.
Mauro, Frédéric. "Political and Economic Structures of Empire, 1580–1750." In Bethell, *Colonial Brazil,* 39–66.
Maury, Matthew Fontaine. *The Amazon, and the Atlantic Slopes of South America. A Series of Letters Published in the National Intelligencer and Union Newspapers, under the Signature of Inca.* Washington DC: Franck Taylor, 1858.
Maxwell, Wright & Co. *Commercial Formalities.* Baltimore MA: Sherwood, 1842.
McCreery, David. *Frontier Goiás, 1822–1889.* Stanford CA: Stanford University Press, 2006.
Meade, Teresa, and Gregory Alonso Pirio. "In Search of the Afro-American 'Eldorado': Attempts by North American Blacks to Enter Brazil in the 1920s." *Luso-Brazilian Review* 25, no. 1 (1998): 85–110.
Medeiros, Regina Del Negri. "American Brazilian English." *American Speech* 57, no. 2 (1982): 150–52.
Menchi, Helena Quintana. "Os Confederados e o ciclo econômico do café: Interação e integração Americana no interior de São Paulo." Faculdade de Arquitetura e Urbanismo, Curso de Pos-Graduação, Universidade de São Paulo, Brazil, 2008.
Merchants and Manufacturers Association, Baltimore, Maryland. *A reciprocidade commercial: Baltimore e Brazil; Um compendio de informações úteis relativas aos interesses mútuos da República do Brazil e da cidade de Baltimore, Estados Unidos da America.* Baltimore MA: A. Hoen, 1891.
Metcalf, Alida C. *Go-Betweens and the Colonization of Brazil, 1500–1600.* Austin: University of Texas Press, 2005.
Mitchell, S. A. "Matthew Fontaine Maury." *Science, New Series* 73, no. 1902 (1931): 632–34.

Moffit, John, and Santiago Sebastian. *O Brave New People: The European Invention of the American Indian*. Albuquerque: University of New Mexico Press, 1996.

Montgomery, Michael B., and Cecil Ataide Melo. "The Language." In Dawsey and Dawsey, *Confederados*, 176–90.

Murray, Edmundo. "William Scully (d. 1885) Irish Journalist and Businessman in Rio de Janeiro." *Irish Migration Studies in Latin America* 4, no. 3 (2006): 175–76.

Nascimento, Abdias do. *O genocídio do Negro Brasileiro: Processo de racismo mascarado*. Rio de Janeiro: Paz e Terra, 1978.

Nash, Roy. *The Conquest of Brazil*. 1926. Reprint, New York: AMS Press, 1969.

Nathan, Carlos. *Exposição que faz o contador público ao commercio do Rio de Janeiro*. Rio de Janeiro: Typographia Indústria Nacional de Cotrim e Campos, 1864.

Neeley, Mary Ann, ed. *The Works of Matthew Blue, Montgomery's First Historian*. Montgomery AL: New South Books, 2010.

Nobles, Melissa. *Shades of Citizenship: Race and the Census in Modern Politics*. Stanford CA: Stanford University Press, 2000.

Oliveira, Lucia Lippi. *O Brasil dos imigrantes*. Rio de Janeiro: Jorge Zahar Editor Ltda, 2001.

Olson, Sherry H. *Baltimore. The Building of an American City*. 1980. Rev. and exp. bicentennial ed. Baltimore MA: Johns Hopkins University Press, 1997.

Padoveze, João Leopoldo F. *Boletim*. Fraternidade Descendência Americana. Accessed August 10, 2018. http://fdasbo.org.br/site/noticias/page/2/.

Pang, Laura Jarnagin. "The State and Agricultural Clubs of Imperial Brazil, 1860–1889." PhD diss., Vanderbilt University, 1981.

Park, Charles E. "The Development of the Clipper Ship." Worcester MA: American Antiquarian Society, 1929. https://www.americanantiquarian.org/proceedings/44806834.pdf.

"Patriotism of the American Colony in Brazil." *Confederate Veteran* 25, no. 9 (1917): 392.

Pearson, Samantha. "Demand for American Sperm Is Skyrocketing in Brazil: Explosive Growth Spurred by More Wealthy Single Women and Lesbian Couples Turning to U.S. Donors." *Wall Street Journal*, March 22, 2018. https://www.wsj.com/articles/in-mixed-race-brazil-sperm-imports-from-u-s-whites-are-booming-1521711000.

Perkins, Edwin J. "Financing Antebellum Importers: The Role of Brown Bros. & Co. in Baltimore." *Business History Review* 15, no. 4 (1971): 421–51.

Phipps & Co. *Cypher Code Compiled by Messrs. Phipps & Co. for Their Own Use and for the Use of Messrs. J. L. Phipps & Co. of New York Liverpool Phipps & Co.* Liverpool: Phipps, 1880.

Pommeranz, Kenneth, and Steven Topik. *The World That Trade Created: Society, Culture, and the World Economy, 1400 to the Present*. Armonk NY: M. E. Sharpe, 1999.

Prefeitura de Linhares. "A Cidade. História, Linhares: Government of Espirito Santo." Prefeitura de Linhares (website). http://www.linhares.es.gov.br/historia/.

Priori, Mary Del. *Histórias da gente Brasileira. colônia.* Vol. 1. São Paulo: LeYa Editora, 2016.
Raeders, Georges. *D. Pedro II e o Conde de Gobineau (correspondências inéditas).* Vol. 109. São Paulo: Companhia Editôra Nacional, 1938.
Ralston, Richard D. "The Return of Brazilian Freedmen to West Africa in the 18th and 19th Centuries." *Canadian Journal of African Studies* 3, no. 3 (1969): 577–93.
Ravenstein, Ernest G. "The Laws of Migration." *Journal of the Royal Statistical Society* 48, no. 2 (1885): 167–227.
Reclus, Élisée. *The Earth and Its Inhabitants: South America. Amazonia and La Plata.* Vol. 2, edited by A. H. Keane. New York: D. Appleton, 1893.
Ribeiro, Alan dos Santos. "The Leading Commission-House of Rio de Janeiro. A firma Maxwell, Wright & Co. no comércio do império do Brasil (c.1827–c.1850)." PhD diss., Universidade Federal Fluminense, Niterói. 2014.
Ribeiro, Felipe Landim Mendes. "Ibicaba revisitada outra vez: Espaço, escravidão e trabalho livre no Oeste Paulista." *Anais do Museu Paulista* 25, no. 1 (2017): 301–57.
Ridings, Eugene W. "Class Sector Unity in an Export Economy: The Case of Nineteenth-Century Brazil." *American Historical Review* 58, no. 3 (1978): 432–50.
———. "Interest Groups and Development: The Case of Brazil in the Nineteenth Century." *Journal of Latin American Studies* 9, no. 2 (1977): 225–50.
Rios, José Artur. "Assimilation of Emigrants from the Old South in Brazil." *Social Forces* 26, no. 2 (1947): 145–52.
Rizzolli, Simone. *A imigração Norte-Americana na cidade de Americana e região e suas influências sócio-culturais e linguísticas.* Monografia, São Paulo: Centro Universitário Adventista de São Paulo, Faculdade Adventista de Educação, 2002.
"Robert Cicero Norris." *Confederate Veteran* 21, no. 8 (1913): 401.
Rood, Daniel. "Bogs of Death: Slavery, the Brazilian Flour Trade, and the Mystery of the Vanishing Millpond in Antebellum Virginia." *Journal of American History* 101, no. 1 (2014): 19–43.
———. *The Reinvention of Atlantic Slavery: Technology, Labor, Race, and Capitalism in the Greater Caribbean.* New York: Oxford University Press, 2017.
Roosevelt, Theodore. "Brazil and the Negro." *Outlook* 106 (1914): 409–11.
Rosi, Bruno Gonçalves. "James Cooley Fletcher, o missionário amigo do Brasil." *Almanack* (Universidade Federal de São Paulo) 5, no. 1 (2013): 62–80.
Russell-Wood, A. J. R. "The Gold Cycle circa 1690–1750." In Bethell, *Colonial Brazil,* 190–243.
Rutter, Frank R. *South American Trade of Baltimore.* Edited by Herbert B. Adams. Baltimore MA: Johns Hopkins University Press, 1897.
Saba, Roberto. "American Mirror: The United States and the Empire of Brazil in the Age of Emancipation." PhD diss., University of Pennsylvania, 2017.

Sampaio, Maria Clara Sales Carneiro. "Emancipação, expulsão e exclusão: Visões do Negro no Brasil e nos Estados Unidos nos anos 1860." *Revista de história da África e de Estados da diáspora Africana* 2, no. 3 (2009): 7–30.

Sansone, Livio. *Blackness without Ethnicity. Constructing Race in Brazil.* New York: Palgrave MacMillan, 2003.

Sauer, Carl O. "The Morphology of Landscape." *University of California Publications in Geography* 2, no. 2 (1925): 19–53.

Scharf, Col. J. Thomas. *The Chronicles of Baltimore. Being a Complete History of "Baltimore Town" and Baltimore City from the Last Period to the Present Time.* Baltimore MA: Turnbull Brothers, 1874.

Schein, Richard H., ed. *Landscape and Race in the United States.* New York: Routledge, 2006.

Scheper-Hughes, Nancy. *Death without Weeping: The Violence of Everyday Life in Brazil.* Berkeley: University of California Press, 1994.

Schiller, Nina Glick, Linda Basch, and Cristina Szanton Blanc. "From Immigrant to Transmigrant: Theorizing Transnational Migration." *Anthropological Quarterly* 68, no. 1 (1995): 48–63.

Schley, David. "A Natural History of the Early American Railroad." *Early American Studies* 13, no. 2 (2015): 443–66.

Schuster, Sven. "Envisioning a 'Whitened' Brazil: Photography and Slavery at the World's Fairs, 1862–1889." *Estudios interdisciplinarios de America Latina y el Caribe* 26, no. 2 (2015): 17–41.

Schwarcz, Lilia Moritz. *As barbas do imperador: D. Pedro II, um monarca nos trópicos.* São Paulo: Companhia das Letras, 1998.

———. *O espetáculo das raças: cientistas, instituições e a questão racial no Brasil, 1870–1930.* São Paulo: Companhia das Letras, 1993.

Schwartz, Stuart B. "Plantations and Peripheries, c. 1580–c. 1710." In Bethell, *Colonial Brazil,* 67–140.

———. *Slaves, Peasants, and Rebels: Reconsidering Brazilian Slavery.* Chicago: University of Illinois Press. 1992.

Shalhope, Robert E. "Race, Class, Slavery, and the Antebellum Southern Mind." *Journal of Southern History* 37, no. 4 (1971): 557–74.

Sharrer, G. Terry. "Flour Milling in the Growth of Baltimore, 1750–1830." *Maryland Historical Magazine* 71, no. 3 (1976): 332–34.

———. "The Merchant-Millers: Baltimore's Flour Milling Industry, 1783–1860." *Agricultural History, Symposium on the History of Agricultural Trade and Marketing* 56, no. 1 (1982): 132–50.

Sheriff, Robin E. *Dreaming Equality: Color, Race, and Racism in Urban Brazil.* New Jersey: Rutgers University Press, 2001.

Silva, Andrée Mansuy-Diniz. "Imperial Re-Organization, 1750–1808." In Bethell, *Colonial Brazil*, 244–83.

Silva, Antonio Gutemberg da. "Entre a Cruz e a Estrela de Davi: Problematizando as identidades Judaicas no Brasil Imperial." Thesis, Programa de Pós-Graduacao em História, Centro de Humanidades, Unidade Acadêmica de História e Geografia, Campina Grande. Paraíba: Universidade Federal de Campina Grande, 2013.

Silva, Célio Antonio Alcantara. "Confederates and Yankees under the Southern Cross." *Bulletin of Latin American Research* 14, no. 3 (2014): 370–84.

Simmons, Charles Willis. "Racist Americans in a Multi-Racial Society: Confederate Exiles in Brazil." *Journal of Negro History* 67, no. 1 (1982): 34–39.

Skidmore, Thomas E. *Black into White: Race and Nationality in Brazilian Thought.* Oxford, UK: Oxford University Press, 1974.

———. *Brazil: Five Centuries of Change.* New York: Oxford University Press, 1999.

———. "Brazilian Intellectuals and the Problem of Race, 1870–1930." Occasional Paper 6. Graduate Center for Latin American Studies, Vanderbilt University, Nashville TN, 1969.

Smith, Geoffrey Sutton. "The Navy before Darwinism: Science, Exploration, and Diplomacy in Antebellum America." *American Quarterly* 28, no. 1 (1976): 41–55.

Smith, T. Lynn. *Brazil. People and Institutions.* 4th ed. Baton Rouge: Louisiana State University Press, 1972.

Sodré, Nelson Werneck. *História da imprensa do Brasil.* 4th ed. Rio de Janeiro: MAUAD Editora Ltda., 1999.

Sousa, Ricardo Alexandre Santos de. "A extinção dos Brasileiros Segundo conde Gobineau." *Revista Brasileira de história da ciência* 6, no. 1 (2013): 21–34.

Southern Poverty Law Center. "Groups Southern Poverty Law Center" (website). Accessed August 10, 2018. https://www.splcenter.org/fighting-hate/extremist-files/groups.

Southey, Robert. *History of Brazil.* Vol. 1. 1822. Reprint, New York: Lenox Hill Push & Dist. (Burt Franklin), 1970.

Stein, Stanley J. *Vassouras, a Brazilian Coffee County, 1850–1900: The Roles of Planter and Slave in a Plantation Society.* 1958. Reprint, Princeton NJ: Princeton University Press, 1985.

Sternberg, Hilgard O'Reilly. "'Manifest Destiny' and the Brazilian Amazon: A Backdrop to Contemporary Security and Development Issues." *Yearbook, Conference of Latin Americanist Geographers* 13, no. 1 (1987): 25–35.

Strait, John B. "Geographical Study of American Blues Culture." *Journal of Geography* 109, no. 1 (2010): 30–39.

Strait, John B, Alan P. Marcus, and Libby Jackson. "Students Experience the Blues Culture during Field Study in the Mississippi Delta Region." *Perspective. National Council for Geographic Education* 41, no. 1 (2011): 6–9.

Sutherland, Daniel E. *The Confederate Carpetbaggers*. Baton Rouge: Louisiana State University Press, 1988.

———. "Looking for a Home: Louisiana Emigrants during the Civil War and Reconstruction." *Louisiana History: The Journal of the Louisiana Historical Association* 21, no. 4 (1980): 341–59.

Tannenbaum, Frank. *Slave and Citizen. The Negro in the Americas*. New York: Alfred A. Knopf, 1947.

Tate, William. "A Robert E. Lee Letter on Abandoning the South after the War." *Georgia Historical Quarterly* 37, no. 3 (1953): 255–56.

Thornton, J. Mills, III. *Politics and Power in a Slave Society: Alabama, 1800–1860*. Baton Rouge: Louisiana State University Press, 1978.

Toussaint-Samson, Adèle. *A Parisian in Brazil. The Travel Account of a Frenchwoman in Nineteenth-Century Rio de Janeiro*. Edited by June E. Hahner. Translated by Emma Toussaint. 1891. Reprint, Wilmington DE: Scholarly Enterprises, 2001.

Tuan, Yi-Fu. "Humanistic Geography." *Annals of the Association of American Geographers* 66, no. 2 (1976): 266–76.

Vorenberg, Michael. "Lincoln and the Politics of Black Colonization." *Journal of the Abraham Lincoln Assassination* 14, no. 2 (1993): 22–45.

Wagley, Charles, and Marvin Harris. "A Typology of Latin American Subcultures." *American Anthropologist* 57, no. 3 (1955): 428–51.

Wahlstrom, Todd W. *The Southern Exodus to Mexico: Migration across the Borderlands after the American Civil War*. Lincoln: University of Nebraska Press, 2015.

Wallis, Brian. "Black Bodies, White Science: Louis Agassiz's Slave Daguerreotypes." *American Art* 9, no. 2 (1995): 38–61.

Ward, Carolyn Smith. *An American-Brazilian Odyssey: The Story of the Miller and Hall Families*. Charlotte NC: Printed by the author, n.d.

Warfield, J. D. *The Founders of Anne Arundel and Howard Counties, Maryland: A Genealogical and Biographical Review from Wills, Deeds and Church Records*. Baltimore MA: Kohn & Pollock, 1905.

Weaver, Blanche Henry Clark. "Confederate Emigration to Brazil." *Journal of Southern History* 27, no. 1 (1961): 33–53.

———. "Confederate Immigrants and Evangelical Churches in Brazil." *Journal of Southern History* 18, no. 4 (1952): 446–68.

Wilkie, Richard W. "'Sense of Place' and Selected Conceptual Approaches to Place." *CRIT: Journal of the American Institute of Architecture Students* 55, no. 1 (2003): 29–33.

Williams, Mary Wilhelmine. *Dom Pedro the Magnanimous, Second Emperor of Brazil*. Chapel Hill: University of North Carolina Press, 1937.

Wolnisty, Claire M. "Austral Empires: Southern Migration to Central and South America, 1850–1877." *Madison Historical Review* 11, no. 1 (2014): 2–14.

———. *A Different Manifest Destiny: Southern Identity, Citizenship, and Survival in Nineteenth-Century South America.* Lincoln: University of Nebraska Press, 2020.

Wright, John Kirtland. *Human Nature in Geography: Fourteen Papers, 1925–1965.* Cambridge MA: Harvard University Press, 1966.

———. "Terra Incognitae: The Place of the Imagination in Geography." *Annals of the Association of American Geographers* 37, no. 1 (1947): 1–15.

Wye Parish. "Wye Parish: History; St. Luke's Chapel." Wye Parish: Old Wye Church & St. Luke's Chapel (website). Accessed August 3, 2018. http://www.wyeparish.org/history.php.

INDEX

A aurora Paulista (newspaper), 113, 206n83
Abney, Joseph, 198n21
Abrantes, Marquês de (Miguel Calmon du Pin e Almeida), 59, 112–13, 121, 138–39
absentee landownership, 100
Adams, John Quincy, 46
Africa, repatriation to, 137–38
Agassiz, Cecile Braun, 212–13n96
Agassiz, Elisabeth Cabot Cary, 147, 212–13n96; *Journey in Brazil*, 147, 212n77
Agassiz, Louis, 9, 139, 143, 146–51, 161, 212–13n96; *Journey in Brazil*, 147, 212n77
Agency Office for Colonization, 66
agriculture: agricultural societies, 112–13; Brazilian knowledge of, before Confederados arrival, 112–14, 205–6n73, 206n77; crops introduced by Confederados, 27, 28; immigrant contribution to knowledge in, 26–27, 106–7, 111–12; and landownership, 99–100; and literacy, 117; plows, 113, 114, 206n73, 206–7n83; soil conditions, 31, 64, 82, 86, 109, 113, 140, 206n73, 206–7n83; success in Santa Bárbara, 163–64; sugarcane cultivation, 6–7, 71–72, 100, 107, 109. *See also* coffee cultivation; cotton cultivation; flour; labor
Aguiar, José Corrêa de, 153
Alden, Dauril, 37
Aleijadinho, 132
Almeida, Caetano Furquim de, 153
Almeida, Inácio Alves de, 112
Almeida, Miguel Calmon du Pin e (Marquês de Abrantes), 59, 112–13, 121, 138–39
Amazon, 88, 138, 139–43, 147, 149, 152, 159
Americana, xv, 25, 31, 170, 180, 191n50
American Colonization Society, 137
American missionary schools, 28–29, 118, 166–71, 216n43, 216n57
Amerindians, 20, 134, 140, 192n58
Anderson, Benedict, 24, 173–74
Andrews, George Reid, 103
Anglo-Brazilian Times (newspaper): advertisements, 67, 111; establishment, 69; promotion of suitable lands for settlement, 16, 69–70, 72, 79–80; reports on U.S. emigration, 66, 68, 76
A reciprocidade commercial: Baltimore e Brazil, 36

237

Arthur, Henry G., 198n21
Ash, Benjamin, 78–79
A Sociedade Central de Imigração, 124
A Sociedade Promotora de Imigração, 124
Assis, Machado de, 132
Associação Auxiliadora de Colonização e Imigração para Província de São Paulo, 124
Atlanta Constitution (newspaper), 118
Aubertin, John James, 52, 109
Austrian immigrants, 105
Avelar Broteros, Isabel Dabney de, 108
Azambuja, Joaquim Maria Nascentes de, 63–64, 71, 83–84, 129

Bacon, John E., 198n21
Bahia, 68, 73, 123
Bahia and São Francisco Railway Company, 119
Baird, James R., 168
Baker, John Martin, 36, 46, 47
Baldwin, D. A., 53
Baltimore and Baltimorean entrepreneurs: advantages of trade relationship with Brazil, 35–37; Brazil connection, overview, xii, 9–10; coffee imports, 35, 36, 38, 44; credit lines to finance trade, 39–40; flour exports, 35–36, 37, 41–42, 44, 194n31; and Freemasonry membership, 53–55; immigration enterprise, 33; Jacob Humbird connections, 51–53; maritime trade expertise, 35–36; personal connections among, 40–41, 43; publications promoting trade relationship with Brazil, 38, 194n29; structure of international commercial firms, 38–39; Wright family connections, 44–51
Baltimore and Ohio (B&O) Railroad, 33

Baltimore Sun (newspaper), 10, 15, 64, 89, 150, 183
Bandel, John M., 45
banks: and credit, 39–40, 115; Territorial Bank proposal, 122
Baptist missions, 166, 168
Barbanti, Maria L. S. H., 166
Barbosa, João Bernadino Vieira, 51
Barbosa, Rui, 151
Barnsley, George Scarborough, 85, 86
Barreto, Tobias, 132
Barros, Antônio Paes de, 109
Barros Leite, Genebra de, 108
Bastos, Aureliano Cândido Tavares: collaborations with James Cooley Fletcher, 148, 153, 161; as Freemason, 54; influenced by contemporary scientific thought, 151–52; and International Immigration Society, 68, 80, 152–53; legacy, 153–54; *O valle do Amazonas*, 153; racial ideology, 152, 153; relationship with Louis Agassiz, 146, 148, 152; in Thayer Expedition, 147
Bastos, José Tavares, 84, 161
Bates, Henry Walter, 157
Beirne, Francis F., 36
Belgian immigrants, 105
Bell, Whitfield J., Jr., 141
Benevides, José Maria Correá de Sá e, 73
Bethell, Leslie, 104, 128
Bias, K. E., 170
Bierrenbach brothers, 111
Bill Aberdeen (1845), 103
binary racial optics, 19–21, 131, 134–36, 192n62
Birckhead, Elizabeth Hunter, 40
Birckhead, Hugh, 40
Birckhead, James, 33, 38, 40–41
Birckhead, Solomon, 33
Birth of a Nation (film), 24, 192–93n70

Blackford, A. L., 168, 169
blackness, 21, 134, 136, 184
black populations: black resistant groups, 134, 178; disenfranchised, 131, 184–85; and polygenesis, 147–48; prohibited from entering Brazil, 129, 139; and racialized rhetoric of Brazilian elite, 210–11n50; and "racial paradise" depictions, 19, 136, 154; social advancement of free, 132–33, 135. *See also* slaves and slavery
Blow, Henry, 87
Blue, John H., 74
Boas, Franz, 182
Bocaiúva, Quintino, xii, 67, 68, 76, 80, 129
Boles, Isaac, 198n21
Bolsonaro, Jair, 184
Bonifácio, José, 165
Bookwalter, Anna Miller, 174–75
Bookwalter, LeRoy King, 174–75
Booth, John Wilkes, 189n6
Bowen, William, 72, 84–86
Brackenridge, H. M., 215n14
Brannon, Peter A., 17
Brannstrom, Christian, 102
Brasher, Jordan Paul, 178
Brazil: exotic trope, 158–59; geographical makeup, 30–31; population, 35, 115, 123, 124
Brazilian World (newspaper), 76–77
British abolition movement, 8, 103
British colonialism, 152
British Honduras, U.S. emigration to, 58
British immigrants, 177, 217n76
Brito, Francisco de Paula, 133
Broome, Colonel, 66
Brown, Alexander, 194–95n36
Brown, George, 39
Brown, George Stewart, 40, 195n36
Brown, James, 195n36

Brown, John A., 195n36
Brown, William, 194–95n36
Brown Bros. & Co., 39–40, 195n36
Brunson, W. H., 198n21
Bryan, B. C., 198n21
Burlamaque, Frederico Leopoldo César, 112–13, 121, 205n73
Burton, Richard Francis: *Exploring the Highlands of Brazil*, 92–93
Butler, A. P., 198n21

California, 37
Campbell, Will D., xiv
Campinas, 62, 162, 168, 169, 170
Campo (Cemitério do Campo): Carter's visit to, 179–80; Confederate symbolism in, 134, 177–79; development and maintenance of grounds, 175–76; Freemason symbolism in, 165; as site of memory and belonging, xi, 23, 174, 177, 179, 180
Campo, churches in, 168–69
Canada, U.S. emigration to, 130
Cananéia: connection to Brazilian elites, 80, 82; emergence of settlements in, 74; first Americans in, 78–79; geography, 31, 80–81
cannibalism, 158, 159, 214n9
Carlton, Edward, 172
Carter, Jimmy, 179–80
Carwile, John R., 198n21
Castiço, Fernando, 153
Castles, Stephen, 22
Catholic Church, 160, 165, 170
cemeteries: British, 217n76; private vs. public, 34, 63. *See also* Campo (Cemitério do Campo)
Chamberlain, George W., 168
Chambers, Edward J., 47
citizenship, 60, 171

civilizing project, 160
Clark, S. J. M., 198n21
Clay, Henry, 137
Clemens, Samuel, 143
clipper vessels, 36
Cloutier, J. E., 72
Cockburn, Alexander, 140–41
coffee cultivation: agricultural implements, 111; benefits, 108–9; commodity boom, 7–8, 123–24; exports from Rio to Baltimore, 35, 36, 38; growing American demand for, 43–44, 195n47; labor for, 103–4, 108, 110
Colégio Batista Brasileiro, 166
Colégio Internacional, 118, 166, 167, 169, 170
Colégio Piracicabano, 29, 167
Colégio Rangel Pestana, 167
Coleman, Hutton & Co., 38, 39
Columbus, Christopher, 158, 159, 214n9
commerce. *See* trade and commerce
Comte, Auguste, 155
Confederacy: Brazil as unofficial ally, 59–60; Confederate flag and memorials, 177–79, 183; postbellum socioeconomic conditions, 60, 127, 131–32
Confederados: Brazil's appeal to, 59–60, 127; compared to "city immigrants," 76–77; contributions of, 27–30; loyalty to United States, 171–72; mass return to United States, 87–88, 89–90; misconceptions of, xv, 25–27; numbers, 10–11; publications by, 15–16; scholarship on, 2–4, 16–18; sense of belonging, 174, 180; sociocultural background, 1–2, 11–14; U.S. press characterization of, 77–78. *See also* migration process; Protestantism; settlements
Confederados, descendants of: citizenship, 171; family reunions, 133, 178, 179; publications, 16–17; stance on race, 133–34
Cooke, A. P., 88
Corbin, Spotswood Wellford, 141
Correio mercantil (newspaper), 83, 92
Correio Paulistano (newspaper), 27
Cosgrove, Denis, 173
Cotegipe, João Maurício Wanderley, Barão de, 87, 132
cotton cultivation: Confederados success in, 163; cotton gins, 26–27; exports from Brazil, 101–2; exports from U.S. South, 131; in Mississippi Delta, xiii–xiv; as native to Brazil, 25; potential in Brazil, 52, 64, 71–72
Coulter, Theresa, 175
Coxe, Ferdinand, 79, 200n88
credit (financial), 39–40, 115
Creswell, Tim, 23
Crisp, John H., 163–64
crop cultivation. *See* agriculture
Cunha, Euclides da, 154
Currie, A. W., 89
Cussen, Henrique George, 94

Daily Dispatch (Richmond VA newspaper), 78, 135
Danish immigrants, 14
Darvil, George, 172
Darwinian evolution, 143, 147, 155
Davies, Surekha, 158
Davis, Jefferson, 78, 141
Davis, Thomas J., 198n21
Dawsey, Cyrus B., 4, 17, 133, 159, 166, 179
Dawsey, James M., 4, 12, 17, 133, 159, 166
Dawsey, John C., 176, 177
Dean, Warren, 109
DeCourcy family, 45
degeneracy, racial, 144–45, 146, 148, 152
deportation and repatriation, 137–39

deterministic ideology, 142–43, 149–51, 182
disenfranchisement, 131, 184–85
Domm, John, 14, 89
Dom Pedro Segundo Railway Company, 119–20
Dunn, Ballard S.: background, 14; *Brazil, the Home for Southerners*, 15–16, 71, 161; as controversial, 209n25; criticism of Charles Nathan, 91–92; disillusionment with United States, 125; Iguape settlement, 71, 72, 73, 74; on Jacob Humbird, 51–52, 120; on plows, 114; political influence, 70–71
Durisoe, T. B., 198n21
Dutch immigrants, 14
Dyer, James, 85

economy: credit, 39–40, 115; in postbellum South, 60, 127, 131–32; and transition to federal republic, 125. *See also* trade and commerce
education: American missionary schools, 28–29, 118, 166–71, 216n43, 216n57; Brazilian schools, 117, 123; and illiteracy, 116–18, 160
Edwards, William Henry, 157
El Dorado, 159
elite families: in Confederado settlement areas, 80, 81–82; and intermarriage, 108; and landownership, 98–100
Ellicott Company, 42
Ellicott family, 42–43
Elliott, Lillian Elwyn (Joyce), 3, 58, 105, 158, 190n7
Elliott, L. E. *See* Elliott, Lillian Elwyn (Joyce)
Ellison, Andrew, Jr., 34, 121
Emerson, William C., 168
Emigrant's Hotel, 66

Emory, Mary Bourke: *Colonial Families and Their Descendants*, 44
Engelberg, Johan Conrad, 111
engenho system (plantations/mills), 100
England, U.S. emigration to, 130
environmental determinism, 142–43, 149–51, 182
Escola Americana, 166
Escola de Agricultura de Piracicaba, 27
Escola de Missão, 166
Escola Presbeteriana, 166
Espírito Santo, 71–72, 123
Estrada de Ferro Dom Pedro II, 120
Estrada de Ferro Maúa, 119
eugenics, 150
evolutionary theory, 143, 147, 155
exotic trope, 158–59
Expanded Metropolitan Complex (Macrometropolis), 30
Ezell, Christopher P., 89

family reunions, 133, 178, 179
Feijó, Antonio, 165
Felício, Rodrigo Ferreira, 153
Fenley, Hiram, 171
Ferguson, Green, 89
Ferguson, Sarah Bellona Smith, 16, 17
financial assistance, 63–64, 66, 68, 71, 83, 91
Fish, Hamilton, 88
Fletcher, James Cooley: background, 161; on black intellectual figures, 132–33; *Brazil and the Brazilians* (with Kidder), 1, 15, 159, 160, 200n88; on Brazil land rights, 140; Brazil trip facilitated by Robert Clinton Wright, 50; collaborations with Tavares Bastos, 148, 153, 161; on Joseph Maxwell funeral, 48; mentioned, 148, 153; relationship with Louis

Fletcher, James Cooley (*cont.*)
   Agassiz, 146; on Rio de Janeiro, 1; in Thayer Expedition, 9, 161; on Vergueiro plantation, 108, 109
flour: Baltimore as major exporter of, 35–36, 37, 44, 194n31; growing Brazilian demand for, 41–42, 43, 194n31, 195n47; shipment methods, 203n137
Forbes, William, 55
Ford, Henry, 181
Franklin, Benjamin, 54
Fraternidade Descendência Americana, 133–34, 175–76, 179
free labor, 110
Freemasons and Freemasonry: and Baltimore-Brazil connection, 53–55; lodges, 54, 55, 164, 197n104; network in Brazil, 4, 14, 78, 165; racial views, 144; symbols, 165
Freyre, Gilberto, 3, 12, 146, 160, 182, 209n26

Gaddis, John Lewis, xvi
Galvão, José C., 67
Gama, Luís da, 132
Gama, Manuel Jacinto Nogueira da, 105
Gammon, S. R., 170
Gardner, W. J., 198n21
Garnett, Charles M., 120
Gaston, James MacFadden: on Charles and George Nathan, 94; commercial interests, 125; *Hunting a Home in Brazil*, 16; medical practice, 200n77; on plows, 114; on prohibition of blacks and slavery, 129; search for suitable lands, 61–62, 70, 81; settlement, 74; on sociocultural similarities with Brazilians, 13, 62–63; on transportation for emigrants, 91; visit to Vergueiro plantation, 109, 110

Gazette & Comet (newspaper), 1, 93–94
geographical imagination, concept of, 23–24, 173–74
German immigrants, 14, 33, 52, 105–6, 110, 130, 144, 176
Germany, Nazi, 146
Gibbon, Lardner, 142
Glover, Charles, 198n21
Gobineau, Joseph Arthur de, 144–46, 151; *Essai sur l'inégalité des races humaines*, 145
Golden Law (1888), 104
Gold Rush, Brazilian, 7, 98–99
Gone with the Wind (film), 23–24
Gould, Stephen Jay, 148, 156
government, Brazilian: criticized for inadequate provisioning, 85–86, 88–89; facilitation of U.S. emigration, 63–64, 66–68, 71, 83–84, 91, 123
government, U.S.: property rights, 71; transportation of emigrants back to United States, 87–88
Graham, Richard, 112, 119, 207–8n111
Graham, William H., 39, 73, 195n36
Grandin, Greg, 181
Grant, Ulysses, 87
Gravois, James M., 17
Griggs, William Clark, 17
Gugliotta, Alexandre Carlos, 152
Guillet, John, 74
Gunter, Basil Manly, 71
Gunter, Charles Grandison: and Ballard Dunn's proposed settlement, 70; Brazilian citizenship, 60; compared to "city immigrants," 76; relationship with Charles Nathan, 95; settlements, 71, 73, 74, 82–83
Gunter, Horace, 71
Gussi, Alcides Fernando, 128
Guyot, Arnold, 139, 142–43, 147, 212n83

Hale, Grace Elizabeth, 131
Hall, Charles Moses, 174
Hall, Hervey, 128, 168
Hall, Lizzie Miller, 174
Hancock, John, 54
Harris, Marvin, 21
Harter, Eugene C., 17, 179–80
Hartley, Diogo "James," 75
Harvard University, 146–47, 150–51
Hastings, Lansford W., 31, 72, 74, 86–87;
   The Emigrant's Guide to Brazil, 87
Haupt, Herman, 153
Hawthorn, Frank, 172
Hawthorne, A. T., 168
Hecht, Susanna, 140–41
Henderson, Nannie, 169
Herndon, William Lewis, 142–43
Hill, Lawrence F., 9, 17, 124, 130
Hitler, Adolf, 146
H. M. Lane & Co., 110–11
Ho, Enseng, xi
Hobsbawm, Eric, 125, 190n9
Horne, Gerald, 18, 127, 191n50
Houston, Elsie, 29
Houston, Sam, 29
Hughes, Calvin, 72
Hughes, Edward, xii
Humbird, Elinor McKee, 51
Humbird, Jacob, 16, 51–53, 120–21
Humbird, John Alexander (brother of Jacob Humbird), 53
Humbird, John Alexander (son of Jacob Humbird), 53
Humboldt, Alexander von, 212n83, 214n3
Hunter, William, 40

Iguape: connection to Brazilian elites, 80, 81, 82; emergence of settlements in, 71, 72, 73, 74; failure of McMullen-Bowen settlement, 83–86; geography, 31, 80–81
illiteracy, 116–18, 160
imagining, concept of, 23–24, 173–74
immigration agents, 65, 67, 70, 74–75, 84–85, 91, 93–94
Immigration Restriction League (Boston), 150
immigration societies, Brazilian, 67–68, 124
immigration societies, U.S., 61
indentured laborers, 8, 108, 110
Indigenous populations, 20, 134, 140, 192n58, 192n62
Inhaúma, Visconde de, 165
Instituto Agrícola de Campinas, 27
Instituto Baiano da Agricultura, 113
Instituto Imperial Fluminense da Agricultura, 113
Instituto Sergipano da Agricultura, 113
intermarriage. *See* miscegenation
International Immigration Society, 68, 80, 105
Irajá, Conde de, 165
Irish immigrants, 14, 69
Italian immigrants, 89, 104, 105, 110, 124

Jackson, Andrew, 137
Jackson, Thomas "Stonewall," 141, 164, 183
James, William, 147, 161
Japanese immigrants, 20, 106
Jarnagin, Laura, xv, 11, 12–13, 18, 48, 55–56, 94, 125, 128, 196n88
Jefferson, Mark, 4, 93
Jenkins, Hugh, 45
Jennings, W. D., 198n21
João VI of Portugal, 38, 105, 204n30
Johnson, H. B., 98
Jones, Charles Fenley, 29
Jones, Cicero, 171, 172
Jones, George, 172

Jones, Judith MacKnight, 22; *Soldado, descansa! Uma epopéia norte americana sob os céus do Brasil*, 16
Jones, Julia Norris, 118
Jones, Leonard Yancey, 29
Jones, Robert, 172
Jones, W. C., 72
Jones, William Francis, 47
Jones, Yancey, 172
Jornal do commercio (newspaper), 26
Juárez, Benito, 59
Juparanã, Lake, 80

Kalley, Robert R., 169
Kelsey, Vera, 17
Kemper, Charlotte, 170
Key, Francis Scott, 137
Keyes, Julia L., 16
Kidder, Daniel Parish: background, 160–61; on black intellectual figures, 132–33; *Brazil and the Brazilians* (with Fletcher), 1, 15, 159, 160, 200n88; on Brazil land rights, 140; on Catholic Church, 160; on Joseph Maxwell funeral, 48; on Rio de Janeiro, 1; *Sketches of Residence and Travel in Brazil*, 15, 160; on Vergueiro plantation, 108; work with James Spaulding, 169
kinship networks, 40–41, 43, 48–49, 101–2
Kirk, Mary Videau, 169
Kirtland, John, 24
Koster, Henry: *Travels in Brazil*, 101
Koster, John Theodore, 101–2
Krähenbühl (manufacturer), 26

labor: free, 110; indentured, 8, 108, 110; racialized, 136. *See also* slaves and slavery
Lamert, Ester, 96
landownership, 97–100, 119

Lane, Edward, 168, 169, 170
Lane, Horace, 74
Lane, Horace Manly, 14, 72, 110–11, 200n70
language, 28, 167, 170–71
Law of the Free Womb (1871), 104
Law of the Sexagenarian (1885), 104
Ledo, Gonçalves, 165
Lee, Rita, 29
Lee, Robert E., 78, 141, 183
Lei Caó (1989), 219n7
Lei das Sesmarias (1375), 99
Lei Eusébio de Queirós (1850), 103, 129
Leopoldina Railway Company, 120
Lesser, Jeffrey, 137
Liberia, 137
Lidgerwood, William Van Vleck, 14, 111
Lincoln, Abraham, 138
Linhares: connection to Brazilian elites, 80, 81–82; emergence of settlements in, 71, 74; failure of Gunter settlement, 82–83; geography, 31
literacy, 116–18, 160
Livingstone, David N., 155
Livingstone, Edward, 46
Lock, Ernest, 172
Lock, Lee Rowe, 172
Lost Cause ideologies, 131–32
Lowe, John, 60

Machado, Domingos da Costa, 162
Maia, José da, 27
Majewski, John, 34, 141
Mandeville, John, 158
Manifest Destiny, 9, 142, 143
Marshall, John, 137
Martins, Margarida da Graça, 162
Martius, Carl F. P. von, 147
Marx, Karl, 212n83
Maryland Colonization Society, 137
Maury, James, 101

Maury, Matthew Fontaine: *The Amazon, and the Atlantic Slopes of South America*, 212n77; Amazonian settlement plan, 88, 138, 139–41, 142, 149, 152; commercial voyage durations, 37; cotton cultivation attempt, 101, 102; deterministic ideology, 142–43
Maximillian, Emperor of Mexico, 58–59, 141
Maxwell, Joseph (José), Sr., 46, 47, 48–49, 196n88
Maxwell, Joseph, Jr., 47
Maxwell, Maria Rosa de Sousa, 48
Maxwell, Rev., 172
Maxwell, Silva & Companhia, 48
Maxwell, Wright & Co.: Baltimore-Brazil relationship, overview, 9–10; coffee imports, 38; commercial vessel numbers, 35; credit lines, 39–40; establishment, 47; flour exports, 44; headquarters–branches structure, 39; personal connections among partners, 48–49
May, William, 46
Mays, Benjamin F., 198n21
McAlpine, N. B., 171
McCann, William, 171
McCul, John, 73
McEwin, D. F., 198n21
McFadden, Edgar, 172
McFadden, John, 171
McFadden, Julian, 172
McFadden, Leroy, 172
McFadden, Sarah, 174
McFadden, William, 174
McMullen, Frank, 60, 70, 72, 74, 83–85
Medeiros, Regina Del Negri, 28
Menchi, Helena Quintana, 163
Meriwether, Robert, 61–62, 63, 70, 95, 119, 198n21

Metcalf, Alida C., 20
Methodist missions, 28–29, 167, 169
Mexico, U.S. emigration to, 58–59, 128, 129, 130, 141
migration process: Brazilian government as facilitator, 63–64, 66–68, 71, 83–84, 91, 123; and emigration enthusiasm, 74–75, 78; immigration agents as facilitators, 65, 67, 70, 74–75, 84–85, 91, 93–94; newspapers as facilitators, 67, 69–70, 79–80; passports, 60–61, 66; and press characterization of emigrants, 76–78; search for suitable lands, 61–63, 64; Wright family as facilitators, 50, 51, 52, 62. *See also* settlements
migration theory, 21–22
Miller, Gena, 174
Miller, James Williamson, 89, 117–18, 174, 175
Miller, John, 175
Miller, Mark J., 22
Miller, Robert, 175
Miller, Sarah, 117–18, 174, 175
Miller, William, 175
Minas Gerais, 68, 123
Minchin, Edward, 171
Minchin, Joseph Long, 171, 172
miscegenation: as beneficial to society, 153, 182; between Confederados and Brazilians, 132, 133; and degeneracy, 144–45, 146, 148; as paradox, 154–55; prominence of, 20, 154; unfamiliarity to northeastern Americans, 38
missionary schools and churches, 28–29, 118, 166–71, 216nn43–44, 216n57
Mississippi Delta, xiii–xiv
mixed races, 20–21, 78, 134–35, 144
Moffit, John, 158

Monroe, James, 137
Monrovia settlement, 137
Morais, Ana Maria, 29
Morais, Prudente de, 29, 167
Morais Barros, Adelaide Benvinda da Silva Gordo de, 29
Morais Barros, Pedro, 29
Morgan, G. W., 198n21
Morrill, Richard, 189n7
Morton, George Nash, 168, 169
Müller, Franz, 14
Murray, Edmundo, 69
Muslims, 116

Nabuco, Joaquim, 54, 104
Nascimento, Abdias do, 19
Nathan, Charles: background, 14, 90, 96, 202n118; criticized by Ballard Dunn, 91–92; descendants, xii; as Freemason, 54, 55; and International Immigration Society, 68, 80; obituary, 95–96; promotion of flour trade, 95, 203n137; in Richard Francis Burton's publication, 92–93; and Santa Bárbara settlement, 163–64; and search for suitable lands, 81; Territorial Bank proposal, 122; transportation arrangements for emigrants, 75, 91, 93–95
Nathan, Emma Goodman, 96
Nathan, George, 68, 94–95
Nathan, Henry, 94
Nathan, Joseph, 94, 96
nationhood, 24, 137, 156, 173–74, 182, 184
Nazi Germany, 146
Newman, Annie Ayres, 167
Newman, Junius C., 168–69
Newman, Mary, 167
newspapers: facilitation of U.S. emigration, 67, 69–70, 79–80; opposition to U.S. emigration, 77–78, 135

New World imagery, 158–59
New York City, immigrants from, 75–76
New York Herald (newspaper), 65, 70, 88, 149
New York Times (newspaper), 1, 34, 77–78, 120
Nielsen, Niels, 14
Norris, Clay, 171
Norris, Manuel, 128
Norris, Olímpia, 128
Norris, Robert Cicero, 29, 54, 128, 162, 164, 171
Norris, William Hutchinson: burial, 165; connection to W. H. D. C. Wright, 55–56; descendants, 29; "founder" designation, 25; as Freemason, 54, 164; Santa Bárbara settlement, 12, 72, 74, 89, 162, 164, 174
North German Lloyd Co., 33

O auxiliador da indústria nacional (journal), 112, 206n73
O commercio (newspaper), 26, 113
O diário de S. Paulo (newspaper), 27
O diário do Rio de Janeiro (newspaper), 27, 68, 94, 106, 113, 163
Oliveira, Carlos Alberto de, 219n7
Oliver, Anthony Thompson, 175
Oliver, Beatrice, 175
Oliver, Inglianna, 175
Oliver, Mildred, 175
Olympio, Sylvanus, 138
Ottoni, Theóphilo, 105

Padoveze, João Leopoldo F., 133–34
Pang, Laura J., 112
Pará, 68, 72, 74
Paraná, 68, 74
Paranaguá, 80, 81
Partridge, J., 171

Partridge, James R., 88
passports, 60–61, 66
Patapsco, 42
Patrocínio, José do, 104, 132
Paula e Sousa, Antônio, 61, 70–71, 81
Pecher, Eduardo, 153
Pedro I, Emperor of Brazil, 198n9
Pedro II, Emperor of Brazil: abdication, 125; bestowal of elite titles, 81, 82; as Confederate ally, 59–60; as emperor, 6, 59; as Freemason, 54, 59; promotion of immigration, 123, 124, 149; promotion of scientific exploration and research, 142; relationship with Ballard Dunn, 70; relationship with Joseph Arthur de Gobineau, 144, 145–46; relationship with Louis Agassiz, 146, 148–49; relationship with Robert Clinton Wright, 34, 50; visits to elite port cities, 80, 82; visit to Campinas, 170; visit to United States, 122–23
Pedroso, Antônio Pereira Barreto, 112, 121, 205n73
Pentecostals, 170, 217n59
Pernambuco, 73, 123
Pestana, Rangel, 167
Phipps companies, 38–39, 44
Pierce, Thomas, 45
Piracicaba, 167, 170
Pitts, Fountain E., 169
place: as concept, 23–24, 173. *See also* Campo (Cemitério do Campo)
plows, 113, 114, 206n73, 206–7n83
Polish immigrants, 105
Polo, Marco, 158
polygenesis, 147–48
population in Brazil, 35, 115, 123, 124
Portuguese colonialism, 98–100, 114–15, 152, 154

Portuguese immigrants, 105
Portuguese language, 28, 167, 171
Presbyterian missions, 166, 168, 169–70
press. *See* newspapers
Protestantism: "civilizing" project, 159–60; continued influence in Brazil, 216–17n59; establishment of schools and churches, 28–29, 118, 166–71, 216nn43–44, 216n57; publications and influence of leaders, 15–16, 160–62; science and evangelicalism, 147, 155. *See also* Dunn, Ballard S.; Fletcher, James Cooley; Kidder, Daniel Parish
Pugh, Catherine E., 183
Pulaski Citizen (newspaper), 75
push/pull factors, 21–22
Pyles, Ezekiel B., 171
Pyles, Franklin, 171
Pyles, Grover G., 171
Pyles, Oscar, 172
Pyles, Richard, 118
Pyles, Ross, 175
Pyles, Samuel M., 168
Pyles, William, 171

Quillen, Elijah H., 168

race: binary racial optics, 19–21, 131, 134–36, 192n62; blacks prohibited from entering Brazil, 129, 139; in Brazilian elite rhetoric, 210–11n50; in Confederados scholarship, 2–3, 4; and Confederate flag, 177–79; current ideological stances, 136, 184–85; and deterministic ideology, 143, 149–51, 182; mixed, 20–21, 78, 134–35, 144; and nationhood, 24, 137, 156, 182, 184; official color divide absent in Brazil, 19, 132–33, 135; and polygenesis, 147–48; in

race (*cont.*)
  postbellum U.S. South, 131–32; racism condemned by Confederados descendants, 133–34; segregation, 131, 132, 150; as term, 190n5; U.S. public perception of Brazilians, 77, 78; U.S. vs. Brazilian ideological framework, 126–27, 135–36; white superiority, 136–37, 144–45, 148–51, 152–53, 155, 156, 184. *See also* black populations; miscegenation
railway systems: in Brazil, 53, 89, 115–16, 119–21, 170, 207–8n111; in United States, 33, 37, 43, 53, 207–8n111
Ralston, William Pultney, 109
Ransom, John Crowe, 167
Ransom, John James, 167
Ratzel, Frederick, 212n83
Ravenstein, Ernst Georg, 22
Rebello, José Silvestre, 46, 47
Rebouças, André, 132
Recife, 80
Reclus, Élisée, 81, 212n83
Reconstruction Era, 131–32
Reese, Thomas B., 198n21
religion. *See* Protestantism
repatriation and deportation, 137–39
reunions, family, 133, 178, 179
Revere, Paul, 54
Revista de imigração e colonização, 16
Ribeira de Iguape region, 80–81
Ridgely family, 54
Ridings, Eugene W., 107, 122
Rio Branco, Barão do, 154
Rio das Velhas, 73
Rio de Janeiro: advantages of trade relationship with Baltimore, 35–37; beauty of, 1; cemeteries in, 34; Freemason lodges in, 55; illiteracy rates, 116; population, 35, 123; as port city, 37–38, 80; Protestant missions in, 166, 168, 169, 170; publications promoting trade relationship with Baltimore, 38, 194n29; railway system, 119; slave imports to, 104; structure of international commercial firms, 38–39; U.S. consuls in, 46–47
Ritter, Karl, 212n83
Roberts, Milnor, 120–21
Rodrigues, Nina, 154
Rood, Daniel, 41
Roosevelt, Theodore, 210–11n50
Roston Dutton & Co., 44
Rowly, Charles N., 72
Rudge, George, 47, 49
Rudge, John, 48–49
Rudge, Maria Amalia Maxwell, 49
Rudge, Sofia Maxwell, 49
Russell-Wood, A. J. R., 7
Russian immigrants, 105

Saba, Roberto, 110
Sabóia, Vicente Cândido Figueira de, 145
sailing vessels, 37, 203n137
Salvador, 80
Sampaio, Maria Clara Sales Carneiro, 138
Santa Bárbara d'Oeste: agricultural success in, 163–64; and Americana confusion, xv, 25, 180, 191n50; Confederado families in, 163; establishment of settlement in, 74, 162; Freemasons in, 164–65; geography, 31; as most successful settlement, 4, 74, 90, 157; Protestant missions in, 166, 168, 169, 170; sociocultural background of Confederados in, 11–14. *See also* Campo (Cemitério do Campo)
Santa Catarina, 68
Santarém, 31, 74, 86–88

Santos, 80
São Luís, 80
São Paulo: agricultural knowledge, 27; coffee boom, 123–24; conurbation, 29–30; geography, 31; illiteracy rates, 116; language, 28; plantation sizes, 13; population, 123; Protestant missions in, 166, 168, 169, 216n44; railway system, 119–20; settler population, 68; slave imports to, 104; soil type, 109. *See also* Santa Bárbara d'Oeste
São Paulo Railway Company (Ingleza), 119–20
São Pedro, 68
Sauer, Carl O., 182
Schemann, Ludwig, 146
Scheper-Hughes, Nancy, 19
Schley, David, 35, 43
schools: American missionary, 28–29, 118, 166–71, 216n43, 216n57; Brazilian, 117, 123
Schuster, Sven, 154
scientific thought: of Arnold Guyot, 142–43; and evangelicalism, 147, 155; of Joseph Arthur de Gobineau, 144–46; legacy in Brazil, 136–37, 154–56, 182–83; of Louis Agassiz, 146–51; of Matthew Fontaine Maury, 139–41, 143; Tavares Bastos influenced by, 151–52
Scully, William, 14, 68, 69–70, 80, 122, 153
Sebastian, Santiago, 158
segregation, racial, 131, 132, 150
sense of belonging, 174, 176–77, 180
Sentell, John, 198n21
sesmarias system (law of redistribution of lands), 99
settlements, 79; Amazon, 88, 138, 139–43, 149, 152; challenges, overview, 82, 88–89; emergence of, 70–74; failure of Gunter settlement, 82–83; failure of Hastings settlement, 86–88; failure of McMullen-Bowen settlement, 83–86; search for suitable lands, 61–63, 64. *See also* Cananéia; Iguape; Linhares; Santa Bárbara d'Oeste; Santarém
Seward, William H., 138
Shaler, Nathaniel Southgate, 150
Sharrer, G. Terry, 42
Shaw, D. L., 198n21
Shaw, Hugh A., 61–62, 63, 119, 198n21
Shippey, William Francis (Frank), 60, 198n16
Silva, Antonio Gutemberg da, 94
Silva, Miguel Antonio da, 205n73
Silva Prado, Antônio da, 81
Simmons, Charles Willis, 127
Simonton, Ashbel Green, 168, 169
slaves and slavery: abolished, 19, 89, 104, 153; and Amazonian settlement plan, 138, 139, 140; Brazilian defense of, 122, 126; education and literacy, 116, 122; and factors in U.S. emigration to Brazil, 127–30; immigrant labor as replacement, 8, 52, 105–6, 108, 110, 121–22, 124; import statistics, 103–4; repatriation and deportation, 137–39; scholarship on Brazilian, 127–28, 209n26; and sugarcane cultivation, 100; trafficking prohibited, 8, 103, 129; unfamiliarity to northeastern Americans, 38
Slave Trade Suppression Act (1845), 103
Smith, T. Lynn, 3, 17
Sociedade Auxiliadora da Indústria Nacional, 112
Sociedade Círculo Agrícola de São João de Cacaria, 112–13, 121

sociocultural conditions: background of Confederados, 1–2, 11–14; illiteracy, 116–18, 160; intellectual stifling, 114–15; landownership, 97–100; racialized upward mobility, 136. *See also* elite families; race; slaves and slavery

soil conditions, 31, 64, 82, 86, 109, 113, 140, 206n73, 206–7n83

Sousa, Ricardo Alexandre Santos, 146

Sousa Coutinho, Rodrigo de, 81–82, 206n77

Sousa Coutinho family, 48, 54, 82

Sousa Queirós, Antônio de, 109

Sousa Queirós, Augusto de, 109

Sousa Queirós, Luís António de, 108

Sousa Queirós, Vicente de, 108

Sousa Queirós family, 108

Southern Colonization Society (South Carolina), 61, 198n21

Southey, Robert: *History of Brazil*, 81, 101

Souza Queirós, Nicolau de, 108

Spanish immigrants, 105

Spaulding, James, 169

Spix, Johann Baptist von, 147

Steagall, Martha Temperance, 13, 93

steamers, 37, 75, 203n137

Stein, Stanley J., 7, 103

Sternberg, Hilgard O'Reilly, 140

Strait, John B., xiii, 189n9

Stuart, J. E. B., 141

sugarcane cultivation, 6–7, 71–72, 100, 107, 109

Swain, M. S., 74

Swann, Thomas, 50

Swiss immigrants, 105

Tannenbaum, Frank, 209n26

Taubaté, 170

Terrell, James Ulrich, 171

Territorial Bank, 122

textile factories, 109

Thayer, Nathaniel, 147

Thayer Expedition, 9, 147

Thomas, Phillip Francis, 46

Thomas, Robert P., 168

Thompson, Ogden, 73

Tordesilhas, Treaty of (1494), 80

Torreão de Barros, B. F., 65

Totten, Silas S., 72

Toussaint-Samson, Adèle, 158

trade and commerce: advantages of Baltimore-Brazil relationship, 35–37; commodity booms in Brazil, 6–8, 100, 190n11; cotton exports, 101–2, 131; credit lines to finance, 39–40; growing commodity demands, 41–44, 194n31, 195n47; and interest in Amazon, 140, 142; and kinship networks, 40–41, 43, 48–49, 101–2; publications promoting Baltimore-Brazil relationship, 38, 194n29; structure of international firms, 38–39. *See also* Maxwell, Wright & Co.

transnational livelihoods, 102

transportation: arrangements and cost for emigrants, 63–64, 66, 68, 71, 75, 83, 91, 93–95; inadequate regional, 82, 86, 102, 115–16, 119; railway system in Brazil, 53, 89, 115–16, 119–21, 170, 207–8n111; railway system in United States, 33, 37, 43, 53, 207–8n111; steamers and sailing vessels, 37, 75, 203n137

Tuan, Yi-Fu, 23, 173

Turkish immigrants, 106

Twain, Mark, 143

Tyson, James Ellicott, 43

Tyson, Martha Ellicott, 43
Tyson, Nathan, 42, 43

Ukrainian immigrants, 105
União de Negros pela Igualdade (UNEGRO), 134, 178
U.S. South. *See* Confederacy

Van Buren, Martin, 46
Veazey, Sarah DeCourcy, 150
Vergueiro, José, 108, 109
Vergueiro, Nicolau Pereira de Campos, 107–8, 109
Vergueiro & Cia., 108
Vergueiro's Ibicaba plantation, 108, 109, 110
Vespucci, Amerigo, 80, 159
Vianna, Oliveira, 154
Vincent, Annie Lou, 170
Vitória, 80

Waddell, Phillip, 118
Wagley, Charles, 21
Wagner, Richard, 146
Wahlstrom, Todd W., 18, 34, 129, 141
Waldseemüller, Martin, 159
Wallace, Alfred Russel, 157
Wallis, Brian, 147
Wall Street Journal (newspaper), 136
Ward, Caroline Smith, 157, 180; *The Story of the Miller and Hall Families*, 16–17
Ward, Henry Veazey, 150
Ward, Robert DeCourcy, 150
Warren, Joseph, 54
Washington, George, 54
watermelons, 27
Watson, Tilman, Jr., 198n21
Watts, Martha Hite, 29, 167
Weaver, Blanche Henry Clark, 17, 117, 127, 166

Webb, James Watson, 59, 138–39
Weisbrod, Elizabeth J., 17
Wessinger, John, 171
West Africa, 137–38
Whitaker, Joseph E., 171, 172
whiteness, 21, 131, 134–35, 136
white superiority, 136–37, 144–45, 148–51, 152–53, 155, 156, 184
Whitridge, William, 45
Whittaker, Joe, 27
Whittaker, Orville, 89
Wilkie, Richard W., xii–xiii, 189n7
Williams, William M., 198n21
Willmot, Clement, 109
Willmot, George, 109
Wise, W. S., 179
Wolnisty, Claire M., 127, 128
Woman's Missionary Society, 167, 170
women: documentation of Confederados, 16–17; as educators, 28, 167, 169; and miscegenation, 154
Wood, William Wallace, 65, 109
World Fairs, 154
World War I, 171–72
Worthrop, George, 171
Wright, Anna Selina Anderson, 50
Wright, Brown & Co., 40
Wright, Carlota Marquês Lisboa, 51
Wright, Caroline Louisa, 46
Wright, Clintonia, 46
Wright, Daniel Giraud, 44–45
Wright, Eliza Lea Warner, 46, 49
Wright, Ella Lee, 46
Wright, Gustavia, 46
Wright, Gustavus, 46
Wright, John Kirtland, 173, 183
Wright, John Skinner, 47
Wright, Mary Tidmarsh DeCourcy, 45
Wright, Nathaniel, 45
Wright, Robert, 45–46

Wright, Robert Clinton: connection to William H. Norris, 55–56; correspondence with W. H. D. C. Wright, 49; facilitation of U.S. emigration, 50; mentioned, 149; partner at Maxwell, Wright & Co., 47; political influence, 34, 44, 47, 50; railway development, 43, 50; relationship with Brazilian government, 34
Wright, Sarah DeCourcy, 46
Wright, Solomon, 45
Wright, Victoria Louisa, 46
Wright, William Henry DeCourcy (W. H. D. C.): committed to asylum, 49; death and burial, xii, 49–50; family, 46, 199n25; as Freemason, 54–55; mentioned, 150; partner at Maxwell, Wright & Co., 47; political involvement in Brazil, 44, 46–47; relationship with Birckheads, 40–41
Wright, William Turbutt, 44, 51, 62, 121
Wright family, 44–51, 196n71

www.ingramcontent.com/pod-product-compliance
Ingram Content Group UK Ltd.
Pitfield, Milton Keynes, MK11 3LW, UK
UKHW031021241224
452752UK00002B/27